D0560955

C O N F E S S I O N S I N D I A L O G U E

A Survey of Bilateral Conversations among
World Confessional Families 1959--1974

by
NILS EHRENSTRÖM and GÜNTHER GASSMANN

Third, revised and enlarged edition by
NILS EHRENSTRÖM

Sponsored by the Conference of Secretaries of
World Confessional Families in cooperation with
the Secretariat on Faith and Order of the
World Council of Churches

World Council of Churches, Geneva 1975

First edition	1972
Reprint	1973
Third, revised and enlarged edition	1975

Faith and Order Paper No. 74

ISBN: 2-8254-0500-0
© 1975 by World Council of Churches, Geneva
Cover picture by John Taylor
Printed in The Netherlands by Krips Repro BV, Meppel

FOREWORD

The ecumenical movement and the search for Christian unity find expression in many forms and ways. The rapid growth of bilateral dialogues between various confessional traditions has been one of the outstanding ecumenical developments of the last decade.

For several years now, secretaries of "world confessional families" have been meeting annually in Geneva to consider matters of mutual interest. This "Conference of Secretaries of World Confessional Families" has proved to be a useful means of consultation though it has no official deliberative character; it has no constitutional position or administrative status. It has, however, provided a mutually beneficial forum for the exchange of views and news, sharing experiences and common concerns, and has proved to be a ready instrument for concerted planning in specific instances.

Since most world confessional families are actively engaged in various bilateral dialogues, the Conference decided some years ago to give concrete expression to its interest in this growing venture. It has been becoming increasingly evident that the potential outreach of these various conversations is being limited by lack of effective communication between the various dialogues themselves on the one hand and on the other between these and the respective opinion-forming and policy-making bodies of the churches involved.

To help facilitate the flow of information, the Conference decided at its November 1969 meeting to sponsor a comparative and evaluative study of the conversations in which world confessional traditions are directly or indirectly involved. Since these bilateral conversations have a bearing upon the ongoing ecumenical theological discussion, the Faith and Order Secretariat of the World Council of Churches offered its cooperation and administrative help. An initial report was published in 1972, covering the decade 1962-1971. It is indicative of the growing volume and importance of these dialogues that it has been found necessary to issue a new, revised and enlarged edition.

The Survey contains a synoptic systematisation of a wealth of hitherto unrelated and often unknown material. In providing profiles of the individual dialogues and offering perceptive observations, the authors have made an important contribution to the clarification of the present ecumenical situation. Their analysis will be of interest to all those who are committed to furthering the cause of unity. The reader will want to give special attention to the concluding recommendations.

We wish to express our appreciation to the authors, especially Professor Nils Ehrenström who edited this new edition of the Survey. We are deeply grateful that he has made available his rich ecumenical experience for this task. We extend our gratitude also to the contributors to the chapter on Worship, and to all those who made this study project possible by supplying information, documents and needed advice.

John Howe
Secretary General
Anglican Consultative Council

Chairman
Conference of Secretaries
of World Confessional Families

B.B. Beach
Secretary, Northern Europe - West Africa Division
General Conference of Seventh-Day Adventists

Secretary
Conference of Secretaries
of World Confessional Families

Lukas Vischer
Director
Secretariat of the Commission on Faith and Order
of the World Council of Churches

Information and suggestions concerning the development of bilateral conversations will be welcome and should preferably be addressed to the office of your world confessional family as well as to the Secretariat on Faith and Order, 150, route de Ferney, 1211 Geneva 20, Switzerland.

TABLE OF CONTENTS

INDEX OF CONVERSATIONS[1]

Recorded in the Descriptive Accounts

1. The titles are listed according to confessional families in alphabetical order. An abbreviation symbol without qualifying geographical reference denotes a world level conversation (e.g. A-L).

I
INTRODUCTION

Bilateral conversations between Christian confessions and communions have been growing apace in the past decade. Multilateral activities of various kinds as well as church union negotiations already have a long history behind them and belong to the established features of the ecumenical scene. To be sure, bilateral conversations too are not without historical antecedents; but as a worldwide movement they constitute a new phenomenon, drawing strength from an unprecedented concurrence of ecumenical and confessional tides. In particular, world confessional families were in the past rarely directly involved in theological conversations with each other; now a vast network of relationships has grown up and in certain countries the national and international conversations find a fruitful complement in local dialogue groups. Agreements are being established which concretise and reinforce the parallel convergences occurring in the ecumenical movement at large. If acted upon, they would decisively advance the drive towards mutual recognition among now separated communions.

For several reasons there is still little information generally available about these conversations. But their very existence raises a host of questions about their purpose, nature and results, which need to be clarified if they are to assume their proper place within the larger universe of ecumenical endeavours.

How is the purpose of these conversations conceived and on what patterns are they structured? What concerns and intentions are revealed in the choice of subjects? What methods of theologising do they employ? What have they accomplished thus far? What authority and weight do the conversations and their results carry? How are the various conversations correlated, if at all? And how are they, in turn, coordinated with the multilateral dialogues and with church union negotiations? What should be the role of world confessional families and the Faith and Order Commission in regard to the bilaterals? What should be done to implement their findings more effectively in the teaching and practice of the churches, both nationally and locally?

To provide answers to questions such as these requires a process of fact-finding, synoptic appraisal, and projection of concerted strategies, which still remains to be undertaken. The present Survey may be seen as a first step toward such an enterprise.

Scope of the Survey. The Survey is purposely designed as a "guide book" which may be useful for those who want a quick bird's-eye-view of this new area of ecumenical dialogue, and also for those who wish to undertake a more thorough study of the theological and ecclesiastical problems involved and therefore would welcome some indications of focal issues, changing configurations, and existing resource materials. Such a synoptic survey cannot, of course, be expected to show forth the delineaments of a pan-Christian *sympnoia*. But it should at least help to deepen the awareness of problems, alternative answers, and nascent convergences, which deserve the attentive consideration of the churches.

According to the initiating decision of the Conference of Secretaries of World Confessional Families, the Survey was to focus on "those bilateral conversations, whether world-wide, regional or national, which are sponsored by world confessional families or their agencies". However, in the course of the study a number of other conversations were added, which, because of their intrinsic value or their close relationship to one or more of the former, deserve inclusion in any survey of the field. In the present edition the scope has been further extended to include additional official dialogues about which information has been obtained. As a result the number of dialogues recorded has risen from 26 to 46. But beyond this, there exist scores of bilaterals of which no concrete reports are available or which are still in the planning stage.

The accounts of the individual dialogues follow a common pattern, but in order to avoid an excessive schematisation, the variety of dialogues as well as of informational materials remains reflected in the mode of presentation.

The term bilateral can of course refer to the relation of two parties in a debate, or two sides of an issue, as is the case, for instance, in the question of mixed marriages. In the present Survey the term is used principally to denote "theological conversations undertaken by offically appointed representatives of two Churches, two traditions, or two confessional families, with purposes ranging from promoting mutual understanding to achieving full fellowship".[1]

---

1. *Faith and Order, Louvain 1971. Study Reports and Documents* (Faith and Order Paper No. 59; World Council of Churches, Geneva 1971), p. 230.

No attempt has been made to present a comprehensive picture of all the various aspects of bilateral conversations, placing them in their theological and ecumenical context, nor to offer an analysis in depth of how particular problems have been framed, argued, and resolved in the discussions. This would have required far more time and space than available, and the analysis would, even so, have yielded but an incomplete and uneven picture of the state of the debate largely because of the confidential nature of much of the material. Important documents, being provisional statements subject to possible revision in later stages of a dialogue or requiring ecclesiastical approval before release, were not accessible for this study or, if made available, were not for quotation.

The cross-conversational synopses in Chapter V are illustrative and therefore selective. They are limited in three ways. They single out six subjects central to the bilaterals, leaving aside conversations which focus on other subjects. They draw chiefly on international and world level conversations and further certain national dialogues of substantial achievement. Finally, the analysis is based in the main on the joint statements in which dialogue groups sum up their conclusions or the trends of the discussion, since these statements provide the most tangible evidence of the accomplishments of a group. Ample use has been made of characteristic quotations in order to suggest something of the flavour of individual documents.

When several conversations are referred to in a given context, these are ranged in alphabetical order, using the nomenclature adopted.

The Survey covers the period from 1959 to 1974. In a few instances, advance information has been supplied about meetings or publications projected for 1975 and 1976.

History of the Study. The Conference of Secretaries of World Confessional Families has for some years been considering the need for a comparative and evaluative study of this kind. At its annual meeting in Geneva, November 19-21, 1969, the Conference decided to sponsor such a study which would include

"1. a survey of bilateral conversations,
2. a theological evaluation of their findings, and
3. suggestions to the World Confessional Families and the World Council of Churches, in particular its Faith and Order Commission, con-

cerning the future of these conversations and ecumenical strategy in general".[1]

The Faith and Order Commission was asked to assume administrative responsibility for the project, and Dr. Nils Ehrenström, professor emeritus of Ecumenics at Boston University, USA, now in Geneva, and Dr. Günther Gassmann, research professor at the Institute for Ecumenical Research in Strasbourg, France, were invited to undertake the study. At the meeting of the Conference, November 18-20, 1970, they presented a tentative outline which was approved in substance and subsequently revised and developed. A Preliminary Report was submitted to the Faith and Order Commission at its triennial meeting at Louvain, Belgium, in August 1971, where it was extensively discussed in a committee on "Church Union Negotiations and Bilateral Conversations". Welcoming the study, the Commission noted its close relation to its own projected inquiry into concepts of unity and models of union, and instructed its secretariat to "provide a clearing house for the exchange of information and materials concerning bilateral and multilateral conversations, establish a repository of such materials, and prepare periodical surveys of the developing trends of such conversations".[2]

When the Conference of Secretaries of World Confessional Families held its next annual meeting in Geneva, November 29 - December 1, 1971, it had before it a complete draft of the Survey. The Conference authorised its publication after due revision and endorsed its concluding recommendations.

In view of the evolving importance of the bilaterals, it was decided to continue the study and to publish in due course an updated and enlarged edition. Apart from the Survey, the general role of the

---

1. The project was not entirely without forerunners. Already some years earlier the Department of Faith and Order of the National Council of Churches of Christ in the USA had begun to include in its annual report a brief summary of bilateral conversations held in the States during the preceding year. The department also produced an extensive bibliography on these conversations, listing individual papers, reports, and publications up to 1969. The staff of the Bishops' Committee for Ecumenical and Interreligious Affairs of the National Conference of Catholic Bishops in the USA had prepared a similar bibliography covering conversations sponsored by the committee.

2. Cf. Report V on "Church Union Negotiations and Bilateral Conversations", <u>Faith and Order, Louvain 1971</u>, pp. 230-38.

bilaterals was discussed in the broader context of the place and role of the world confessional families in the ecumenical movement at Faith and Order meetings in Salamanca, Spain, 1973, and in Accra, Ghana, 1974, and likewise at the annual meetings of the Conference of Secretaries of World Confessional Families the same years. In conjunction with its latest meeting the Conference convened a special consultation, December 9-11, 1974, to undertake for the first time an overall assessment of the bilaterals under three aspects: the implementation of bilateral findings in various areas of church life; bilateral dialogue and theological advance; the future of the bilaterals and the bilaterals of the future.[1]

During their work, the authors have been in close consultation with the Director of the Faith and Order Secretariat, Dr. Lukas Vischer, and have had the benefit of assistance and advice also from numerous officers of world confessional families, denominational ecumenical secretariats, and bilateral dialogue groups, including many of those mentioned in the Directory and in the accounts of individual conversations. By supplying documents and reports on the dialogues and by scrutinising relevant sections of the manuscript, they helped make the study a truly collaborative enterprise.

---

1. For the recommendations adopted by the meetings referred to, see below pp. 256ff.Other evaluations of specific groups of bilaterals are mentioned on pp. 138f.

II

DESCRIPTIVE ACCOUNTS OF THE CONVERSATIONS

The accounts are divided in two groups: (A) conversations at the world level, usually sponsored by world confessional families, and (B) conversations at regional and national levels.

A. CONVERSATIONS AT THE WORLD LEVEL

1. Anglican-Lutheran .... A-L

"Anglican-Lutheran International Conversations" sponsored by the Lambeth Conference and the Lutheran World Federation

Meetings

I. Oxford, England, September 7-11, 1970
Authority and Freedom[1]

II. Løgumkloster, Denmark, March 29 - April 2, 1971
The Nature and Mission of the Church

III. Lantana, Florida, USA, January 2-7, 1972
The Ministry

IV. Pullach nr. Munich, Germany, April 4-8, 1972
Word and Sacrament; Final Report

The Context. Without having a detailed and adequate knowledge of each other, Anglicans and Lutherans nevertheless felt always that there were no grave theological differences standing between them. The frequent encounters between the two communions within the ecumenical movement and the informal conversations between individual Anglican and Lutheran Churches revealed, however, a distinct difference in the doctrine and form of the ministry and differing attitudes towards the role of theology and confession, Scripture and tradition, spirituality, etc. These differences became decisive issues when Anglican and Lutheran Churches in recent times met one another in church union negotiations.

---

[1] For each meeting the principal theme and occasionally the various topics included on the agenda are indicated.

Background. The impetus for this dialogue was mainly provided by the church union negotiations in South India and East Africa. Here the theological and ecclesiological problems at stake (especially the different concepts of the ministry) could obviously not be satisfactorily settled at the purely local level. They seemed to have implications which directly affected the relationship of the negotiating churches to their respective world organisations - to which they felt attached by reason of a common confession or a common church order.

History. In 1963 the Commission on World Mission of the Lutheran World Federation (LWF) passed a resolution requesting the setting-up of a study committee for the preparation of worldwide Anglican-Lutheran conversations, especially with respect to the Lutheran and Anglican concepts of the ministry and episcopacy. This proposal received the endorsement of the LWF Commission on Theology that same year. After further deliberations at the Helsinki Assembly of the LWF in 1963 and by the Executive Committee and the two Commissions of the LWF during the following years, a special consultation of the LWF in preparation for the conversations was held in Loccum, Germany, in October 1966.

Contacts with the Archbishop of Canterbury resulted in the appointment of an ad hoc Anglican-Lutheran Committee which met in Berlin (November 1967) and drafted a "Memorandum" proposing that the Lambeth Conference and the Executive Committee of the LWF authorise "the appointment of a representative 'Anglican-Lutheran Commission'". The sub-committee of the Lambeth Conference (1968) which dealt with the proposals of the Memorandum recommended the acceptance of the initial initiative of the LWF and accordingly the holding of Anglican-Lutheran conversations. This recommendation was accepted by the Lambeth Conference. The Executive Committee of the LWF, meeting shortly afterwards, consideredthe Memorandum in its turn and took the same decision.

Terms of Reference. In the Memorandum of 1967 it was stated that the "Anglican-Lutheran Commission" should

"(a) conduct a world-wide Anglican-Lutheran dialogue;
(b) consider other contacts and areas for practical cooperation;
(c) report regularly to their respective appropriate authorities".

This was accepted by the Lambeth Conference and by the LWF Executive Committee in 1968.

In addition, the sub-committee of the Lambeth Conference, taking up a suggestion of the Memorandum, recommended that the "conversations should begin by discussing the general mission of the Church in the world and only afterwards proceed to questions of doctrine and order, though major issues should be faced as soon as possible". The Lambeth Conference decided also that these conversations "should be held on four occasions over a two-year period".

Appointment and Composition of the Group. The Anglican delegation was appointed by the Archbishop of Canterbury in consultation with the Primates and Metropolitans of the Churches of the Anglican Communion in 1969, and the Lutheran delegation by the officers of the LWF in the same year.

Among the nine Lutheran and ten Anglican participants (including the two secretaries) were eight bishops or church presidents, nine professors of theology, one archdeacon and one church official. Ten of the participants came from Europe, six from North America and three from Asia and Africa. Both groups represented different positions of theological thinking and church life within the two confessional families. The World Council of Churches had appointed a permanent observer (a Presbyterian).

Characteristics of the Conversations. From the outset the commission set as its aim to examine the conditions for "mutual recognition and fellowship between the two churches" in the context of the general mission of the Church to the world. To provide an adequate theological basis, the commission explored five broad areas: sources of authority, the Church, the word and the sacraments, apostolic ministry, worship. The findings of successive meetings were summed up in provisional statements and then revised and integrated into a formal report, released in 1972. The report also includes "personal notes" by the two co-chairmen, explaining its highlights in the language germane to each of the two communions.

The document registers substantial agreements on the subjects explored, with certain qualifications concerning the historic episcopate. The existing differences are held to reflect differing historical developments and thus not to be ultimately divisive. The historic episcopate remains a controversial issue (as it does within the

Anglican Communion itself), but the gap between the differing positions has been greatly narrowed down by a common acknowledgement that apostolic mission and episcopacy are more basic and inclusive realities than apostolic succession in the form of the historic episcopate. "Thus apostolicity pertains first to the gospel and then to the ministry of word and sacrament ..." and "the succession of apostolicity through time is guarded and given contemporary expression in and through a wide variety of means, activities and institutions ..." Both communions are exercising the essential function of "oversight", though in varying forms. It is concluded that the beliefs of each tradition in the matter, while now in part incompatible, nevertheless do not prevent mutual recognition.

In consequence the report urges a mutual recognition among Anglican and Lutheran churches as "a true communion of Christ's body possessing a truly apostolic ministry". Although the Anglican participants cannot foresee "full integration of ministries (full communion) apart from the historic episcopate", this does not in their view preclude increasing intercommunion. The Lutherans on the other hand insist that their churches are free to accept the historic episcopate, but it "should not become a necessary condition for interchurch relations or church union".

Co-chairmen

The Rt. Rev. Ronald R. Williams, Bishop of Leicester, England (Anglican)

The Most Rev. Gunnar Hultgren, Archbishop emeritus of Uppsala, Sweden (Lutheran)

Co-Secretaries

The Rev. Canon R.M. Jeffery, London, England

The Rev. Canon M.M. Hamond Moore, The Archbishop of Canterbury's Counsellors on Foreign Relations, Palace Court, 222 Lambeth Road, London SE1 7LB, England

Prof. Dr. Günther Gassmann, Institute for Ecumenical Research, 8, rue Gustave-Klotz, 67 Strasbourg, France

An official Joint Working Group, with three members and secretaries from each side, was commissioned by the Anglican Consultative Council and the LWF Executive Committee in 1973 to evaluate the responses of the churches and to further the implementation of the practical recommendations in the report, including increased intercommunion. This group will start its work in 1975.

Publications

Anglican-Lutheran International Conversations. The Report of the conversations 1970-1972 authorised by the Lambeth Conference and the Lutheran World Federation. London: S.P.C.K., 1973. Price 40p. Also in Lutheran World XIX, 4, 1972, 387-399; Lutherische Rundschau XXII, 1972, 505-525.

Lutheran-Episcopal Dialogue: A Progress Report. Cincinnati, Ohio: Forward Movement Press, 1972. Price 50¢. (Includes also the report of the International Dialogue.)

2. Anglican-Old Catholic ....A-OC

"Anglican-Old Catholic Theological Conferences" sponsored by the Anglican and the Old Catholic Communions

Meetings

I. Berne, Switzerland, April 10-12, 1972
Exchange of Information about Interchurch Dialogues in which Both Churches are Engaged

II. Oxford, England, June 25-29, 1973
The Meaning of Full Communion

III. Lucerne, Switzerland, September 14-18, 1974
On the Way to the Unity of the Church: The Bonn Agreement as Now Understood

The so-called Bonn Agreement of 1931 put the stamp of official approval on the long standing fraternal contacts between the Anglican and the Old Catholic Communions. By this agreement "Each Communion recognizes the catholicity and independence of the other, and maintains its own" and agrees "to permit members of the other Communion to participate in the Sacraments". This is the background for the official decision taken in 1971 to coordinate the Anglican and the Old Catholic dialogues with Orthodox, Roman Catholic and Lutheran partners and to spell out the implications for the Bonn Agreement. Like the Joint Committee between the LWF and the WARC, this new venture thus represents another attempt to establish interconnecting links between two confessional families and thereby multiply the fruitfulness of the dialogues.

The Anglican participants are appointed by the Archbishop of Canterbury and the Old Catholic ones by the International Bishops' Conference. No formal commission has yet been constituted but a steering committee is being set up to shape further plans, including preparations for the next conference to be held in September 1977 on the subject of Authority.

3. Anglican-Orthodox ....A-O

"The Commission for Anglican-Orthodox Joint Doctrinal Discussions" sponsored by the Anglican Consultative Council and the Inter-Orthodox Commission for the Dialogue with the Anglicans

In the early 1960s, the Anglican and Orthodox authorities agreed to resume the series of consultations which had been initiated in 1930. At the Third Pan-Orthodox Conference at Rhodes in 1964 it was decided to establish an Inter-Orthodox Theological Commission for the Dialogue with the Anglicans, composed of delegated representatives of the various Orthodox Churches. The Commission has held four meetings.[1]

I. Belgrade, Yugoslavia, September 1-15, 1966

The conference drew up a detailed list of four categories of possible subjects for discussion: (1) subjects on which agreement has been reached between the Anglican and some of the Orthodox Churches; (2) subjects that have been examined but on which no full agreement has as yet been reached; (3) subjects that have not been fully examined; (4) subjects which must be examined immediately at the opening of the dialogue with the Anglicans.

Whereas earlier Anglican conversations had been conducted with various local churches separately, the policy was now laid down "that only Pan-Orthodox, and not bilateral[2], conversations on the subjects of the second, third and fourth categories will take place with the Anglicans".

---

1 The first full meeting of the Joint Commission took place only in 1973, but since in this case the exceptionally thorough preparations on both sides form an integral part of the proceedings, they deserve full recording here.

2 That is, involving individual Orthodox Churches.

II. Chambésy/Geneva, Switzerland, October 1-7, 1970

The agenda focussed on the subjects which had been listed in the fourth category at the Belgrade Conference: (1) the manner in which the Anglican Church conceives of its union in faith with the Orthodox Church; (2) whether union of the Anglican Church with the Orthodox Church is possible, having regard to the intercommunion on which the Anglican Church has decided and is now practising with certain Lutherans, as well as with the Confessions which took part in the South India Scheme; (3) the manner in which the decisions to be taken in this current dialogue will bind the whole Anglican Communion; and (4) the authority of the Thirty-Nine Articles and of the Book of Common Prayer in the Anglican Communion.

III. Helsinki, Finland, July 7-11, 1971

The subjects discussed were: (1) the Holy Spirit as Interpreter of the Gospel and Life-giver in the Church Today; (2) the Nature of Christ's Redeeming Work in the Cross and the Resurrection; (3) Interpretation of the Anglican Theory of "Comprehensiveness"; (4) Modern Problems in the Anglican Church.

IV. Chambésy/Geneva, Switzerland, September 7-11, 1972

The Orthodox Commission made final plans for the joint meeting of members of both commissions held immediately afterwards.

On its side, the Anglican Commission for Joint Doctrinal Discussions with the Orthodox Church has held two full meetings, apart from regional meetings in 1968 and 1970.

I. Jerusalem, Israel, September 15-19, 1969

The subjects discussed were: Comprehensiveness and the Mission of the Church; the Thirty-Nine Articles; Anglican Understandings of the Holy Eucharist; the <u>filioque</u>; the Minister of the Eucharist. The commission concurred in the proposals set forth by the Orthodox, but recommended the inclusion of two further concerns: (1) a consideration of questions of a pastoral, liturgical and spiritual nature, "so that we may together investigate how our doctrine is expressed in the life and worship of our Churches and in the search for holiness"; and (2) a consideration of the urgent and difficult questions involved in the presentation of the faith in the world today.

II. Haywards Heath, England, July 26-30, 1971

The meeting continued the discussion of the previous subjects, and also prepared a statement outlining the Anglican position in response to the four questions raised by the Orthodox Commission in 1970.

These preliminary consultations on both sides, though independent, were not carried out in complete separation, but involved an intermittent "dialogue by correspondence" in the form of an exchange of information and clarification of uncertain points.

From September 11-14, 1972, Anglican and Orthodox subcommissions met for the first time at Chambésy/Geneva to make final arrangements. The meeting reaffirmed an earlier proposal that the conversations should not be limited to doctrine but include questions of church life and worship as well. It further recommended a broadening of the doctrinal dialogue to include "all the truths of Christian faith, in the hope that, under the guidance of the Holy Spirit, the members will achieve unity of faith".

The first meeting of the full Commission for Anglican-Orthodox Joint Discussions was held at:

Oxford, England, July 6-13, 1973

Comprehensiveness and the Mission of the Church; the Holy Spirit as Interpreter of the Gospel and Giver of Life in the Church Today; the Redemptive Work of Christ on the Cross and in the Resurrection.

As indicated, the group based its deliberations on three introductory papers which had already been considered and revised in the preparatory stage. Considerable progress was noted, especially in the discussion of the redemptive work of Christ, which brought to light the common traditions of the two Churches. With respect to the other subjects, it was felt that the Anglican notion (strange to Orthodoxy) of comprehensiveness and the Orthodox view of the work of the Holy Spirit outside the Church and of the limits of the Church required deeper probing. In addition to these papers, the group discussed the Anglican answers to the four questions previously raised by the Orthodox.

The second full meeting of the joint commission will be held in 1976. Meanwhile three sub-commissions are preparing materials on: (a) Inspiration and Revelation in the Holy Scriptures; (b) The Church as the Eucharistic Community, including the role of the epiclesis in the eucharistic liturgy; the relation between the sacramental body of Christ and the Church as the mystical body of Christ; the apostolicity of the ordained ministry and the catholicity of faith as a ground for eucharistic communion; and (c) the Authority of the Councils, including the relationship between the Scriptures and the decisions of the Councils; the problem of the infallibility of the Councils; the filioque; and the dogmatic status of the Seventh Council.

Co-Chairmen

The Rt. Rev. A.K. Runcie, Bishop of St. Albans, England (Anglican)
The Most Rev. Athenagoras, Archbishop of Thyateira, London (Orthodox)

Co-Secretaries

The Rev. Canon M.M. Hamond Moore, The Archbishop of Canterbury's Counsellors on Foreign Relations, Palace Court, 222 Lambeth Road, London SE1 7LB, England
The Rev. Fr. Kallistos Ware, 15 Staverton Road, Oxford OX2 6X2, England

Publications

Position papers and reports on the meetings have appeared in such publications as Het Christelijk Oosten, Eastern Churches News Letter, Episkepsis, The Greek Orthodox Theological Review, The Journal of the Moscow Patriarchate, One in Christ, Sobornost, Theology, St. Vladimir's Theological Quarterly.

4. Anglican-Roman Catholic .... A-RC

"Anglican-Roman Catholic International Commission (ARCIC)" sponsored by the Anglican Consultative Council and the Vatican Secretariat for Promoting Christian Unity

Meetings

I. Windsor, England, January 9-15, 1970
Fundamentals of the Faith; Authority; Church, Intercommunion and Ministry; Eucharist

II. Venice, Italy, September 21-28, 1970
Church and Ministry; Church and Authority; Church and

Eucharist; the Relation of Men and Women; the Making of Moral Judgments

III. Windsor, England, September 1-8, 1971
The Eucharist - Joint Statement

IV. Gazzada, Italy, August 30 - September 7, 1972
Ministry and Ordination

V. Canterbury, England, August 28 - September 6, 1973
Ministry and Ordination - Joint Statement

VI. Grottaferrata/Rome, Italy, August 27 - September 5, 1974
Authority

Background. Vatican II certainly opened up new opportunities for better relations between the Roman Catholic Church and the Churches of the Anglican Communion, but it was more specifically the visit of the Archbishop of Canterbury to Pope Paul VI in March 1966 which led to the inauguration of an official dialogue between the two communions. In their "Common Declaration" of March 24, 1966, the Pope and the Archbishop gave thanks to Almighty God for the new atmosphere of Christian fellowship between the two Churches, and declared their intention to inaugurate a serious dialogue.

History. It was as a result of this Declaration that a Joint Preparatory Commission was set up. This commission, composed of twenty-five members, held three meetings: Gazzada (Italy), January 1967, Huntercombe Manor (England), September 1967, and Malta, January 1968. The report of the Joint Preparatory Commission (usually called the "Malta Report") was submitted to the Archbishop of Canterbury and the Pope. It was printed ("strictly confidential") in preparation for the Lambeth Conference 1968 ("Documents on Anglican-Roman Catholic Relations"). The report contains an outline of basic agreements between the two Churches and makes a number of recommendations. These include such practical suggestions as joint use of church buildings, sharing facilities for theological education, joint worship services, and cooperation in different fields. Further, a series of controversial and important theological questions, such as theology of marriage and mixed marriages, intercommunion, recognition of ministries, ecclesiology, and authority, were proposed as topics for serious theological examination. Finally it was recommended that the Preparatory Commission be replaced by a Permanent Joint Commission, to which two joint sub-commissions should be attached, the one dealing with the question of intercommunion and the related matters of Church and ministry, the other taking up the question of authority.

In a letter to the Archbishop of Canterbury (June 1968), Cardinal Bea informed the Archbishop that the Pope had accepted the proposals of the Malta Report, especially with regard to the appointment of a Permanent Joint Commission. In August 1968, the Lambeth Conference recommended "the setting up of a Permanent Joint Commission, for which the Anglican delegation should be chosen by the Lambeth Consultative Body (or its successor) and be representative of the Anglican Communion as a whole". The new commission, later renamed "Anglican/Roman Catholic International Commission", had its first session in Windsor in January 1970.

Terms of Reference. In the letter of Cardinal Bea as well as in the Report of the Lambeth Conference the broad theological topics enumerated in the Malta Report were recommended for study by the new commission or its sub-commissions. The Lambeth Report added that these future conversations should be conducted with due regard to the multiplicity of conversations in progress with other churches. Moreover, there should be close contact and mutual exchange of information with Anglican-Roman Catholic conversations in different parts of the world.

Appointment and Composition of the Group. The Anglican delegation was appointed by the Archbishop of Canterbury in consultation with the Primates and Metropolitans of the Churches of the Anglican Communion. The Roman Catholic delegation was appointed by the Secretariat for Promoting Christian Unity. Among the nine Anglican and nine Roman Catholic members there are six bishops, ten professors of theology, one (lay) professor of history, and one church official. Ten members come from Europe, six from North America, one from Australia and one from Africa. There are two secretaries, usually a few consultants and regularly an observer from the World Council of Churches. The members of the commission represent different theological positions within the two churches.

Characteristics of the Work. After an initial introductory discussion, the commission concentrated its ensuing work on three main topics: Eucharist, Ministry, and Authority. From the beginning the commission declared its intention to work towards the organic unity of the two Churches. An attempt was made to include an examination of moral questions in the second meeting, but after some discussion the group returned to the main topics. The work of the commission has so far been marked by a diversity of positions (even within the two delegations), and a way to more significant agreements has been sought by means of intensified and long discussion. The commission has also kept in close contact with Anglican-Roman Catholic conversations in other parts of the world. In order to give as much publicity as possible to the work of the commission and to encourage the cooperation of wider circles in both Churches, the preliminary reports of the September 1970 meeting as well as the later joint statements on Eucharist and Ministry were widely disseminated.

The September 1971 meeting achieved a remarkable breakthrough. It not only considered a more preliminary and moderate aim, called "limited communion", but also devoted its work in groups entirely to the question of the eucharist, using the draft of a preparatory sub-commission. A consensus was reached on the two critical issues which had been points of dissension between the two communions: affirmation of the real presence, without using substantialist categories, and an equally firm insistence on the "once-for-all" of Christ's sacrifice. The eucharistic "anamnesis" is understood as making this sacrifice effective in the present, and inviting the believers' self-offering in faith. The result of this effort was an Agreed Statement on Eucharistic Doctrine. "We believe that we have reached substantial agreement on the doctrine of the Eucharist ... It is our hope that in view of the agreement which we have reached ... this doctrine will no longer constitute an obstacle to the unity we seek." The statement was published at the end of 1971 after permission had been granted by the Pope and the Archbishop of Canterbury.

The meeting in September 1971 also welcomed a proposal for a large-scale sociological study on attitudes, etc. of Roman Catholics and Anglicans towards one another.

The next two meetings were devoted to the question of the ministry, a small subcommission again preparing an outline. The so-called Canterbury Statement on Ministry and Ordination, published in December 1973, marks another major milestone in Anglican-Roman Catholic relations. These relations have long been vitiated by the debate around the Bull "Apostolicae Curae" (1896), in which Leo XIII declared the Anglican orders to be "absolutely null and utterly void". It was inevitable that the question of how to overcome this stumbling block should arise, but the report makes merely a passing reference to the problem without even mentioning the Bull and simply concludes that new developments in thinking about the ministry have put the issue in a new context.

Instead of continuing the old debate in its established terms, the commission adopts a fresh approach by exploring the common ground of beliefs about the nature of the Church's ministry. "Agreement on the nature of Ministry is prior to the consideration of the mutual recognition of ministries." Thus the report discusses the unity and diversity of ministerial services in the New Testament Church, the distinctive role and function of the ordained ministry in relation to the common priesthood of all believers, the divinely inspired emergence of the three-fold pattern of order, the meaning of ordination and of apostolic succession. It is the conviction of the commission that, in its consensus on essential matters, "both Anglican and Roman Catholic will recognise their own faith". The commission is now engaged in a similar investigation of the thorniest subject of all - the shape of authority in a united church, including a consideration of the Petrine office and its functions.

More deliberately and extensively than any other bilateral dialogue, the Anglican-Roman Catholic one has generated discussion of its statements throughout the two world communions at national and sometimes parish levels, and its work has greatly benefited from the volume of reactions received. A number of church bodies have responded officially. Joint dialogue groups are sharing in this work of reception and co-operation in an impressive range of countries: Australia, Belgium, Canada, East Africa, France, Ireland, Japan, Malawi, New Zealand, Papua New Guinea, Scotland, South Pacific, USA, Wales[1].

Co-Chairmen

The Rt. Rev. H.R. McAdoo, Bishop of Ossory, Ferns and Leighlin (Anglican)

The Rt. Rev. Alan C. Clark, Bishop of Northampton, Elmham (Roman Catholic)

---

1 See Colin Davey, "Report on the Current Work of National A/RC Dialogues and A/RC Relations in the Countries Concerned 1972-73", One in Christ X, 1, 1974, 71-85. Some of the national dialogues are reported below in chapter II B.

Co-Secretaries

The Rev. Colin Davey, since 1974 the Rev. Christopher Hill, Assistant Chaplain, Archbishop of Canterbury's Counsellors on Foreign Relations, Palace Court, 222 Lambeth Road, London SE1 7LB, England

The Rt. Rev. Mgr. W.A. Purdy, Staff Member, Secretariat for Promoting Christian Unity, 00120 Vatican City, Vatican

Publications

"The Venice Conversations" (i.e. reports of the September 1970 meeting), Theology LXXIV, February 1971, 49-67; The Catholic Mind, April 1971, One in Christ VII, 2-3, 1971, 256-276

Agreed Statement on Eucharistic Doctrine. London: S.P.C.K., 1972; ARC-DOC I, 1972, pp. 47-50; also published, for example, in the January 1972 issues of One in Christ, Theology, The Clergy Review, Documentation Catholique, Okumenische Rundschau, April 1972

Ministry and Ordination: A Statement on the Doctrine of the Ministry Agreed by the Anglican/Roman Catholic International Commission, Canterbury 1973. London: S.P.C.K., 1973. Price 12p. (Appended to the official text is an account of the work of the commission, with bibliographical references to commentaries on the two agreed statements, published by commission members, and to individual papers which have appeared in periodicals); published also, for example, in: One in Christ, Theology, Documentation Catholique, Okumenische Rundschau.

Commentaries on the Eucharist and Ministry statements have been published by three members of the commission: Julian W. Charley, The Anglican/Roman Catholic Agreement on the Eucharist with an Historical Introduction and Theological Commentary, and Agreement on the Doctrine of the Ministry ... with Theological Commentary and 'Notes on Apostolic Succession' (Grove Books, Bramcote, Notts, England); Alan C. Clark, Agreement on the Eucharist: The Windsor Statement with an Introduction and Commentary, and Ministry and Ordination ... The official text, together with introduction and commentary (Catholic Information Office, Avante House, 9 Bridge Street, Pinner, Middlesex, England); and Fr. Herbert Ryan SJ, in Worhip, January 1972 and January 1974.

ARC-DOC I and II. Documents on Anglican/Roman Catholic Relations, compiled by the Bishops' Committee on Ecumenical and Interreligious Affairs, in co-operation with the Joint Commission on Ecumenical

Relations, 1972 and 1973. United States Catholic Conference, Publications Office,1312 Massachusetts Avenue, N.W., Washington, D.C. 20005. $ 1.00 each.
Alan C. Clark and Colin Davey, eds., Anglican-Roman Catholic Dialogue: The Work of the Preparatory Commission. London/New York/Toronto: Oxford University Press, 1974. UK £1.00. (The volume contains relevant reports and a selection of papers.)

5. Baptist-Reformed ....B-R

"Baptist-Reformed Theological Conversations" sponsored by the Baptist World Alliance and the World Alliance of Reformed Churches

Meetings

I. Rüschlikon, Switzerland, December 14-17, 1974
The Distinctive Elements of the Baptist and Reformed Heritages Today; The Baptist and Reformed Perspectives in Understanding the Gospel

Background. The question of an official dialogue was first raised at the 1969 meeting of the Executive Committee of the WARC. Because of the forthcoming union with the International Congregational Council effected the following year, the matter was deferred to 1971 when the Executive Committee, endorsing the idea, requested the Department of Theology to explore the possibilities further. The ensuing consultations with Baptist leaders resulted in a joint proposal to launch a dialogue, which, for organisational and financial reasons, would initially take the form of a pilot study in the European context "without prejudice to other areas of the world". This staff proposal was approved by the executive committees of both world bodies in the summer of 1972, and the following year a definite plan was adopted.

As factors motivating a dialogue, the planning memorandum notes the rootage of both traditions in a common history running back through the Reformation period to the New Testament, the great influence of Calvin and Zwingli on Baptist thinking, and, on the other side, the mounting concern in many Reformed churches about the doctrine and practice of baptism. Both traditions share "a common emphasis on the normative source of Holy Scripture, the witness to Jesus Christ as Saviour and Lord, and the sovereignty of grace". The doctrines of baptism and of church structures are seen as the principal areas of tension.

Aim and Organisation. The initial aim is twofold: to provide the member churches with information on the present theological positions of the two traditions with a view to overcoming the still existing differences; and to explore the respective convictions about baptism "in a way which illuminates their relation to, and consequential nature within, a total understanding of theology and of the Church's task today".

The study will be carried out by a Joint Commission, composed of three permanent representatives, together with one ad hoc consultant and one staff member, from each side. After a series of four yearly meetings, a full report will be submitted for evaluation by the executive committees of the two world bodies.

Co-Chairmen

Dr. Rudolf Thaut, Vice-President, Baptist World Alliance, Hamburg, Germany, (Baptist)

Professor Martin Cressey, Cambridge, England (Reformed)

Co-Secretaries

Dr. C. Ronald Goulding, Associate Secretary, Baptist World Alliance, 4 Southampton Row, London WC1B 4AB, England

The Rev. Richmond Smith, Secretary of the Department of Theology, WARC, 150, route de Ferney, 1211 Geneva 20, Switzerland.

6. Congregational-Presbyterian (ICI-WARC)..........................C-P

Merger Conversations between the International Congregational Council (ICI) and the World Alliance of Reformed Churches Holding the Presbyterian Order (WARC)

Background. On August 20, 1970, at the General Uniting Council held in Nairobi, Kenya, the International Congregational Council and the World Alliance of Reformed Churches Holding the Presbyterian Order formally united to constitute the World Alliance of Reformed Churches (Presbyterian and Congregational). This is the first instance of bilateral dialogues leading to a merger of two world confessional families as such, and it thus represents a category of its own in this Survey.

In the union documents a number of factors are indicated which contributed to this development. The two bodies were increasingly overlapping and interlocking. At the national level, numerous

Congregational and Presbyterian churches had joined in united churches or were looking toward closer fellowship or full union. Four united churches possessed membership in both bodies. The World Council of Churches provided another platform of rapprochement as 61 of the Alliance's 101 members and 17 of the International Congregational Council's 21 members were members also of the World Council of Churches. Both groups had increasingly become aware of their historical affinities and their common doctrinal and social emphases deriving from the Geneva Reformation.

History of the Merger. After some years of informal discussions, definite conversations with a view to merger were initiated in 1960. An extensive programme of study and consultation was developed having as its aim "(a) a fuller understanding of past relationship between Congregationalists and (in particular) Presbyterians, and this to the end that the issues which divided them be re-evaluated in the light of present relations of our two families of Churches, (b) an exposition of such essential unity in faith and ecclesiology as exists between us ..., (c) a common understanding of our joint ecumenical responsibility as Reformed Churches". In 1964 a joint committee was officially appointed to prepare proposals for closer relationships, and two years later a statement of "Principles", proposals for union, and a draft constitution were sent to the member churches which overwhelmingly voted approval.

Characteristics of the New Alliance. The merger was greatly facilitated by the broad commonality of beliefs and practices existing among the affiliated churches and by the fact that neither body required "a strictly defined confessional position of its members ... Nor is membership based on a supposed consensus, except in the most general sense ... The aims of both bodies are not to uphold an historic confessional outlook or polity, but to serve within the ecumenical movement as a whole by providing a place where Churches of like traditions may examine these traditions together and exercise their common witness to the Gospel." This common stance includes a conflation of classic Congregational and Reformed emphases: the headship of Jesus Christ, the localness of the Church, a corporate *episcope* within the Church with government by covenant and constitution and stress on conciliar processes at all levels, and the insistence that "the mission of every 'local' Christian community is defined first of all by Christ's ministry to the whole world ..." ("Principles", nos. 11 & 13).

The Alliance takes its stand "within the one Church, Catholic and Reformed", and the Constitution's Article II provides the best commentary on this intention:

> Any Church which accepts Jesus Christ as Lord and Saviour; holds the Word of God given in the Scripture of the Old and New Testaments to be the supreme authority in matters of faith and life; acknowledges the need for the continuing reformation of the Church catholic; whose position in faith and evangelism is in general agreement with that of the historic Reformed confessions, recognising that the Reformed tradition is a biblical, evangelical and doctrinal ethos, rather than any narrow and exclusive definition of faith and order, shall be eligible for membership. United Churches which share this understanding of the nature and calling of the Church shall be eligible for membership.

Publications

The merger documents are on file in the offices of the World Alliance of Reformed Churches in Geneva.

7. Lutheran-Reformed (LWF-WARC)................................L-R

"The Lutheran-Reformed Joint Committee" sponsored by the Lutheran World Federation and the World Alliance of Reformed Churches

First Series

Meetings

I. Geneva, Switzerland, January 28-29, 1970
The Continuing Dialogue between the two World Bodies; "Concord" as a Model of Church Fellowship; the Practical Implications of a Theological Consensus; the Role of the two World Organisations in the Life of the Younger Churches; a Closer Working Relationship

II. Geneva, February 3-5, 1971
The Present Relationship between Lutheran and Reformed Churches; the Mutual Understanding of the two Confessional Bodies of their Ecumenical Commitment and their Role in the Future Development of the Ecumenical Movement; the Attitude of the two Confessional Bodies towards the Idea of a "Universal Council"

III. Basle, Switzerland, November 14-16, 1972
The Relationship between the Central Affirmation of the Christ-Event as Justification and the Social Commission of

the Church; Evaluation of the Confessional Approach in the Search for the Unity of the Church

IV. Cartigny/Geneva, July 17-21, 1973

Joint Statement on the Relationship between the Proclamation of the Gospel and the Social Task of the Church; the Relationship between Koinonia and Doctrinal Consensus; the Implications of the Leuenberg Agreement; the Role and Purpose of Confessional Families

Background. The establishment of a Joint Committee is to be seen as the logical fruit of several convergent developments in recent years. The historical and confessional closeness of these two branches of the Reformation movement is being rediscovered. Together with the WCC Commission on Faith and Order, the Lutheran World Federation and the World Alliance of Reformed Churches jointly initiated the interchurch conversations in Europe resulting in the Leuenberg Agreement on a regional interchurch fellowship. In the larger ecumenical movement, Lutherans and Reformed constantly observe that the differences between them "turn out to be opposition within a common position which is not to be found in the same way between other churches".

In 1967, the LWF and WARC set up a joint committee to evaluate the conversations held in Europe and North America. At its first meeting in Geneva in January 1968, this ad hoc committee spelled out its conviction that "the time has already overtaken the Lutheran and Reformed Churches when they must draw closer together in the ecumenical movement both in order to contribute to it as fully as possible the evangelical heritage of the Reformation and to learn from all the other churches how they may best serve the Gospel in the modern world". It recommended setting up a permanent Lutheran-Reformed Committee, and this proposal was subsequently approved by the executive agencies of both bodies.

Purpose. The main task of the committee is to further the theological consensus between Lutheran and Reformed Churches and to seek ways and means of achieving a closer working relationship between the two world families.

Appointment and Composition of the Group. Appointed by the executive committees of the two world bodies, the committee consists of six members from each side, comprising church leaders and theological professors. An unusually high proportion (five of twelve) are drawn from the Third World.

Work. Under its general mandate, the committee has devoted its meetings to the subjects listed above, usually in pursuance of specific assignments by the two executive committees, to which it submits annual reports. Thus in 1974, the committee was requested to focus on three concerns: to study the ecclesiological and theological implications of the Leuenberg Agreement, with an evaluation of the responses of the churches involved; to confer with the various Lutheran-Reformed dialogue groups concerning a joint examination of the implications of the bilaterals at regional and world levels; and to continue the study of the concept of a universal council.

Co-Chairmen

The Rt. Rev. Dr. Friedrich Hübner, Kiel, Germany (Lutheran)

The Rev. Dr. Jacques Rossel, President of the Basle Mission, Basle, Switzerland (Reformed)

Secretaries

Dr. Peder Højen, Secretariat for Interconfessional Research, LWF, Geneva

The Rev. Richmond Smith, Department of Theology, WARC, Geneva

Second Series

Meeting

I_2 Strasbourg, France, March 17-21, 1975

A new committee, with partly different membership and mandate, is scheduled to begin its work in March 1975.

Co-Chairmen

The Rev. Prof. Dr. Andreas Aarflot, Oslo, Norway (Lutheran)

The Rev. Dr. Jacques Rossel, President of the Basle Mission, Basle, Switzerland (Reformed)

Co-Secretaries

Dr. Daniel F. Martensen, Secretariat for Interconfessional Research, LWF, Geneva

The Rev. Richmond Smith, Department of Theology, WARC, Geneva

8. Lutheran-Reformed-Roman Catholic .... L-R-RC

"Joint Roman Catholic/Lutheran/Reformed Study Commission on 'The Theology of Marriage and the Problem of Mixed Marriages'"

Meetings

I. Strasbourg, France, November 23-26, 1971
Marriage as a Common Human Reality

II. Madrid, Spain, December 4-9, 1972
Sexuality and Anthropology in Contemporary Thought; The Sacramentality of Marriage

III. Basle, Switzerland, October 22-27, 1973
Indissolubility of Marriage

IV. Strasbourg, France, December 2-7, 1974
Indissolubility: The Distinctive Approaches of the Christian Traditions with Regard to Broken Marriages

Background. The question of mixed marriages has been and still remains one of the most sensitive points of friction between the Roman Catholic Church and other communions because of the canonical requirements concerning valid marriage and the upbringing of the children. As these requirements pose fundamental questions about the nature of the Church and the theology of marriage and family life, it was natural that the problem should arise also in the bilateral dialogues. In some it appears as one topic among several on the agenda, in other instances it is the sole object of a joint commission appointed to review pastoral practices in light of the improving ecumenical climate. The Roman Catholic-Lutheran-Reformed commission may be taken as a representative example of the latter. In its composition, it moreover illustrates a growing trend to regard kindred communions - in this case Lutheran and Reformed - as one partner in a bilateral dialogue, thereby avoiding wasteful duplication.

History. The Roman Catholic-Lutheran Working Group which met twice in Strasbourg (August 1965 and April 1966) proposed not only a study commission on "The Gospel and the Church", but also a study commission on "The Theology of Marriage and the Problem of Mixed Marriages". Because of certain developments within the Catholic Church (the Episcopal Synod in 1967 and the Encyclical "Humanae Vitae" of July 1968), the creation of such a commission was deferred. In order to prepare for the dialogue, the Executive Committee of the LWF in 1968 and the officers of the LWF in January 1969 invited the World Alliance of Reformed Churches to be associated with the LWF in "... a joint consultation between Reformed and Lutherans to study preparations for a possible joint dialogue with the Roman Catholic Church on the theology of marriage and the problem of mixed marriages". The Executive Committee of the WARC in 1969 responded positively to this invitation and in November 1969 and March 1970 two consultations were held at Cartigny/Geneva. A third consultation took place in Rome in December 1970, now involving representatives of the LWF and the WARC as well as representatives of the Roman Catholic Church. Proposals were worked out concerning the programme and the practical implementation of the future dialogue.

Terms of Reference. A three year period (1971-73) with four meetings and a commission with six permanent members from each side (i.e. six LWF/WARC and six Roman Catholic representatives) were proposed. The main subjects for discussion were to be: (1) Marriage as a common human reality, (2) A sacramental reality, (3) Indissolubility, and (4) Ecclesiastical regulations. At the conclusion of the three year period a final report would be produced designed for widespread diffusion after submission to the authorities on each side.

Appointment and Composition of the Group. The three delegations were appointed by the Executive Committees of the LWF and the WARC and by the Secretariat for Promoting Christian Unity. The whole group consists of four lay people, including three women, and twelve theologians (four professors and eight pastors or church officials). All participants, except one Asian, come from Europe or North America.

Work of the Commission. Conscious of the cultural and social diversity of forms of marriage, the group started with a psychological, sociological and religious analysis of the contemporary marriage crisis. Against this background, it sought to take hold of the universal characteristics and criteria of marriage. The discussion of its sacramentality led back to the rupture at the Reformation time between conflicting understandings of grace and sacrament; however, a deeper reflection on the christological foundation of the means of grace revealed that many of the traditional differences were merely verbal. On the matter of indissolubility, the participants unanimously affirmed "the permanence and lifelong character of marriage ... on the ground of the Christian Gospel in the gift of Christ and his grace", but the sharp divergences on the meaning of indissolubility and on divorce and remarriage will require further study. A shared pastoral responsibility for broken marriages was advocated.

The reports of the successive meetings have not been made public, but will be incorporated in an overall report scheduled to appear in 1976.

Co-Chairmen

Prof. Dr. Dietrich Rössler, Tübingen, Federal Republic of Germany (Lutheran)

Dr. Rachel Henderlite, Austin, Texas, USA (Reformed)

Mrs. Jacqueline Stuyt, London, England (Roman Catholic)

Co-Secretaries

Prof. Dr. Harding Meyer, Institute for Ecumenical Research, 8, rue Gustave-Klotz, 67 Strasbourg, France

The Rev. Richmond Smith, Department of Theology, WARC, 150 route de Ferney, 1211 Geneva 20, Switzerland

The Rev. Pierre de Contenson, Secretariat for Promoting Christian Unity, 00120 Vatican City, Vatican

9. Lutheran-Roman Catholic ....L-RC

"The Joint Lutheran/Roman Catholic Study Commission on 'The Gospel and the Church'"

First Series

Meetings

I. Zürich, Switzerland, November 26-30, 1967
The Gospel and the Church

II. Båstad, Sweden, September 15-19, 1968
World and Church under the Gospel

III. Nemi, Italy, May 4-8, 1969
Structures of the Church

IV. Cartigny/Geneva, Switzerland, February 22-26, 1970
Gospel and Canon Law

V. Malta, February 21-25, 1971
Preparation of a Final Report

Background. Though the traditional controversial questions between Catholics and Lutherans are still of concern, they appear now in a different perspective because of theological developments in both traditions, the emergence of the modern world view and new insights in natural science, historical research, and biblical exegesis.
Vatican II strengthened and encouraged already existing theological interchanges between the two communions and opened up a variety of new

contacts in different areas. The report of the Working Group (see below) states that "special and official relations are necessary between the Roman Catholic Church and the Lutheran Churches. The common origin of both Churches and the particular history of their relations to each other account for the specific responsibility which they acknowledge for each other".

History. The contacts between the Council fathers and theologians on the one hand, and the observers of the Lutheran World Federation on the other which arose during the years of the Council, resulted in a series of conversations between representatives of the Secretariat for Promoting Christian Unity and the Lutheran World Federation. They led to the formation of a "Roman Catholic-Lutheran Working Group" authorised by the Roman Catholic Church in June and by the Lutheran World Federation in July, 1965. This group met twice in Strasbourg (in August, 1965 and in April, 1966).

The group decided that a serious theological dialogue between the two communions should be undertaken and seven problem areas were outlined for the projected conversations. In order to begin this dialogue, the creation of two joint study commissions was suggested, one of which was to take up the theme "The Gospel and the Church" and the other the theme "The Theology of Marriage and the Problem of Mixed Marriages".

In July 1966, the Executive Committee of the Lutheran World Federation approved the joint report of the Working Group. The approval of the report by the Holy See had been announced shortly before. Following these actions the study commission on "The Gospel and the Church" was formed in 1967 and had its first meeting that same year.

Terms of Reference. Apart from proposing the establishment of the two study commissions, it was recommended in the Working Group report that "the respective staffs of the Secretariat for Promoting Christian Unity and the General Secretariat of the Lutheran World Federation shall facilitate the work of these commissions (which can be composed of seven members on each side) and the proper reporting to their respective authorities". It was emphasised that the deep differences between the two churches should not be overlooked. However, the commission was not expected to study the theological controversies of the 16th century as such, but to examine the confessional differences "in the light of contemporary biblical theology and church history as well as of perspectives opened up by the Second Vatican Council".

Appointment and Composition of the Group. The members of the joint study commission on "The Gospel and the Church" were appointed in 1967 by the Secretariat for Promoting Christian Unity and by the LWF officers. Among the seven Roman Catholic and six Lutheran members of the commission there were twelve professors of theology and one bishop. Ten of them were Europeans, three came from the USA. There were usually two advisors on each side and two secretaries present. The Secretariat for Promoting Christian Unity was represented by its President (Cardinal Willebrands) or his deputy; the Lutheran World Federation was represented by its General Secretary or its Associate General Secretary. The World Council of Churches was represented at all meetings by an observer.

Characteristics of the Work. The commission took its departure at the very point where the 16th century schism once occurred, namely, the meaning of the Gospel and its soteriological and ecclesiological consequences. Drawing on contemporary convergences in biblical and theological scholarship - notably the thoroughgoing historical concreteness of both the Gospel and Christian faith and the inherent interrelation of Church and world - the group was able to break open a host of rigid stereotypes, discovering unexpected pearls of agreement. These are recorded in the final report, sometimes called the "Malta Report", released in January 1972. The authority of the Word of God in and over the Church is affirmed. The doctrine of justification and sanctification is reconceived in its original New Testament setting, correcting the polemical misconceptions persisting in Lutheran as well as Roman Catholic teachings.

Similarly, substantial agreements or convergences are registered on the doctrine of the eucharist, especially as regards the understanding of its sacrificial character and the real presence of Christ and, in some measure, also on the ministry and order of the Church. Basic to this is a common acknowledgement of the diversity of charisms and ministries in the New Testament period, and of the historicity of church structures. It is indicative that the commission, reviewing the basic concordances attained, raises the startling question "whether the remaining differences must be viewed as hindrances to church fellowship". As a result the commission recommended that the respective authorities of the two Churches should consider the possibility of an official mutual recognition of ministries and the possibility of allowing acts of intercommunion on specific occasions. On the last point, however, four Roman Catholic members felt obliged to express reservations in separate statements.

Among the disputed theological subjects which will have to be tackled in the light of the consensus discerned in the Gospel, the report mentions the relationship of Gospel, Church, and faith to the sacraments; the relation of nature and grace and of law and Gospel; the magisterium; and Mariology. The stumbling block of papal primacy is touched upon. The Lutherans did not a priori exclude the office of the papacy as a visible sign of the communion of the churches "insofar as it is subordinated to the primacy of the gospel by theological reinterpretation and practical restructuring".

Co-Chairmen

Prof. Dr. Einar Molland, Oslo, Norway (Lutheran)

Prof. Dr. Walter Kasper, Tübingen, Germany (Roman Catholic)

Co-Secretaries

Prof. Dr. Harding Meyer, Institute for Ecumenical Research, 8 rue Gustave-Klotz, 67 Strasbourg, France

Dr. August B. Hasler, then staff member, Secretariat for Promoting Christian Unity, Vatican City, Vatican

Publications

"Report of the Joint Lutheran/Roman Catholic Study Commission on 'The Gospel and the Church'", Lutheran World XIX, 3, 1972; Lutherische Rundschau, July 1972

Harding Meyer, Luthertum und Katholizismus im Gespräch: Ergebnisse und Stand der katholisch-lutherischen Dialoge in den USA und auf Weltebene. (Ökumenische Perspektiven, 3) Frankfurt/Main: Verlag Otto Lembeck, Verlag Josef Knecht, 1973

H. Meyer and A. Hasler, "The Joint Lutheran/Roman Catholic Study Commission on 'The Gospel and the Church'", Lutheran World XVI, 4, 1969, 363-379 and XVIII, 2, 1971, 161-187; Lutherische Rundschau XIX, 1969, 467-488 and XXI, 1971, 208-240

Second Series

"Roman Catholic-Lutheran Joint Working Group"

Meetings

I_2 Geneva, Switzerland, March 20-24, 1973
Survey of Lutheran-Roman Catholic Relations; Programme Planning

II_2 Rome, Italy, January 8-12, 1974
The Ministry in Interconfessional Dialogue; the Theology of Liberation and the Structures of the Church

Following decisions by the Lutheran World Federation and the Vatican Secretariat for Promoting Christian Unity, a second round of discussions was launched in 1973. A new group was set up with different membership and with the following mandate: (a) to promote the reception of the Malta report among the Lutheran Churches and Roman Catholic Episcopal Conferences and to arrange for an evaluation of the responses in 1975; (b) to carry forward the investigation of specific questions arising from the earlier dialogue. These would include the significance of the world for the self-understanding and mission of the Church, the ordering of the ministry with special attention to the episcopal and Petrine ministries and their connection with eucharistic celebration, and the doctrine of the eucharist (which had not been dealt with in the Malta Report).

Co-Chairmen

Prof. Dr. George Lindbeck, Yale Divinity School, New Haven, Conn., USA (Lutheran)

The Most Rèv. Hans L. Martensen, Bishop of Copenhagen, Denmark (Roman Catholic)

Co-Secretaries

Dr. Peder Høјen, LWF, Geneva (1973-74),and (since 1974)
Prof. Dr. Vilmos Vajta, Institute for Ecumenical Research, 8, rue Gustave-Klotz, 67 Strasbourg, France (Lutheran)

Staff member, Secretariat for Promoting Christian Unity, Vatican City, Vatican (Roman Catholic)

10. Methodist-Roman Catholic..............................M-RC

"Joint Commission of the Roman Catholic Church and the World Methodist Council"

First Series

Meetings

I. Ariccia/Rome, Italy, October 15-19, 1967
Mutual Presentations; Sanctification; Practical Cooperation

II. London, England, August 31-September 4, 1968
Eucharist; Authority

III. Rabat, Malta, September 15-19, 1969
Ministry; The Church in the Contemporary World

IV. Lake Junaluska, N.C., USA, August 24-28, 1970
Christian Home and Family

Background. Among the bilateral conversations between the Roman Catholic Church and other churches at the world level, the Methodist-Roman Catholic conversations occupy a special position insomuch as the Methodist churches do not have their origin in a break with the Roman Catholic Church. Therefore, these two communions do not look back at a history of theological controversies and mutual condemnations as is the case of the churches of the Reformation. "From the outset we recognized that Roman Catholic-Methodist dialogue had a singular advantage - there is no history of formal separating between the two churches, none of the historical, emotional problems consequent on a history of schism. When speakers reflected at Ariccia on 'how a Roman Catholic looks at Methodism' and 'how a Methodist looks at Roman Catholicism' (each theme was treated twice, once by an American and once by an Englishman) it was made clear, without any glossing over difficulties, that there were yet more solid grounds for affinity. First among these was the central place held in both traditions by the ideal of personal sanctification, growth in holiness through daily life in Christ"("Report", nos. 6-7). "It is because we have become aware of the exceptional affinities between Roman Catholics and Methodists in that religion of the heart which is the heart of religion, that we believe in the future of Roman Catholic-Methodist relations" (ibid., no. 129). The very fact that Roman Catholics and Methodists are working side by side in many parts of the worlds, and the problems to which this co-existence gives rise, provided a further motive to try and secure better relationships between the two communions.

History. As a result of initiatives taken after Vatican II and decisions made at the World Methodist Council in London, August 1966, a dialogue was inaugurated between groups representing the World Methodist Council and the Roman Catholic Church. This Joint Commission held its first meeting in 1967.

Appointment and Composition of the Group. The group consisted of 20 members, ten from each side. There were six bishops, six professors of theology, the others were church officials or pastors and one Roman Catholic layman. With three exceptions (Vatican, Ireland and Nigeria) all the members came from the USA and Great Britain. Cardinal Willebrands took part in the first two meetings. There were advisors present at all meetings.

Programme. The Joint Commission made it clear from the beginning that it would not limit itself to doctrinal discussions. In addition to traditional questions like authority, eucharist and ministry, present-day problems were taken up (secularisation) and the field of inquiry was extended to spirituality, sanctification and Christian life. A special feature was an agreement on several practical proposals (worked out at the first meeting) for submission to the highest authorities of the Roman Catholic Church and the World Methodist Council. These ranged from exploring possibilities of cooperation in the training of ministers to the possibilities of joint efforts in the fields of world peace, development, family, poverty, race, and immigration. A third development was the organisation of three smaller consultations in 1968, 1969 and 1970 in preparation for the meeting of the full commission.

A "Report of the Joint Commission between the Roman Catholic Church and the World Methodist Council, 1967-1970" was published in 1971 (the "Denver Report"). Here the work of the commission is summarised and evaluated under a number of headings, including "Christianity and the Contemporary World", "Spirituality", "Christian Home and Family", "Eucharist", "Ministry", "Authority" and "The Way Ahead". In this last section, proposals are made for the future. In order to ensure an efficient structuring of the programme, a small joint "central committee" was suggested to take general responsibility for relations between the two communions. Its other areas of concern would include the stimulation of cooperation and dialogue at national and local levels, and the coordination and review of ongoing and future theological dialogues in the perspective of the total ecumenical picture, including other dialogues and church union schemes. The committee would also make sure that proper and effective channels for information and communication are developed with regard to all aspects of Methodist-Roman Catholic relations.

Co-Chairmen

The Rt. Rev. William R. Cannon, Atlanta, Ga., USA (United Methodist)

The Most Rev. John Murphy, Archbishop of Cardiff, Wales (Roman Catholic)

Publication

"Report of the Joint Commission between the Roman Catholic Church and the World Methodist Council, 1967-1970", 1971, Book of Proceedings of the Twelfth World Methodist Conference. Nashville: The Methodist Publishing House, 1972

Second Series

Meetings

I_2 Rome, Italy, December 10-14, 1972
Reorganisation and Planning

II_2 Reuti, Switzerland, October 1-5, 1973
Salvation Today, with Special Reference to the Bangkok Conference

III_2 Venice, Italy, September 30-October 4, 1974
Evangelisation, with Special Reference to the Roman Catholic Episcopal Synod in Rome; Prevenient Grace, Conversion, Salvation Today; Spirituality; Eucharist; Mixed Marriages; Methodist Involvement in Church Union Plans

IV_2 Bristol, England, September 8-12, 1975

A new commission was set up in 1972 to implement the recommendations of the Denver Report, with the commission itself carrying out studies on "Common Witness and Salvation Today", "Authority and Leadership", "Spirituality", "Eucharist and Ministry" (with special consideration of the parallel A-RC statements), "Theology of Marriage and Mixed Marriages". In pursuing these inquiries, the commission is collaborating with national groups in various countries. A comprehensive report will be submitted to the respective authorities in 1976.

Co-Chairmen

The Rt. Rev. William R. Cannon, Atlanta, Ga., USA (United Methodist)

The Rt. Rev. Michael Bowen, Bishop of Arundel and Brighton, England (Roman Catholic)

Co-Secretaries

The Rev. Dr. Lee F. Tuttle, General Secretary, World Methodist Council, Lake Junaluska, N.C. 28745, USA

The Very Rev. Mgr. William A. Purdy, Secretariat for Promoting Christian Unity, Vatican City, Vatican.

11. Old Catholic-Orthodox ....OC-O

"Mixed Orthodox-Old Catholic Commission" sponsored by the Pan-Orthodox Conference and the International Conference of Old Catholic Bishops

During the past hundred years, Old Catholics and Orthodox have been engaged in a long series of conversations, based on doctrinal and liturgical kinship and a common rejection of the papal claims of the First Vatican Council. It is estimated that some ninety attempts at a rapprochement have taken place during that period. Occasionally Orthodox theologians have voiced their personal conviction that there exists no dogmatic obstacle preventing intercommunion and eventual union. The hopes of the Old Catholic Church have not materialised, however. In the Orthodox view, there still remain several critical differences or at least ambiguities, which must be cleared up before any formal recognition can occur.

Following the decision of the Third Pan-Orthodox Conference at Rhodes in 1964, an Inter-Orthodox Commission for the Dialogue with the Old Catholics was established. It has met three times:

I. Belgrade, Yugoslavia, September 1-15, 1966
II. Chambésy/Geneva, Switzerland, October 16-24, 1970
III. Bonn, Federal Republic of Germany, June 22-30, 1971

The parallel International Commission of the Union of Utrecht for the Dialogue between Orthodox and Old Catholics, set up by the International Conference of Old Catholic Bishops, has held one meeting:

Bonn, Federal Republic of Germany, April 19-20, 1971

In response to the desire expressed by the Belgrade Conference for elucidation of divergences that had been noted, the International Conference of Old Catholic Bishops issued three declarations which state the Old Catholic beliefs about Revelation and its traditioning, Church and sacraments, the principle of unity, the filioque clause in the Nicene Creed, and primacy in the Church. Full agreement with the Orthodox position in these matters was claimed. In its subsequent meetings in Chambésy and Bonn, the Orthodox Commission expressed its satisfaction with the orthodoxy of these declarations and pursued its study of questions it felt required deeper study: the teaching of the Old Catholics on the unity of the Church; the canonicity of the Old Catholic hierarchy; the Holy Eucharist as a propitiatory sacrifice; the intercommunion of the Old Catholics with other churches; the manner in which the union between the two Churches is conceived. The outcome of the Bonn meeting was a recommendation that the preparations were sufficiently advanced to allow the opening of dialogue between the two commissions, and that the first meeting be held in 1972.

As a final preliminary step the two commissions met at Penteli/Athens, Greece, July 5-14, 1973, first separately and then jointly, to conclude the preparations and to outline a programme for the forthcoming official dialogue. It will include subjects requiring further clarification in six areas: theology, christology, ecclesiology, soteriology, sacramental doctrine, and eschatology. The first two-week meeting of the Mixed Theological Commission, scheduled for July 1975, will be devoted to the first three areas. When the examination of the whole complex of dialogue themes has been completed, the signed documents will be presented to the heads of the local Orthodox and Old Catholic Churches for appraisal and decision.

A major crux in the establishment of a full ecclesial koinonia is likely to be the Orthodox attitude to the (existing or prospective) eucharistic communion of the Old Catholic Church with the Anglican and Roman Catholic Churches.

Co-Chairmen

The Rt. Rev. Léon Gauthier, Bishop of the Old Catholic Church in Switzerland, Berne (Old Catholic)

The Most Rev. Irenaios, Metropolitan of Germany, Bonn, Germany (Greek Orthodox)

Publications

"Der Primat in der Kirche", Internationale Kirchliche Zeitschrift 60, 1970, 57-59

"Dokumente zum orthodox-altkatholischen Dialog", ibid. 61, 1971, 65-74; 63, 1973, 188-192

Werner Küppers, "Stand und Perspektiven des altkatholisch-orthodoxen Dialogs", ibid. 62, 1972, 87-117; "Der orthodox-altkatholische Dialog nimmt Gestalt an", ibid. 63, 1973, 182-188

J. Kalogirou, "Der altkatholisch-orthodoxe Dialog", ibid. 60, 1970, 338-347

12. Eastern Orthodox-Oriental Orthodox EO-00

The separation between the Eastern Orthodox and the Oriental Orthodox (the Chalcedonian and the non-Chalcedonian) Churches in the fifth century constitutes the first major split within Christendom. Meeting each other at ecumenical gatherings, the representatives of both ecclesial families have increasingly come to realise their kinship and the need for a fresh effort to heal the ancient schism. As a result, a series of unofficial consultations between theologians from both sides was initiated in 1964.

Meetings

I. Aarhus, Denmark, August 11-15, 1964
The Christological Dogma

II. Bristol, England, July 25-29, 1967
The Manhood and Humanity of Christ; Doctrinal Continuity in the Ancient Councils

III. Geneva, Switzerland, August 16-21, 1970
The Recognition of Councils

IV. Addis Ababa, Ethiopia, January 22-23, 1971
The Anathematisation of Controversial Teachers

These unofficial consultations have indicated four principal themes which require an elucidation: (a) Christology, (b) the role and place of certain councils in the life of the Church, (c) the anathematisation or canonisation of certain controversial teachers in the Church, (d) problems of jurisdiction connected with the manifestations of the unity of the Church at local, regional, and world levels.

On the first subject, the group reached the conclusion that "an agreement exists on the essentials of a common Christology", and on the third also concrete solutions were proposed.

Following a decision of the Fourth Pan-Orthodox Conference in 1968, an Inter-Orthodox Theological Commission for Dialogue with the Oriental Orthodox Churches was set up and met for the first time at Addis Ababa, August 18-28, 1971. Having examined the findings of the unofficial consultations, it concluded that the theological preparations were sufficiently advanced to warrant the initiation of an official dialogue. To this end, it recommended that the Orthodox

Churches invite the Oriental Churches to establish a corresponding commission for joint deliberations, and this was done the following year by the Permanent Commission of the Oriental Orthodox Churches. Two subcommittees, one from each side, met at Penteli/Athens, July 30-August 5, 1973, to project a programme and it was decided to focus the further preparations for the official dialogue on the subject "The Person of Christ according to Orthodox Tradition". The aim would be to establish a "formula of concord", expressing the common Christological faith while avoiding the disputed terms of the ancient church.

Publications

"Unofficial Consultations between Theologians of Eastern Orthodox and Oriental Orthodox Churches, August 11-15, 1964 - Papers and Minutes", The Greek Orthodox Theological Review X, 2, Winter 1964-65, 5-160

"Papers and Discussions between Eastern Orthodox and Oriental Orthodox Theologians - The Bristol Consultation, July 25-29, 1967", ibid.XIII, 2, Fall 1968, 121-320

"The Third and Fourth Consultations between Eastern Orthodox and Oriental Orthodox Theologians - The Geneva Consultation and the Addis Ababa Consultation", ibid. XVI, 1-2, Spring and Fall 1971, 1-259

Articles in Episkepsis (Information Bulletin of the Orthodox Centre of the Ecumenical Patriarchate, Chambésy/Geneva) and Proche Orient Chrétien

13. Pentecostal-Roman Catholic ....Pe-RC

"Pentecostal-Roman Catholic Dialogue" sponsored by the Secretariat for Promoting Christian Unity and Pentecostal leaders

Meetings

I. Horgen/Zürich, Switzerland, June 20-24, 1972
   Baptism in the Holy Spirit in the New Testament and its Relation to Regeneration, Sanctification and Charismata

II. Rome, Italy, June 18-22, 1973
   Historical Background of the Pentecostal Movement; the Relation of the Baptism in the Holy Spirit to the Rite of Christian Initiation; the Role of the Holy Spirit and the Gifts in the Mystical Tradition

III. Schloss Craheim, Wetzhausen, Germany, June 10-14, 1974
The Relation of the Action of the Holy Spirit to Church Structures; Water Baptism, Adult and Infant Baptism

Background. This dialogue had its beginning in the contacts made by individual members of the Pentecostal Churches with the Vatican Secretariat for Promoting Christian Unity in 1969 and 1970. Out of these personal contacts came the idea of a representative dialogue. The growth of the neo-Pentecostal movements, not least within the Roman Catholic Church, strengthened the conviction that such encounters at the leadership level would be of mutual benefit. In 1970 and 1971 exploratory meetings were held in Rome which indicated that such a dialogue would be possible, and a small steering committee was appointed to work out a programme of meetings extending over a five-year period.

Purpose. The declared aim is that "prayer, spirituality and theological reflection be shared concerns at the international level in the form of a dialogue between the Secretariat for Promoting Christian Unity and Pentecostal Churches". There are also some participants from neo-Pentecostal movements within the Anglican and Protestant churches. The dialogue is focussed on "the meaning for the Church of fullness of life in the Holy Spirit" in both its experiential and theological dimensions. Emphasis is placed on exchange of information and experience and on deepening, in prayer and common witness, the already existing unity in Christ. Problems of structural union are explicitly left aside.

Status and Composition of the Group. The dialogue presents some unusual features. On the Roman Catholic side, it is officially sponsored by the Secretariat for Promoting Christian Unity, which also appoints the Roman Catholic members. As the World Pentecostal Conference on the other side possesses constitutionally no authority in the matter, the Pentecostal participants are appointed by individual churches or in other ways. Both classical and neo-pentecostalist movements are represented in the group, which includes nine Pentecostal and seven Roman Catholic members.

Programme. The plan foresees a series of five annual meetings. In addition to the subjects of the first three meetings listed above, the dialogue will study psychological and sociological dimensions of Pentecostalism, its prayer and worship life, and finally the pastoral problems connected with common witness and the danger of proselytism. No consensus statements are produced but "agreed accounts" indicate the trends of the discussion at each meeting. A comprehensive report will be published at the end.

Because of mutual unfamiliarity, much of the time has been devoted to clarifying affinities and differences in matters of spirituality and worship. The personal character of Christian faith and the nurture and sharing of spiritual experience were common concerns, but a distinct polarity of emphases appeared in discussing the relation between the life of the individual Christian and the sacramental life of the Church.

The concluding sentence of the account of the 1973 meeting illustrates the amazing change in mutual attitudes that has occurred within the last few decades: "The participants in the dialogue have become increasingly aware of the growing extent and dimension of the Pentecostal Churches and the charismatic renewal and realize that these movements could have profound repercussions on the renewal of the Churches and progress towards Christian unity".

Co-Chairmen

The Rev. Dr. David du Plessis, World Pentecostal Leader, Oakland, Calif., USA

The Rev. Fr. Kilian McDonnell, OSB, Collegeville, Minn., USA

Co-Secretaries

The Rev. Dr. John McTernan, President, International Evangelical Church, Via Caiovendi 57, Rome, Italy

The Rev. Fr. Basil Meeking, Secretariat for Promoting Christian Unity, Vatican City, Vatican

Publications

"The Roman Catholic-Pentecostal Dialogue", One in Christ 1974, 2. (The whole number is devoted to the subject and contains an account of the dialogue, reports of the two meetings in 1972-1973, and a series of papers presented at those meetings.)

14. Reformed-Roman Catholic.................................. R-RC

"Study Commission on 'The Presence of Christ in Church and World'" sponsored by the World Alliance of Reformed Churches and the Vatican Secretariat for Promoting Christian Unity

Meetings

I. Rome, Italy, April 6-10, 1970
Christ's Relationship to the Church

II. Cartigny/Geneva, Switzerland, March 22-27, 1971
The Teaching Authority of the Church

III. Bièvres/Paris, France, January 31-February 5, 1972
The Presence of Christ in the World

IV. Woudschoten, The Netherlands, February 18-23, 1974
The Eucharist

Background. The World Alliance of Reformed Churches had repeatedly affirmed that it consciously desisted from mounting an international dialogue with Roman Catholics in order to strengthen the potential dialogue between the World Council of Churches and the Roman Catholic Church. The accelerating pace of ecumenical developments, however, led to a revision of this policy. There were several reasons for such a shift. As member churches of the WARC would increasingly engage in national dialogues with Roman Catholic partners, the conversations ran the risk of wasteful duplication unless international exchange of information and correlation was secured by both partners. Moreover, in certain cases the dialogues might be unable to reach definite conclusions by themselves because of the universal nature of the problem under consideration. Also, in many countries there is no national dialogue of this kind, and consequently those countries are deprived of the influence of the conversations proceeding elsewhere. A Reformed-Roman Catholic dialogue at the world level, paralleling other international ones, would therefore be a worthwhile undertaking, helping to strengthen a common witness.

History. Following a decision of the Executive Committee of the WARC in June, 1968, and corresponding actions by the Roman Catholic Church, two consultations of representatives of the WARC and the Secretariat for Promoting Christian Unity were held at Geneva, November 27-29, 1968 and at Vogelenzang (The Netherlands), April 15-19, 1969. The report of these two consultations outlined the justification for a dialogue between the two bodies and a list of subjects. It recommended the setting up of a study commission, having as its main theme "The Presence of Christ in Church and World". This and the other recommendations were accepted by the Executive Committee of the WARC and the

Secretariat for Promoting Christian Unity in summer 1969.

Terms of Reference. In the report of the two consultations it is stressed "that the Reformed-Roman Catholic dialogue on a world level must reflect not only the peculiar tensions between the two traditions, but also their common concern to make manifest the relevance of Christ in the world today". For the conversations themselves, a period of three years (1970-73) with five meetings was proposed. The number of participants would be five on each side. All practical arrangements for the conversations were delineated. At the conclusion of the three year period a final report would be produced, indicating the point of departure, the course pursued, the results, and the questions still unresolved. Apart from serving as a study document in the churches, the report would be submitted to the competent authorities on each side. It should also contain recommendations concerning the possible continuation of the dialogue.

Appointment and Composition of the Group. The two delegations were appointed by the authorities of the WARC and the Secretariat for Promoting Christian Unity. The five Roman Catholic and five Reformed members of the commission are all professors or lecturers in theology. Eight of them are Europeans, two come from the USA. There has been so far one consultant present on each side at each meeting, dependent on the nature of the subject, and also specific representatives from the Third World. The WARC has been represented by its General Secretary and Theological Secretary, the Secretariat for Promoting Christian Unity by its Secretary and a staff member. There is a permanent observer invited from the World Council of Churches.

Characteristics of the Work. The short summaries which were accepted at the first four meetings reveal the wide variety of problems which came up during the discussions. Fundamental subjects such as the Church, Scripture and tradition were prominent, showing many agreements especially in the area of exegetical and historical studies. It was recognised that because the formulation of doctrine is a dynamic developing process, the attitudes of the two sides are no longer as diametrically opposed as at the time following the Reformation and the Council of Trent. It was agreed that the Church has traditionally been described too exclusively in terms of its relation to Christ and fuller reference is needed to the activity of the Holy Spirit; and that the Church, though it does not derive its nature and mission from the world, is still a part of the world and exists for the sake of the world. Discussion on the specific question of understanding the presence of Christ in the world focussed on the theological problem of relating creation and redemption, and therefore the missionary responsibility of the Church in and for the world and the understanding of the Church as the effective sign of Christ's presence in the world. This led to a statement of common concern about the adequacy of the churches for their contemporary tasks. The group affirmed its conviction that the engagement of the Christian community in the world is based on its nature as a worshipping body.

In this context the necessity of a common understanding of the eucharist assumed fresh importance. Drawing on the biblical witness and the testimony of the ancient Fathers, the group moved forward to unexpected convergences concerning the centrality of the eucharist in the life and mission of the Church, the real presence of the Lord, and the meaning of sacrifice. "We believe we have reached a common understanding of the meaning and purpose and basic doctrine of the Eucharist which is in agreement with the Word of God and the universal tradition of the Church."

The fifth meeting, dated for March 1975, will be devoted to the theme of "The Ministry". The final meeting in 1976 is expected to establish an overall report, based on the provisional reports from the annual meetings.

<u>Co-Chairmen</u>

Prof. Dr. David Willis, Berkeley, Calif., USA (Reformed)

The Rev. Fr. Kilian McDonnell, OSB, Collegeville, Minn., USA (Roman Catholic)

<u>Co-Secretaries</u>

The Rev. Richmond Smith, Department of Theology, WARC, Geneva

The Rev. Fr. Pierre de Contenson, Secretariat for Promoting Christian Unity, Vatican City, Vatican

<u>Publications</u>

Press releases in <u>Reformed Press Service</u>, WARC, Geneva, and <u>Information Service</u>, Secretariat for Promoting Christian Unity, Vatican.

B. CONVERSATIONS AT REGIONAL AND NATIONAL LEVELS

1. Church of England - Evangelical Church in Germany (EKD)....................A-Ev/e-frg

Meetings

I. Oxford, England, April 1964
Authority and the Church

II. Bethel, Federal Republic of Germany, March 1966
Word and Eucharist

III. Launde Abbey, England, March 1970
Presentation of the Christian Faith Today: Essentials and Non-Essentials

Upon an initiative of the Archbishop of Canterbury and following a decision by the Council of the Evangelical Church in Germany (EKD) - a federation of Lutheran, United and Reformed Churches - a series of theological conversations between theologians of the Church of England and of the EKD in the Federal Republic of Germany started in 1964. The conversations were official in character, the "foreign offices" of the two churches bearing responsibility for their preparation and implementation.

The conversations were not aiming at a specific goal but intended to contribute to a better knowledge and understanding between the two traditions. The papers and summaries of discussions were published in English and German.

Co-Chairmen

The Rt. Rev. Ronald R. Williams, Bishop of Leicester, England (Anglican)
Professor Dr. Wolfgang Schweizer, Bethel, Federal Republic of Germany (Lutheran)

Publications

Autorität und geistliche Vollmacht (Beiheft zur Okumenischen Rundschau Nr. 1). Stuttgart: Evangelischer Missionsverlag, 1965
Wort und Abendmahl (Beiheft zur Okumenischen Rundschau Nr. 5). Stuttgart: Evangelischer Missionsverlag, 1967
Experiment: Glaube (Beiheft zur Okumenischen Rundschau Nr. 16). Stuttgart: Evangelischer Missionsverlag, 1971
English editions were published by S.P.C.K., London (out of print)

2. Anglican-Lutheran/Australia.............................. A-L/aus

"Anglican-Lutheran Conversations in Australia" sponsored by the Church of England in Australia and the Lutheran Church of Australia

These conversations owe their origin to Resolution no. 59 of the Lambeth Conference of 1968 recommending the initiation of Anglican-Lutheran dialogues. As a result, the Conference of Anglican Bishops in Australia made such a proposal to the Lutheran Church of Australia which met with favourable response. The Lutheran Church of Australia, formed in 1966 through the union of two earlier bodies, maintains "selective fellowship" with the Lutheran Church-Missouri Synod in the USA and is not a member of the Lutheran World Federation. The dialogue, first limited to South Australia, is now constituted on a national basis. The Anglican members are appointed by the Missionary and Ecumenical Council of the General Synod of the Church of England in Australia, and the Lutheran respresentatives by the Commission on Theology and Inter-church Relations of the Lutheran Church of Australia.

Composed of four church leaders and theologians from each side, the group held its initial meeting on March 22, 1972, and issued in 1973 a "Combined Anglican-Lutheran Statement on the Eucharist" dealing with the mode of Christ's presence and with its relationship to Christ's sacrifice once-for-all on the Cross. Both partners affirm the Lord's presence in the entire rite and his "real presence" in the sacramental elements. Transubstantiation and a mere memorialist doctrine are rejected. The gift of Christ's presence must not be dissociated from the sacramental elements or the act of sacramental eating. While the Lutherans avoid any use of sacrificial terminology in order to ensure the primacy of Christ's sacrifice once-for-all over against any human response, both agree that Christ has given the sacrament "as a means by which his atoning work on the cross might be proclaimed and made effective in the life of his saints". As matters requiring further exploration the statement notes the action of the Holy Spirit in relation to the eucharist, the concept of unworthy participation, the relationship between ontological and significatory language, and ministry and eucharist.

Subsequently the group has been studying the question of the ministry and a joint statement will be issued in 1975.

<u>Chairman</u>

The Rt. Rev. Lionel E.W. Renfrey, Assistant Bishop and Dean of Adelaide, Church Office, 18 King William Road, North Adelaide 5006, Australia (Anglican)

3. <u>Episcopal-Lutheran Dialogue/USA</u>............................<u>A-L/usa</u>

Sponsored by the Joint Commission on Ecumenical Relations of the Episcopal Church and the Division of Theological Studies of the Lutheran Council in the USA

First Series

<u>Meetings</u>

I. Detroit, Mich., October 14-15, 1969
   The Meaning and Authority of Scripture in the Life of the Church Today

II. Milwaukee, Wisc., April 7-9, 1970
   The Relationship of the Church's Worship and Sacramental Life to the Unity of the Church

III. New York, N.Y., November 17-19, 1970
   Our Baptismal Unity and its Ecumenical Significance

IV. St. Paul, Minn., April 14-16, 1971
   The Apostolicity of the Church

V. New York, N.Y., November 10-12, 1971
   What Would Be Needed for Full <u>Communio in Sacris</u> between Our Two Churches?

VI. New York, N.Y., May 31-June 1, 1972
   Preparation of Progress Report

Originating in an invitation issued by the General Convention of the Episcopal Church in 1967, the dialogue was initiated under a mandate to explore the "possibilities and problems for a more extended dialogue having more specific fellowship or unity or union goals". The group was composed of nine representatives from each side, including theological professors, church officials, parish clergy and laymen. Among the Lutherans were three members of the Missouri Synod.

Discovering the wide measure of unity already existing between the two communions, the group soon moved beyond its cautious remit to concentrate on the more specific question of realising altar and pulpit fellowship. Agreement was explicitly noted on the following fundamentals of church life and doctrine: (a) The primacy and authority of the Holy Scriptures; (b) the doctrine of the Apostles' and Nicene Creeds; (c) justification by grace through faith as affirmed by both the Lutheran Confessions and the Anglican Book of Common Prayer and Thirty-Nine Articles of Religion; (d) the doctrine and practice of baptism; (e) fundamental agreement on the eucharist, though with some differences in emphasis.

As in other similar dialogues, the divisive theological issue turned out to be the meaning of apostolicity. The problem was resolved by agreeing that the apostolic gospel is mediated and addressed to every new generation in multiple ways and that "within the one church, both the Anglican continuity of the apostolic order, and the Lutheran concentration on doctrine, have been means of preserving the apostolicity of the one church". Each respecting "the right of the other to honor the distinct history which mediates its apostolicity ...", the two communions should recognise each other's ordained ministry and sacramental administration as truly apostolic.

In the matter of intercommunion, the group proposed "Commendation of communicants of each communion to the eucharistic celebrations and gathering around the Word of the other, including intercommunion between parishes or congregations which, by reason of proximity, joint community concerns, and/or activities, have developed such a degree of understanding and trust as would make intercommunion an appropriate response to the Gospel". Contrary to orthodox Lutheran opinion, a full consensus de doctrina is thus not held to be a precondition for increased eucharistic sharing and other forms of ecclesial fellowship.

Co-Chairmen

The Rt. Rev. Richard S.M. Emrich (Episcopal)

The Rev. Dr. O.V. Anderson, Milwaukee, Wisc. (Lutheran), now deceased

Co-Secretaries (also of the second series)

Dr. Peter Day, Executive Council of the Episcopal Church, New York, N.Y.

Dr. Paul D. Opsahl, Division of Theological Studies, Lutheran Council in the USA, New York, N.Y.

Publication

Lutheran-Episcopal Dialogue: A Progress Report. Cincinnati: Forward Movement Press, 1972. Price 50¢

Second Series

A second round of conversations is currently being planned. It will focus on the central question of "What is the Gospel?"

4. Anglican-Orthodox/USA....................................A-O/usa

"Anglican-Orthodox Theological Consultation" sponsored by the Ecumenical Commission of the Standing Conference of Canonical Orthodox Bishops in the Americas and the Joint Commission on Ecumenical Relations of the Episcopal Church

Meetings

I. Greenwich, Conn., September 27-29, 1962
The Nature of the Church

II. New York, N.Y., November 19-20, 1963
Hindrances and Helps in the Progress towards Unity, especially at the Parish Level

III. New York, N.Y., April 15-16, 1964
The Eucharist

IV. New York, N.Y., November 10-11, 1964
The Eucharist; the Goal of the Consultation; Implications of the Second Vatican Council for Anglicans and Orthodox

V. New York, N.Y., March 6, 1965
The "Theotokos" in Anglican Thought; Icons

VI. Brookline, Mass., September 27-28, 1965
Christian Unity, Anglican and Orthodox; Adoption of Guidelines for Ecumenical Relations

VII. Tuckahoe, N.Y., May 27, 1966
Survey of Popular Ideas of Anglican-Orthodox Relations; Principles of Unity; the Consultation on Church Union (COCU)

VIII. Tuckahoe, N.Y., May 25, 1967
Reactions to the Recent Pan-Orthodox Conference at Belgrade; Patriarch Meletios

IX. New York, N.Y., January 24, 1968
The Holy Spirit and the Church; Ecumenical Commitments

X. Tuckahoe, N.Y., October 11, 1968
Secularism in Orthodox Lands and the West; the Orthodox Ecumenical Conference at Chambésy/Geneva

XI. Brookline, Mass., May 9, 1969
The Lambeth Conference; Crisis and Promise in the Ecumenical Movement

XII. New York, N.Y., November 14, 1969
Orthodoxy and Ecumenism in Europe and in America

XIII. New York, N.Y., March 12, 1970
Review of the Aims and Membership of the Consultation

XIV. New York, N.Y., November 13, 1970
Context and Purposes of the Consultation

XV. Tuckahoe, N.Y., February 18-19, 1972
The Mission of the Church in Contemporary Society; the Preparations for the International Anglican-Orthodox Dialogue

XVI. New York, N.Y., June 16, 1972
The C.O.C.U. Plan of Union; the Orthodox View of Ordination of Women

XVII. New York, N.Y., February 10, 1973
The Social Ethos of the Orthodox Church; Church and World in the Orthodox Tradition; Anglican Evangelicalism and Christian Social Ethics

XVIII. New York, N.Y., June 2, 1973
Orthodox Statement on the Proposed Ordination of Women in the Episcopal Church with Episcopal Response; the Gospel Kerygma and the Mission of the Church; Review and Prospect of the Consultation

XIX. New York, N.Y., November 1-2, 1974
Anglicanism and Orthodoxy in the Ecumenical Movement; Sociological and Cultural Conditioning Factors in Anglican-Orthodox Relations; Common Statement of Purpose; Future Programme

The consultation was established in 1962 on the initiative of the Ecumenical Patriarch of Constantinople, Athenagoras I, through Archbishop Iakovos, and of the Episcopal Presiding Bishop, Arthur C. Lichtenberger. As a recent statement of purpose indicates, the consultation presents certain characteristic features which distinguish it from Anglican-Orthodox conversations elsewhere. Only in America do the two traditions share in a common culture in which neither has a majority or dominant role and where they are exposed to the same challenges and needs. The fact, moreover, that conversations or decisions by representatives of either Anglicans or Orthodox in other parts of the world would have their major practical impact in America, is another reason why a serious continuing dialogue is imperative in that continent. The ultimate purpose of the consultation is the full union of the two communions. Its proximate purpose is the encouragement of this end through a consideration of the many serious differences still existing between the two bodies, and the internal problems with which both must contend.

During the 1960's the consultation chiefly served the purpose of mutual explanation and exchange of information. Matters of doctrine, principles of unity, and parish level relations were recurrent features of the discussions. The brevity of the meetings, however, did not allow for any sustained grappling with the issues, eventuating in definite agreements. In 1970 it was decided to focus the meetings for some years on a unifying central theme - the Mission of the Church in America, with increasing attention to its social aspect - and in that context to consider other topics that might also require attention. As presently constituted, the commission includes sixteen Anglican and twelve Orthodox members drawn from the various churches.

The new programme adopted in 1974 aims to strengthen the consultation in three directions. A deliberate effort will be made to assess the progress achieved in Anglican-Orthodox relations over the past century as it bears on current relations. The consultation should serve as a forum for reporting on the achievements of other Anglican as well as Orthodox dialogues so as to enrich the American one. Finally it hopes to relate its theological work more directly to the life and witness of the constituent churches, for example, by calling their attention from time to time to problems of joint concern.

The next meeting in October 1975 is scheduled to discuss three subjects: Tradition and historical-critical method in the two communions; secularism or the relation of the Church, kingdom and world; and the practical meaning of the eucharist.

Co-Chairmen

The Rt.Rev. Jonathan G. Sherman, Bishop of Long Island, N.Y. (Episcopal Church)

The Rt. Rev. Dimitri, Bishop of New Haven and New England (Orthodox Church in America)

Co-Secretaries

The Rev. William A. Norgren, Ecumenical Office of the Episcopal Church, 815 Second Avenue, New York, N.Y. 10017

The Very Rev. Paul W. Schneirla, 8005 Ridge Boulevard, Brooklyn, N.Y. 11209

Publication

"Guidelines on Anglican-Orthodox Relations" (adopted in 1965), Handbook of American Orthodoxy (Cincinnati: Forward Movement Publications 1972), pp. 11-14

5. Anglican-Roman Catholic/Canada............................A-RC/can

"The Canadian Anglican-Catholic Dialogue" sponsored by the Anglican Church of Canada and the Candian Catholic Conference

Meetings

I. Toronto, Ontario (all meetings), November 16, 1971
Discussion of the Work of the Anglican-Roman Catholic International Commission; Assistance in its Study of the Ministry

II. March 18, 1972
Review of Reactions to the A-RC Windsor Statement on the Eucharist and Canadian Follow-up; the Historical Context of Apostolicae Curae

III. October 13, 1972
Discussion of the Work of A-RC on the Ministry

IV. December 1-2, 1972
Preparation of a Statement on the Ministry for A-RC

V. March 2-3, 1973
Continued

VI. May 9, 1973
Review of the Purpose of the Dialogue; Ways of Pastoral Implementation

VII. November 29, 1973

VIII. March 1, 1974

Reaction to the Canterbury Statement on Ministry and Ordination; Planning of Assigned Paper on the Authority of Scripture for A-RC

IX. May 3, 1974

Examination of the Dogmatic Constitution of Vatican II on Divine Revelation

The recorded history of this dialogue goes back to personal "bilateral" conversations beginning in 1965 between Canon H.L. Puxley, the then Director of the Ecumenical Institute of Canada, and Father John J. Keating, the then Director of the National Secretariat for Ecumenism of the Canadian Catholic Conference. The matter was pursued further in the Anglican-Roman Catholic Inter-Church Committee and a preparatory committee was set up which held a meeting in January 1971 to shape a definite proposal for sub-mission to the church authorities.

The group meets three or four times a year. It is composed of sixteen representatives of the two Churches, including bishops, clergymen, ecumenical officers, and theological professors. An observer from the United Church of Canada attends the meetings to serve as a link with the larger ecumenical scene and particularly with the church union conversations involving Anglicans, United, and Disciples of Christ.

As is the case with other A-RC groups, the purpose of the Canadian group is "to move the Churches towards the unity that Christ wills". The group sees as its main task to assist in the work of the A-RC International Commission - a cooperation facilitated by two of its members belonging to both commissions. Thus the group has devoted much of its time to studies relating to the A-RC study of the ministry, contributing an assigned paper on the theological stance of Anglicans and Roman Catholics on ministry at the time of Apostolicae Curae and another on ministerial priesthood in relation to Christ and the Church. For the international meeting in 1974, it produced papers examining the Dogmatic Constitution on Divine Revelation as an authoritative description of the authority of Scripture. Some consideration is also given to the role the group might play in the wider implementation of ecumenical dialogue in Canada. The group is currently being reorganised.

6. Anglican-Roman Catholic/ England ....A-RC/eng

"English ARC", a national Commission jointly sponsored by the Church of England and the Roman Catholic Church in England

Meetings

I. London (all meetings), April 20, 1970
Problem of Mixed Marriages; Future Agenda

II. October 22, 1970
The Eucharist

III. February 26, 1971
The A-RC Venice Papers on Eucharist and Ministry

IV. June 25, 1971
Authority in the Church

V. December 3, 1971
The Blessed Virgin Mary

VI. March 10, 1972
A-RC Agreed Statement on the Eucharist

VII. November 17, 1972
Programme for the English A-RC

VIII. March 20, 1973
Towards a Developing Ecclesiology

IX. August 28, 1973
Meeting with Members of A-RC/usa

X. November 23, 1973
Preliminary Report on the A-RC Canterbury Statement on Ministry and Ordination; Discussion of the Document Mysterium Ecclesiae

XI. March 28-29, 1974
Draft Leaflet on Anglican-Roman Catholic Marriages; Discussion of A-RC Statement on Ministry and Ordination; Discussion of Paper by the Roman Catholic International Theological Commission on "Unity of Faith and Theological Pluralism"

XII. November 29, 1974
Synod of Roman Catholic Bishops 1974: Evangelisation in the Modern World

Background. As a consequence of the desire for closer relations between the two communions, evident during and after the Second Vatican Council, the Archbishop of Canterbury's Commission for Roman Catholic Relations, initially consisting of a number of area convenors, was set up to promote dialogues throughout the country. Somewhat later the Roman Catholic Church established an Ecumenical Commission of England and Wales. At a joint meeting of the two bodies in 1968, it was decided to set up a smaller joint body of sub-committees. The new Joint Commission ("English ARC") held its first meeting in 1970 and it has been meeting since then twice a year in London. Meanwhile a number of diocesan and other local dialogues had been initiated and the Joint Commission was therefore in a position to build on work already in progress.

Composition of the Group. After re-structuring, the Joint Commission is since 1972 composed of a sub-committee of the Board of Mission and Unity of the General Synod of the Church of England and the Church of England Sub-committee of the Roman Catholic Ecumenical Commission of England and Wales. The group numbers fifteen members from each side, including bishops, clergymen, lay persons, church officials and professors of theology.

Terms of Reference. The purpose of the group is defined as follows: "The positive fostering of Roman Catholic and Anglican relations in England, and the co-ordination of future work undertaken for this purpose by our two Churches".

Programme. As its main function is that of stimulation, coordination and support, the commission has not undertaken fixed long-range projects of its own. Taking up the subjects of the A-RC international commission, it discusses these in the religious and theological setting of the country and, serving as one of the area sub-commissions of the international commission, it contributes preparatory statements to its work. In the other direction, English A-RC disseminates information on the development in A-RC relations and interprets their implications for church life. It seeks also to foster consultation and cooperation between the two Churches in such areas as pastoral and evangelistic problems, clergy training, the possibility of team ministries, liturgical texts and practices, joint use of church buildings and other facilities. A jointly prepared study guide has been published on the Canterbury Statement on Ministry and Ordination.

Co-Chairmen

The Rt. Rev. John Trillo, Bishop of Chelmsford (Anglican)

The Rt. Rev. Mgr. B.C. Butler, OSB, Auxiliary Bishop of Westminster (Roman Catholic)

Co- Secretaries

The Very Rev. Canon John Arnold, Board of Mission and Unity, Church House, Dean's Yard, Westminster, London SW1P 3NZ

The Very Rev. Canon Richard L. Stewart, Roman Catholic Ecumenical Commission of England and Wales, 44 Gray's Inn Road, London WC1X 8LR

7. Anglican-Roman Catholic Dialogue/Japan....................A-RC/jap

Meetings

I. Tokyo, April 29, 1972
Planning for Dialogue

II. Tokyo, October 14, 1972
Joint Translation into Japanese of the Windsor Statement on Eucharistic Doctrine of 1971

III. Tokyo, December 16, 1972
Theological, Canonical and Pastoral Aspects of Mixed Marriages

IV. Tokyo, May 19, 1973
Discussion of the Windsor Statement on Eucharistic Doctrine

V. Tokyo, December 8, 1973
Discussion of Modern Theological Trends

The decision to start an official dialogue was taken at a meeting in October 1971, involving the chairmen of the Anglican and Roman Catholic ecumenical commissions. The immediate aim of the group is to further mutual understanding of each other's historical and doctrinal positions but this is set in the wider context of the group's concern with the question of how to communicate the shared Gospel among non-Christian people. Further plans include a study of sacrament and liturgy, a common catechism and common spiritual exercises. The group, numbering six representatives from each side, consists of theological professors together with two bishops.

Co-Chairmen

The Very Rev. Bishop Toshio Koike, Osaka (Anglican)

The Most Rev. Bishop John S. Ito, Niigata (Roman Catholic)

Liaison Persons

The Rev. Fr. Tetsuro Nishimura, Tokyo (Anglican)

The Rev. Fr. Paul Pfister, SJ, Secretary of the Episcopal Commission for Ecumenism, 10-1 Rokuban-cho, Chiyoda-ku, Tokyo 102, Japan (Roman Catholic)

8. Latin American Anglican-Roman Catholic Conversations......A-RC/lam

Meeting

Bogota, Colombia, February 9-14, 1971

Ministry and Eucharist; Authority and Government in the Church; Mixed Marriages; Collaboration, Cooperation and Mutual Help

The immensity of the evangelistic and social mission in Latin America, the realisation of a common heritage and a shared faith, the Anglican-Roman Catholic rapprochement in other parts of the world - this was the background for the Bogota meeting jointly convened by the Anglican Council of Latin America (CALA) and the Ecumenical Commission of the Catholic Episcopate of Latin America (CELAM). The group comprised ten bishops from each side together with some consultants. The first of its kind, the conference opened with presentations of the history and attitudes of the two Churches on the continent and considered major doctrinal and pastoral questions affecting their mutual relationships. The discussions on "Mixed Marriages" and "Collaboration, Cooperation and Mutual Help" were summed up in agreed statements. The recommendations, submitted to the ecclesiastical authorities, urge extensive cooperation not only in the field of welfare and social justice, publications, use of church buildings, but also in evangelisation and forms of worship.

In 1973, the Anglican Council of Latin America and the Ecumenical Commission of the Catholic Episcopate of Latin America appointed a Joint Commission, composed of four members from each side, with the following terms of reference:

1. To serve as a contact organ between CELAM and CALA;
2. To examine the areas of cooperation and collaboration in the continental area;
3. To favour and promote the same cooperation at grass roots level;
4. To study the theological and practical subjects of common concern.

The inaugural meeting is scheduled for 1975.

Correspondent

Father Jorge Mejia, Executive Secretary, Department of Ecumenism of the Catholic Episcopate of Latin America, Pacheco de Melo 2016 4°A, Buenos Aires, Argentina

9. Anglican-Roman Catholic/South Africa ....A-RC/saf

Meetings

.....

.....

X. La Verna, December 10-13, 1973
The Ministry and Authority of the Community's Faith

XI. Irene, May 13-16, 1974
The Authority of God, Father, Son and Holy Spirit; Scripture and Tradition in the Anglican and Roman Catholic Churches; Mixed Marriages

XII. La Verna, December 9-12, 1974
Authority in the New Testament

With the permission of the bishops of both Churches in South Africa, a dialogue group was formed in 1965. Consisting of about ten persons, it met at regular intervals to discuss matters relevant to Anglican-Roman Catholic divergences. In 1969, these conversations were transformed into an official dialogue sponsored by the respective hierarchies. Meetings are held twice a year. The present membership includes eleven bishops, clergymen and theological professors plus an observer from the Church Unity Commission in South Africa.

The conversations had been touching a wide range of subjects, such as authority and freedom, the nature of the Church, priesthood and the ministry, Anglican orders, baptism, the eucharist, intercommunion, marriage, discipline, black theology. Serving as a regional subsidiary, the group has produced papers on eucharist, ministry, and authority for incorporation in the final drafts of the International Commission.

Its deliberations have also issued in a number of other consensus statements and recommendations or referrals to the joint meetings of Anglican and Roman Catholic bishops - relating to the freedom of each participating Church to proceed with union with other Churches; the freedom of each Church to consider the ordination of women to the priesthood; an appeal to the hierarchies to act on reciprocal intercommunion in accordance with the joint statement on the eucharist; cooperation respecting mixed marriages, etc. A number of such recommendations have been adopted by the bishops, including a resolution explaining and encouraging the practice of intercommunion at nuptial masses and wedding anniversaries.

Joint Chairmen

The Rt.Rev. E.G. Knapp-Fisher, Bishop of Pretoria (Anglican)

The Rt. Rev. P. Buthelezi, O.M.I., Bishop of Johannesburg (Roman Catholic)

Joint Secretaries

The Rev. Dr. G.W. Ashby, Rhodes University, P.O. Box 94, Grahamstown, C.P., South Africa (Anglican)

The Rev. Dr. B. Gaybba, Chaplain of University of Cape Town, Kolbe House, 14 Grotto Road, Rondebosch 7700, Cape Town, South Africa (Roman Catholic)

10. Anglican-Roman Catholic/Scotland........................A-RC/scot

"The Joint Study Group of Representatives of the Roman Catholic Church in Scotland and the Scottish Episcopal Church"

Following consultation between episcopal leaders of the two Churches, the group was formed in 1968. The immediate sponsoring bodies are the Inter-Church Relations Committee of the Scottish Episcopal Church and the National Ecumenical Commission of the Roman Catholic Church. Its work is performed in an alternation of plenary sessions, meetings of two regional groups based in Edinburgh and Glasgow, and meetings of the steering committee composed of the four convenors. The group, both clerical and lay, counts some twenty five members. It includes an observer from the Scottish Churches' House at the plenary sessions, helping to relate the dialogue to the total ecumenical scene of the country.

The group is carrying out structured studies of particular subjects. Drawing on the wide measure of agreement already existing between the two Churches, it aims to deepen and define these informal understandings in joint declarations of consensus and to present them to the appropriate authorities for consideration. During the period from October 1968 to May 1969, it produced a common statement on "The Nature of Baptism and its Place in the Life of the Church", which discusses the meaning of baptism, its sociological and ecumenical implications, the requirements for a mutual recognition of baptism, and suggests consultations on the adoption of a common ritual. The document was published with commendation by the Provincial Synod of the Scottish Episcopal Church and the Scottish Roman Catholic Hierarchy. An offical agreement has been concluded about mutual recognition of baptism as administered in both Churches.

The group issued in 1974 a report on "The Ecclesial Nature of the Eucharist", representing an "extensive and thorough agreement on the doctrine of our respective traditions with regard to Eucharist, sacrament and sacrifice". The procedure adopted was to start with an examination of the eucharistic practices of both Churches, to consider their eucharistic theologies in this light, and finally to devote a major section to the ecclesial nature of the eucharist. The manner in which the report interprets the eucharist as the sacrament and the model of the Church, its mission and structures, is a distinctive note. The group is now continuing its study of the eucharist by considering the question of the ministry. It is hoped later to discuss the question of intercommunion.

<u>Chairman</u>

Dr. Robert A. Shanks, 9 Belmont Crescent, Glasgow, W. 2, Scotland

<u>Secretary</u>

The Rev. James Quinn SJ, Church of the Sacred Heart, 28 Lauriston Street, Edinburgh EH3 9DJ, Scotland

<u>Publications</u>

<u>The Nature of Baptism and Its Place in the Life of the Church</u>, 1969. Price 5p. A reprint, with new covers, is planned (price not fixed).

<u>The Ecclesial Nature of the Eucharist</u>, 1974. Price 15p.

Both pamphlets can be ordered from J.S. Burns & Sons, 25 Finlas Street, Glasgow G22 5DS, Scotland.

11. Anglican-Roman Catholic/USA..............................A-RC/usa

"Joint Commission on Anglican-Roman Catholic Relations in the USA (ARC)" sponsored by the Joint Commission on Ecumenical Relations of the Episcopal Church and the Bishops' Committee for Ecumenical and Interreligious Affairs

Meetings

I. Washington, D.C., June 22, 1965
   Preliminary Meeting

II. Kansas City, Mo., February 2, 1966
   The Eucharist, Sign and Cause of Unity

III. Providence, R.I., October 10-12, 1966
   The Minister of the Eucharist

IV. Milwaukee, Wisc., May 24-26, 1967
   The Eucharist

V. Jackson, Miss., January 5-7, 1968
   The Nature, Necessity and Function of the Ministerial Priesthood

VI. Liberty, Mo., December 2-5, 1968
   The Episcopal Symbol of Unity

VII. Boynton Beach, Fla., December 8-11, 1969
   Toward Full Communion and Organic Unity

VIII. Green Bay, Wisc., June 17-20, 1970
   ARC: Achievement and Prognostication; Models for Church Unity; Episcopacy and Priesthood in A Plan of Union of the Consultation on Church Union

IX. St. Benedict, La., January 26-29, 1971
   Hierarchy of Truths; the Primacy of Jurisdiction of the Roman Pontiff

X. Liberty. Mo., June 20-23, 1971
   The Principles of Interpreting Dogmatic Statements; the Exercise of Teaching Authority in the Church

XI. New York, N.Y., January 22-24, 1972
   Doctrinal Agreement and Christian Unity

XII. Cincinnati, Ohio, June 12-15, 1972
Teaching Authority: Correspondences and Differences; the Eucharistic Presence; Comment by the Commission on the Windsor Statement on Eucharistic Doctrine

XIII. Cincinnati, Ohio, March 18-22, 1973
The Purpose or Mission of the Church; the Growing Accord between Roman Catholics and Anglicans

XIV. Vicksburg, Miss., January 6-10, 1974
The Church as a Eucharistic Communion; Response to the Canterbury Statement on Ministry and Ordination

XV. Cincinnati, Ohio, November 10-13, 1974
Authority

The commission, which began its work in 1965, has over the years explored a variety of subjects affecting the relations between the two communions, and the advances made have been recorded in successive statements. Substantial agreement was achieved on baptism, the Church as a eucharistic fellowship, the theology of the celebrant, and the nature of eucharistic sacrifice, transcending the polemical formulations and mutual misunderstandings of the past. Thus the 1967 meeting affirmed "the substantial identity" of the two Churches in the controverted doctrine of eucharistic sacrifice. At its next meeting, considering the necessity and role of the ordained priesthood and its relationship to the common priesthood and role of the laity in the Church, the commission concluded that "there is no basic difference of understanding on these topics. Whatever minor differences of understanding exist, they do not in themselves constitute the barrier to the two churches celebrating and receiving communion together".

The declared goal is "full communion and organic unity", and a statement of "historic significance", emanating from the 1969 meeting, projected a series of possible steps toward this goal, including "the reconciliation of the ordained ministries of the two churches without 'reordination' or 'conditional ordination'". The 1969 document was "gratefully and enthusiastically" accepted by the two sponsoring agencies and its recommendations are being implemented in various ways.

Since then the commission has been engaged in an orderly examination of subjects requiring further clarification and agreement: the Purpose or Mission of the Church; the Church as Eucharistic Communion; Ministry in the Eucharistic Communion; Authority, with attention to the relations of the papacy to different "typoi" (i.e. particular ecclesial communions) within the one Church of Christ. The final report with recommendations is expected to be completed by 1976. On each of the topics there will be produced a consensus statement and a study booklet suitable for local discussion groups.

In January 1972, the commission adopted a methodological document "Doctrinal Agreement and Christian Unity", a set of principles which deserves the attention of all ecumenical dialogue groups as a guide in appraising doctrinal diversity and change.

A notable feature of the commission's work is its efforts to stimulate wide participation in its pursuit of unity by encouraging discussion among clergy and laity of the local implications of the agreements reached, prayer fellowships, intervisitations between Episcopal and Roman Catholic parishes, convenanted parishes, and the like.

Co-Chairmen

The Rt.Rev. Arthur E. Vogel, Bishop of West Missouri, Kansas City, Mo. (Episcopal)

The Most Rev. Charles Helmsing, Kansas City, Mo. (Roman Catholic)

Co-Secretaries

Dr. Peter Day, Ecumenical Officer, Executive Council of the Episcopal Church, 815 Second Avenue, New York, N.Y. 10017

The Rev.Dr. John F. Hotchkin, Executive Director, Bishops' Committee for Ecumenical and Interreligious Affairs, 1312 Massachusetts Avenue, N.W., Washington, D.C. 20005

Publications

ARC-DOC I and II. Documents on Anglican-Roman Catholic Relations, compiled by the Bishops' Committee on Ecumenical and Interreligious Affairs, in cooperation with the Joint Commission on Ecumenical Relations. 1972 and 1973. Publications Office, United States Catholic Conference, 1312 Massachusetts Avenue, N.W., Washington, D.C. 20005. $1.00 each. (The booklets include the joint statements referred to above, the Windsor Statement on the Eucharist, addresses by

Pope Paul VI, Archbishop Ramsey and Cardinal Willebrands, actions by Roman Catholic bishops and the Episcopal General Convention.)
Episcopalians and Roman Catholics: Can They Ever Get Together? Edited by Herbert J. Ryan, SJ, and J. Robert Wright. Graymoor Ecumenical Institute, Graymoor, Garrison, N.Y. 10524, 1973. $2.95.

12. American Baptist-Roman Catholic/USA....................AB-RC/usa
"American Baptist-Roman Catholic Dialogue" sponsored by the American Baptist Convention's Commission on Christian Unity (now Office of Ecumenical Relations of the American Baptist Churches in the USA) and the Bishops' Committee for Ecumenical and Interreligious Affairs
Meetings

I. DeWitt, Mich., April 3-4, 1967
Areas of Theological Agreement

II. Green Lake, Wisc., April 29-30, 1968
Christian Freedom and Ecclesiastical Authority; Believers' Baptism and the Sacrament of Confirmation

III. Schiller Park, Ill., April 28-29, 1969
The Nature and Communication of Grace

IV. Atchison, Kansas, April 17-18, 1970
The Role of the Church as seen by Laymen

V. Detroit, Mich., April 23-24, 1971
Clergy-Lay Issues and Relations in Theological Perspective; Theology of the Local Church

VI. Liberty, Mo., April 13-14, 1972
Church-State Relations in the United States Today

Baptists are rarely participating in bilaterals and church union conversations and it therefore represented something of a historical event when in 1966 the General Council of the then American Baptist Convention accepted a Roman Catholic invitation to join in official conversations. The members of the two committees, comprising the group, were appointed by the Commission on Christian Unity of the American Baptist Convention and by the Bishops' Committee for Ecumenical and Interreligious Affairs.

At the outset if was agreed not to attempt to work towards formal agreements but rather to find mutual enrichment in Christian witness by removing misconceptions and by seeking deeper understanding of the respective religious and doctrinal positions. There has been growing awareness that the different Baptist-Roman Catholic approaches to grace, spiritual liberty and ecclesiastical authority, baptism and confession etc., are not necessarily mutually exclusive but may, at least in part, reflect different ways of expressing one side or the other of an inherent polarity. Convergences of mind have kept appearing in recognising the uniqueness of the Bible as the inspired word of God, while at the same time acknowledging the mutual influence over the centuries between the Scripture and Christian experience; in recognising that "there is no salvation except by the grace through faith that comes as a gift from God"; and in a common concern for the mission of the Church to all men and for religious freedom. On the other hand, the group frankly noted sharp differences persisting in the understanding of the meaning and role of the sacraments (or in Baptist language, ordinances), church membership, and the manner in which the Church's authority is made explicit in the community of faith.

A second assignment was to provide material suitable for use in local dialogues, in order to share with the congregations the understanding and enrichment gained. To this end, the national conversation was suspended in 1972 and plans shaped to encourage dialogues in four pilot areas in the country in 1974. The two interpretative reports mentioned below provide resource material.

Co-Chairmen

Professor Robert T. Handy, Union Theological Seminary, New York, N.Y. (Baptist)

The Most Rev. Joseph Green, Bishop of the Diocese of Reno, Reno, Nevada (Roman Catholic)

Co-Secretaries

The Rev. Dr. Robert G. Torbet, Assistant General Secretary for Ecumenical Relations, American Baptist Churches in the USA, Valley Forge, Pa. 19481

The Rev. Dr. John Hotchkin, Executive Director, Bishops' Committee for Ecumenical and Interreligious Affairs, 1312 Massachusetts Avenue, N.W., Washington, D.C. 20005

Publications

"Towards an American Baptist-Roman Catholic Dialogue: Areas of Theological Agreement from a Baptist Point of View", Foundations: A Baptist Journal of History and Theology X, 2, 1967, 150-172

"Believers' Baptism and the Sacrament of Confirmation", ibid. XI, 2, 1968, 127-147

"Christian Freedom and Ecclesiastical Authority", ibid. XI, 3, 1968, 197-226

"The Nature and Communication of Grace", ibid. XII, 3, 1969, 213-231

"The Role of the Church: The Catholic Laity's View ... A Baptist Layman's View", ibid. XIII, 4, 1970, 334-353

"Toward a Theology of the Local Church; The Catholic Theology of the Local Church", ibid. XV, 1, 1972, 42-71

"Clergy-Lay Issues and Relations", ibid. XV, 2, 1972, 146-162

"Church-State Relations", ibid. XVI, 3, 1973, 261-278

Growing in Understanding. A Progress Report on the American Baptist-Roman Catholic Dialogue, 1972. Price 25¢. Obtainable from the Publications Office, United States Catholic Conference, 1312 Massachusetts Avenue, N.W., Washington, D.C. 20005, or Office of Ecumenical Relations, American Baptist Churches in the USA, Valley Forge, Pa. 19481

After 450 Years - A New Thing! A report on an American Baptist-Roman Catholic Dialogue that began in 1967, by Robert G. Torbet (reprint of six articles in Baptist Leader 1973-74). Price 25¢. Likewise obtainable from Valley Forge.

13. The Christian Church - Roman Catholic/USA................CC-RC/usa

Conversations sponsored by the Council on Christian Unity of the Christian Church (Disciples of Christ) and the Bishops' Committee for Ecumenical and Interreligious Affairs

Meetings

I. Indianapolis, Ind., March 16-17, 1967
Preliminary Meeting

II. Kansas City, Miss., September 25-27, 1967
The Nature of the Unity We Seek

III. St. Louis, Miss., April 29-May 1, 1968
A Responsible Theology for Eucharistic Intercommunion

IV. Washington, D.C., October 16-17, 1968
Mixed Marriages

V. New York, N.Y., April 25-26, 1969
Patterns and Experience of Ministry

VI. Columbus, Ohio, November 3-5, 1970
The Parish Concept in A Plan of Union from the Consultation on Church Union

VII. New York, N.Y., June 8-10, 1971
Baptism and Confirmation

VIII. Indianapolis, Ind., March 8-10, 1972
Post-Baptismal Sin and Reconciliation

IX. Madison, Wisc., June 26-28, 1972
Five Years of Dialogue between Catholics and Disciples; Analysis of Agreements and Differences

X. Pleasant Hill, Ky., May 22-24, 1973
The Church in the New Testament

In the course of its meetings, the group found notable affinities in concern and intent. There was no elaboration of formal consensus statements, but the trends of the discussions with their convergences and divergences were recorded in summary reports. The Catholic emphasis in the Disciples' tradition was for the Roman Catholic participants a discovery, and for the Disciples themselves a rediscovery of their own past. Unity, it was affirmed, does not mean spiritual unity and practical cooperation alone; the will of Christ requires nothing less than "organic constitutional union". Recognising the centrality of the eucharist in the life of both churches, the group explored its function as the central symbol of unity and a means to unity. The meeting on intercommunion declared in its closing statement: "In our respective beliefs and churchly self-understandings and even within the officially expressed statements of our Churches at present we have found sufficient theological justification in principle for some eucharistic sharing."

The distance separating the two traditions became evident, however, in the discussions around such subjects as the hierarchical structure of the Church, the relationship of freedom and authority, and the celebration of the eucharist by a lay elder or by a validly ordained priest. Advancing beyond the level of comparative theology, the group has commenced a joint study of the nature and mission of the Church as witnessed by the New Testament.

The Disciples are now involved, as part of the Reformed delegation, also in other bilateral conversations in North America.

Co-Chairmen

Dr. George G. Beazley, Jr. (till 1973); now Dr. Paul A. Crow, Jr., Indianapolis, Ind. (Christian Church)

The Most Rev. Aloysius J. Wycislo, Green Bay, Wisc. (Roman Catholic)

Co-Secretaries

The Rev. Robert H. Boyte, Associate Ecumenical Officer, Council on Christian Unity of the Christian Church, P.O. Box 1986, Indianapolis, Ind. 46206, USA

Staff member, Bishops' Committee for Ecumenical and Interreligious Affairs, 1312 Massachusetts Avenue, N.W., Washington, D.C. 20005, USA

Publications

"Bilateral Conversations between Catholics and Disciples", September 25-27, 1967; April 29 - May 1, 1968; Mid-Stream VII, 2, Winter 1967-68, 1-91

"Further Bilateral Conversations between Catholics and Disciples", October 16-17, 1970; June 8-10, 1971; March 8-10, 1972; June 26-28, 1972; Mid-Stream XII, 2-3-4, 1973-74, 1-206

An Adventure in Understanding: Roman Catholic-Disciples Dialogue 1967-1973. Publications Office, United States Catholic Conference, 1312 Massachusetts Avenue, N.W., Washington, D.C. 20005

14. Evangelical Church in the Federal Republic of Germany (EKD) - Ecumenical Patriarchate of Constantinople ....Ev-O/frg-c

Meetings

I. Istanbul, Turkey, March 16-19, 1969
The Holy Spirit in the Church and in the Believers

II. Arnoldshain, Federal Republic of Germany, October 4-8, 1971
Christ - The Salvation of the World

III. Chambésy/Geneva, Switzerland, October 2-5, 1973
The View of Man in Orthodoxy and Protestantism

After several years of sporadic discussions on the desirability of a theological encounter, the late Ecumenical Patriarch Athenagoras I seized the occasion of a visit by German Evangelical

Church leaders in 1966 to formally announce the opening of a "dialogue of faith and love". Parallel commissions were set up for the purpose, and it was decided to focus the initial meetings on three cardinal areas: pneumatology, Christology and soteriology, and anthropology. The fourth meeting, scheduled for October 1975, will consider the eucharist. The group comprises some twenty church dignitaries and theological professors.

As a "dialogue of love", these colloquies are primarily intended to promote mutual acquaintance and remove misconceptions, thereby eventually paving the way for a "dialogue of faith" exploring the possibilities of dogmatic and ecclesiological agreement. The published conference reports contain the position papers and summaries of the discussions, but due to the preliminary nature of the exchanges, no attempt is made to define divergences and convergences in agreed statements.

The discussions have covered a wide range of questions as, for example, the role of the Holy Spirit working in and through the Church as interpreter of Scripture, the embodiment of the apostolic continuity in the Church, the relationship of justification and theosis, and diverging views of "good works". The normativity of Holy Tradition, including scriptural tradition, and the appropriate methods of interpretation, emerged as a focal issue. A basic difference appeared here between a typological interpretation, expounding the scriptural foundations of Orthodox faith, and, on the other hand, a historical-critical exegesis seeking to discover the biblical message in its supremacy over later doctrinal interpretations.

The subject of the 1973 meeting is of special interest because of its rarity in bilateral conversations and its outreach to the preoccupations of contemporary man. It placed the evident differences - noticeable for instance in the divergent interpretations of the Old Testament key passage (Gen. 1:26) on man as created in the image of God - in the common context of practical pastoral concerns, and raised general questions about the meaning of human existence, where interconfessional differences are bracketed and reduced by larger interreligious and ideological oppositions.

While the debates remainded inconclusive, some preliminary results were nevertheless registered: (a) elimination of mutual misunderstandings; (b) growth of mutual trust, grounded in a shared liturgical experience; (c) discovery of the spiritual treasures of the partner church and the possibility of their assimilation; (d) awareness of the fact that, within the differing thought structures and divergent formulations, it nevertheless is possible to find equivalents; (e) the tentative securing of a common ground, which later might make it possible to bridge the profound differences (Liebfrauenberg Report, p. 12; cf. below p. 138).

Co-Chairmen

The Rev. D. Adolf Wischmann, former President of the Office of Foreign Relations of the Evangelical Church in Germany, Frankfurt/Main, Federal Republic of Germany (till 1973)

The Most Rev. Irenaios, Metropolitan of Germany, Bonn, Federal Republic of Germany (Greek Orthodox)

Co-Secretaries

Prof.Dr. Hildegard Schaeder (till 1971); Dr. Karl Christian Felmy(1971-7 Kirchliches Aussenamt der EKD, Bockenheimer Landstrasse 109, 6 Frankfurt/Main, Federal Republic of Germany

The Rt.Rev. Augustinus, Bishop of Elea, c/o Greek Orthodox Metropolis of Germany, Niebuhr-Strasse 61, 53 Bonn, Federal Republic of Germany

Publications

Dialog des Glaubens und der Liebe, hrsg. vom Kirchlichen Aussenamt der Evangelischen Kirche in Deutschland (Beiheft zur Okumenischen Rundschau, 11), Stuttgart: Evangelischer Missionsverlag, 1970

Christus - das Heil der Welt (Beiheft zur Okumenischen Rundschau, 22), Stuttgart: Evangelischer Missionsverlag, 1972

Das Bild vom Menschen in Orthodoxie und Protestantismus (Beiheft zur Okumenischen Rundschau, 26),Stuttgart: Evangelischer Missionverlag, 1974

15. Evangelical Church in the Federal Republic of Germany (EKD) - Russian Orthodox Church ....Ev-O/frg-r

Meetings

I. Arnoldshain, Federal Republic of Germany,
October 27-29, 1959 (A I)
Tradition; Justification

II. Zagorsk, USSR, October 21-25, 1963 (A II)
The Work of the Holy Spirit in Worship and Sacraments and in the Ancient Councils

III. Hoechst, Federal Republic of Germany, March 3-8, 1967 (A III)
The Christian View of Reconciliation in Biblical Perspective, in the Work of the Church, and in the Efforts for Peace

IV. Leningrad, USSR, September 12-19, 1969 (A IV)
Baptism; the New Life and Church Membership; The Responsibility of the Baptized for the World

V. Kirchberg/Horb, Federal Republic of Germany, October 20-28, 1971 (A V)
The Risen Christ and the Salvation of the World

VI. Zagorsk, USSR, November 26-29, 1973 (A VI)
The Eucharist

In 1959, an official dialogue was inaugurated between the German Evangelical Church in the Federal Republic of Germany (EKD) and the Russian Orthodox Church, acting through their offices for external relations. The German Evangelical Church is a federation comprising churches of Lutheran, Reformed and United background, but because of the composition of its delegation, the meetings have in fact largely had the character of a Lutheran-Orthodox encounter. As with other Orthodox dialogues, the aim is to reach greater mutual understanding through personal encounters and an exchange of information about the life and thought of the two churches, and by exploring areas of common faith. That the wider ecumenical and international horizons of the encounters are not overlooked is explicitly confirmed in a statement from the 1973 meeting:"... with great satisfaction the partners note the usefulness of this long-term dialogue for the strengthening of fraternal relations between the Evangelical Church in Germany (FRG) and the Russian Orthodox Church, for the ecumenical movement at large and for the growth of mutual understanding and amity between the FRG and the USSR."

Each meeting is generally focused on a central theme, which is treated from the perspective of major theological disciplines and introduced in paired papers from both sides. The conference reports are unusually complete, including, besides ceremonial addresses and sermons, all the papers presented, agreed statements, and lately also extensive digests of the taperecorded discussions. The reports are published in a German series, partly also in Russian periodicals. For the sake of convenience the meetings are usually named and numbered after the place of the first meeting: Arnoldshain (or A) I, etc.

The conversations began with an exploratory re-examination of two subjects traditionally regarded - along with the threefold apostolic ministry - as critical points of division: tradition and scripture, and justification and sanctification. Despite the chasm, convergences became apparent, as for instance in the declaration that "Both Churches recognize one source of salvation: the revelation of Jesus Christ, which through the apostles is communicated to men in oral preaching and in writings. The tradition must not contradict the witness of Scripture. Its concordance with Scripture is the essential criterion of its authenticity" (A I, p. 10). A distinction must therefore be maintained between the tradition of the apostles and Church traditions. As still open questions were noted the scope and authenticity of the apostolic tradition after the fixation of the New Testament canon; how the continuity of the pure apostolic tradition in the Church is to be understood; and the weight to be attached to the criterion of age, alongside the criterion of truth, in distinguishing between apostolic tradition and later decisions of the Church.

The discussion was continued at the second meeting, but now in the larger perspective of the work of the Holy Spirit, especially as it is manifested in the ecumenical councils. Over against the first meeting, the renewed discussion revealed a certain retraction in so much as the divergences now re-appeared with strength. It was admitted that the agreement initially found in regard to Holy Tradition was "only partial", and it was symptomatic that the group on this occasion, in contrast to other subjects, presented its dialectic of agreements and disagreements in the form of parallel and not joint propositions (A II, pp. 29-31). Thus "the Orthodox theologians acknowledge the immutable theological and ecclesiastical importance of the seven ecumenical councils, which, under the cooperation of the Holy Spirit, have expressed the faith of the Church and fixed its canonical order with precise dogmatic definition". The Evangelical theologians fully concurred in the opinion of the Orthodox theologians that God in the ancient ecumenical synods has led the Church on a road on which we all can look back with gratitude. "In the dogmatic discussions of these synods we hear the voice of the Holy Spirit." Both agree that the councils offer no supplemental revelation, but a reaffirmation of the apostolic tradition in face of heresies. The Orthodox participants underscore the point by explicitly rejecting the very possibility of a development of dogma.

Within this convergence, a seemingly slight but in fact profound ecclesiological difference appears in the following proposition: "The Orthodox theologians hold the conviction that the ecumenical councils are organs of the Church, which in like measure reflect as well the consciousness of the Church as the will of God manifested by the Holy Spirit. The Evangelical theologians believe that the activity of these synods is not grounded in the manner in which they were convened, but in the fact that the ecumenical Church hears through them the voice of the Holy Spirit ..." (A II, p. 29).

A second recurring theme embraces the problems of justification and sanctification, grace, reconciliation, where also the ecclesial, societal and cosmic dimensions of reconciliation received due attention. As with the problem of scripture and tradition, so here too the attempt to stake out common ground was accompanied by an elimination of mutual misconceptions. Three propositions outline the scope of the consensus: "We receive justification through grace in faith in the salvation brought through the Lord Jesus Christ. There exists no justification on the ground of good works. The Reformation experience of justification by faith has a far-reaching equivalent in Orthodox liturgy and ascetics" (A I, p. 11; A IV, p. 26). Hereby two ingrained misconceptions were removed:" ... that in Orthodox theology good works are a prerequisite for justification, and that in Reformation theology the New Testament teaching on judgment according to works is rejected".

The following meeting, leaving aside the terms of the 16th century controversy in Western Christinity, shed new light on the subject by focusing on another, more prominent New Testament image, that of reconciliation. A study of the New Testament data proved highly fruitful. Not only did it indicate a substantial concordance, it also made clear to what extent the polarities inherent in the biblical vision later were distorted and absolutised into false dichotomies. The perennial difficulty of relating God's action in Jesus Christ and the believer's - also the non-believer's - "synergy" in the ministry of reconciliation, or the emphasis in the Orthodox tradition on the cosmic objectivity of God's act of reconciling the world with himself contra the preoccupation in Western piety and theology with the conditions of its individual appropriation, are signalised as outstanding examples.

The joint report takes note of two major remaining divergences: the effect of God's reconciling work on persons who do not believe in Jesus Christ, and the related question whether it changes the moral condition of the world apart from faith (A III, p. 23).

The linkage of reconciliation with Christian co-responsibility for world peace is a prominent concern of Russian Orthodox dialogues - and not only on political but ultimately on religious grounds. That this linkage is inherent in the Christian faith is aptly suggested by the title for the 1967 conference - reconciliation. For the Russian term here used for reconciliation primirenie is a derivation of the root mir, meaning peace. Since then the theology and practice of peace has been a recurrent topic, and while divisions of opinion in matters of policy are not reflected in the joint statements, these indicate a general agreement on theological principles governing the peace witness of the churches (e.g. A III, pp. 25f; A IV, pp. 26ff; A V, pp. 25f).

The sacramental life of the Church belongs to the self-evident foundations of any Orthodox dialogue. Viewing the sacraments in the double context of the Church and the world, the group has probed the meaning of baptism as the incorporation in the body of Christ, a re-birth instituting a new way of life. It is recognised that the baptismal rites of both churches are valid and hence unrepeatable acts (A IV, pp. 24ff). Currently, the group is engaged in a study of the eucharist, drawing not only on the doctrinal teachings of the two Churches but on their eucharistic liturgies, hymns and practices, and enriched by the experience of attending each other's celebrations. The 1973 meeting, incidentally, for the first time deliberately linked the dialogue with the wider ecumenical scene by including two presentations of the eucharist in current ecumenical thought and practice.

Of particular note is the attention given to the corporate ecclesial and socio-ethical - dimensions of the eucharist. In each celebration the whole Church participates. And a consensus statement on "The Eucharist and the Transformation of the World" asserts that "the Lord's Supper is a powerful force for the transformation of each Christian, the Christian Church, and through them the surrounding world, for good and for holiness. By the operation of his Holy Spirit, Christ present in the Supper makes the Christian open to every truly good will towards reconciliation, peace and justice, which he encounters in the world" (A VI, p. 26).

Among the issues that remain to be examined, the last report mentions the sacrificial character of the eucharist, and, especially, the qualifications of a valid celebrant. It is the divisive question of apostolic continuity and ministry that here arises on the horizon. This is also a principal reason why the Orthodox Church, despite the growth of mutual appreciation, cannot grant the Reformation churches ecclesial recognition. The occasional references to this crucial ecumenical issue move cautiously forward between the poles of bounded faith and boundless love. While the Evangelical Churches unhesitatingly recognise the Russian Orthodox Church as Church of Jesus Christ, the latter "regards the Christians belonging to the Evangelical Church, born of water and spirit, as members of the body of Christ ... [But] they do not receive the grace, which, in the fulness of the Orthodox Church, is bestowed on its members through the priesthood and which continually manifests itself as the bestowal of the gifts of the Holy Spirit (pre-eminently in the sacraments)." Yet there immediately follows an assertion that "each of us knows that the members of the other Church are living in the assured confidence of sharing, in their Church, in the fulness of promises and gifts which the Lord has given and gives his Church. Hence the problem of unity is a particularly burning one for our churches" (A III, pp. 21f).

Co-Chairmen

The Rev. D. Adolf Wischmann, former President of the office for Foreign Relations of the Evangelical Church in Germany, Frankfurt/Main, Federal Republic of Germany (till 1973)

The Most Rev. Juvenaly, Metropolitan of Tula and Belev, Chairman of the Department of External Church Relations of the Moscow Patriarchate, Moscow, USSR

Co-Secretaries

Prof.Dr. Hildegard Schaeder (till 1971); Dr. Karl Christian Felmy (1971-1975), Kirchliches Aussenamt der EKD, Bockenheimer Landstrasse 109, 6 Frankfurt/Main, Federal Republic of Germany

Staff member, Department of External Church Relations of the Moscow Patriarchate, 18/2 Ryleeva, Moscow G-34, USSR

Publications

Tradition und Glaubensgerechtigkeit. Das Arnoldshainer Gespräch zwischen Vertretern der evangelischen Kirche Deutschlands und der russisch-orthodoxen Kirche vom Oktober 1959. Studienheft 3. Hrsg. vom Aussenamt der Evangelischen Kirche in Deutschland. Witten: Luther Verlag, 1961

Vom Wirken des Heiligen Geistes. Das Sagorsker Gespräch über Gottesdienst, Sakrament und Synoden ... 1963. Studienheft 4. Witten, 1964 (The minutes of the discussions at this conference appeared in Evangelische Theologie, 1965, Heft 9.)

Versöhnung ... 1967. Studienheft 5. Witten, 1967

Taufe - Neues Leben - Dienst ... 1969. Studienheft 6. Witten, 1970

Der auferstandene Christus und das Heil der Welt ... 1971. Studienheft 7. Witten, 1972

Die Eucharistie ... 1973. Studienheft 8. Bielefeld: Luther Verlag, 1974

Reports of the conferences, agreed theses, and various position papers are also published in Bogoslovskie Trudy (Moscow), The Journal of the Moscow Patriarchate, Stimme der Orthodoxie (Berlin) and Informationen aus der Orthodoxen Kirche (Kirchliches Aussenamt, EKD, Frankfurt/Main)

16. Federation of Evangelical Churches in the German Democratic Republic - Russian Orthodox Church ....Ev-O/gdr-r

Meetings

I. Zagorsk, USSR, July 8-11, 1974

The Orthodox-Protestant Dialogue in the Context of the Ecumenical Movement; Preaching Today; the Church in a Socialist Society

On the occasion of the visit of Protestant church leaders from the German Democratic Republic in Moscow in 1972, Metropolitan Nikodim proposed the initiation of a theological dialogue between the two churches on the general theme of "Tradition and Situation". The matter was further clarified at a counter-visit the following year. The outcome was an agenda envisaging an exchange of information about the life of the two Churches and their cooperation in the ecumenical movement, and a theological exploration of common problems arising from the encounter of the Christian tradition with the present situation. The fact that the participating churches were living in socialist countries was pointed out as a special reason for such an exchange also at the official level.

The three sub-topics of the first meeting were presented by a speaker from each side and the trends of the discussion recorded in agreed summaries. The opening session turned largely around the theological foundations for the peace efforts which the Russian Orthodox Church is pursuing, in part jointly with other religions, and, more generally, the distinctive role of the Church.

In the discussion on preaching, a contrast appeared between two hermeneutical approaches: one shaped by the living tradition of the Church, centering in the liturgy, and another influenced by the historical-critical method in biblical studies. But a substantial consensus was nevertheless expressed in the succinct theses on the subject: " (1) The proclamation of the Gospel to all creatures has been commissioned to the Church by the Lord for all times. The proclamation continues the work of the apostles. Its abiding content is the Lord Jesus Christ, for us crucified, risen and exalted ... (2) The witness to Christ is effected through the life of the whole Church and of all its members. (3) The sermon addresses itself to man of today."

Finally, the group exchanged experiences about the problems confronting the two Churches in a new society, in which, freed from an age-long confusion of church and state, they have to learn to live in sole dependence on their Lord. This does not justify a life of withdrawal, on the contrary: "Christians must work so that every man can achieve the full development of his personality and so that in all circumstances freedom, brotherhood and the inviolable dignity of every man is the basis of social life".

Co-Chairmen

The Rt.Rev. Werner Krusche, Magdeburg, German Democratic Republic

The Most Rev. Juvenaly, Metropolitan of Tula and Belev, Chairman of the Department of External Church Relations of the Moscow Patriarchate, Moscow, USSR

Co-Secretaries

Dr. Günther Schulz, Naumburg, German Democratic Republic

Mr. A.S. Buievsky, Department of External Church Relations of the Moscow Patriarchate, 18/2 Ryleeva, Moscow G-34, USSR

Publications

The conference proceedings will be published in book form by the Evangelische Verlagsanstalt, Berlin 1976. The major documents will appear also in the journal Die Zeichen der Zeit, 1975. In the absence of primary sources, the present account is based on an unpublished report by Günther Schulz.

"Résumé of the Reports ...", The Journal of the Moscow Patriarchate, 1974, 10, 70-72; also in Stimme der Orthodoxie, 1974, 10, 39-56

17. Finnish Lutheran-Russian Orthodox Theological Conversations ....L-O/f-r

Sponsored by the Evangelical Lutheran Church of Finland and the Russian Orthodox Church

Meetings

I. Turku, Finland, March 19-22, 1970
The Eucharist as Manifestation of the Unity of Believers; the Theological Foundations of the Churches' Peace Efforts

II. Zagorsk, USSR, December 12-16, 1971
The Eucharist, especially its Sacrificial Nature; Justice and Violence

III. Järvenpää, Finland, May 23-28, 1974
The Doctrine of Eucharist and Priesthood; the Christian Teaching of Salvation; the Churches' Service to the World Today

The dialogue has grown out of the official visits that have been made between representatives of the two Churches, and in 1967 it was decided to include in the visitations programmes a prepared theological discussion of doctrinal and socio-ethical subjects. The group is composed of some fifteen church leaders and theologians. The first meeting included three invited observers from the small Orthodox Church of Finland, which belongs to the Constantinople jurisdiction; at the second meeting the group was enlarged by professors from the Zagorsk Spiritual Academy, and the third included six observers from the Orthodox Church of Finland and the Ecumenical Council of Finland (Baptist, Methodist, and Roman Catholic). Position papers and agreed statements are published in Finnish and Russian theological journals.

The programme is centered around two poles: the eucharist and peace. According to the 1970 meeting, "The unity in the eucharist is the deepest manifestation of the oneness of the Church"; but precisely for this reason intercommunion is inconceivable. For " ... the eucharist cannot be used as a tool to bring about unity"; it is the sacramental act of communion within the one Church. The achievement of doctrinal consensus is therefore a precondition of eucharistic sharing (Turku Report, Lutheran World XIX, 3, 1972, 289). The following meeting pursued the examination of the two doctrines held to be divisive - the mode of Christ's presence in the eucharist and its sacrificial character. Agreement was confirmed on basic points: the centrality of the eucharist in the saving work of the Holy Spirit, bestowing forgiveness of sins and sanctification; the real presence of Jesus Christ "in the fullness of his person as God and man"; the once-for-all sacrifice of Calvary. As doctrinal differences were noted the Orthodox belief in the permanence of Christ's eucharistic presence in bread and wine beyond the act of celebration, and the reluctance of the Lutheran partner to interpret the eucharist in sacrificial terms so as not to detract from the uniqueness of Calvary. Continuing the study of the eucharist, the 1974 meeting took up the question of the valid celebrant in relation to apostolicity which was defined as "the continuity in the Church of the Gospel teaching and the Sacraments as they were instituted by Christ and proclaimed by the Apostles by the action of the Holy Spirit". Accordingly it was maintained that "The Eucharist, ordained by Christ, may be celebrated only by persons in Holy Orders" and that its validity does not depend on the moral qualities and spiritual state of the celebrant but "only on the due performance of the sacramental act". Further studies will explore the meaning of apostolic succession and the significance of the fact that it from the beginning involved "both the continuity of correct apostolic teaching and the succession of the laying on of hands".

The statement on the Christian teaching of salvation, spanning the arc from creation to the eschatological fulfilment, is essentially a summary of New Testament teachings on the subject; its consensus demonstrates again the unifying power of common Bible study. In an assessment of the Bangkok Conference, 1973, on "Salvation Today", the group concurred in its emphasis on human liberation, justice and peace, but insisted that "the real 'triumph of salvation' comes when man is reconciled with God and his fellowman in Jesus Christ, and especially when the Church celebrates the eucharist".

The continuing discussions on peace and war spell out the responsibility of Christians and churches to strive together, and with all people of good will, "against the exploitation of their fellowman, the degrading of the value of man, racial discrimination and all forms of discrimination, hunger, poverty, injustice, and against everything which is a threat to world peace and normal life". A special point is made of grounding the Christian peace efforts in God's redemption of mankind in Jesus Christ.

Co-Chairmen

The Most Rev. Martti Simojoki, Archbishop of Finland, Helsinki (Lutheran)

The Most Rev. Vladimir, Archbishop of Dmitrov (Orthodox)

Publications

Papers and agreed statements are published in Teologinen Aikakauskirja (Helsinki) and Bogoslovskie Trudy (Moscow) VII, 1971, pp. 212-249 and XI, 1973, pp. 162-209; partly also in The Journal of the Moscow Patriarchate, Stimme der Ostkirche (Berlin), and Informationen aus der Orthodoxen Kirche (Kirchliches Aussenamt, EKD, Frankfurt/Main)

"A Report on the Summary of the Finnish Lutheran - Russian Orthodox Discussions", by Maunu Sinnemäki, Lutheran World XIX, 3, 1972, 288-292

"The Third Theological Conversations between the Russian Orthodox Church and the Evangelical Lutheran Church of Finland", The Journal of the Moscow Patriarchate, 1974, 10, 61-69

18. Lutheran-Orthodox/USA..................................L-O/usa

"Lutheran-Orthodox Consultation" sponsored by the USA National Committee of the Lutheran World Federation and the Standing Conference of Canonical Orthodox Bishops in the Americas

Meetings

I. New York, N.Y., November 17-18, 1967
   Scripture and Tradition

II. New York, N.Y., March 21-22, 1969
   Scripture and Tradition

Background. When these conversations were first announced, it was explained that they would "pick up an unfinished task of history". In the 16th century, Lutheran and Orthodox churchmen did in fact engage in a series of bilateral conversations exploring such subjects of common concern as Scripture and tradition, justification and sanctification. These produced no results. Since the Second World war, however, as earlier indicated, Lutheran-Orthodox dialogues of various kinds have been undertaken in Europe, stimulating a similar effort in the United States.

Composition of the Group. The project was initiated by the USA National Committee of the Lutheran World Federation and the invitation was accepted by the Standing Conference of Canonical Orthodox Bishops in the Americas in October 1965. The group consisted of seven theologians from each side, together with some staff consultants. The participants were drawn from six Orthodox and three Lutheran churches, including the Missouri Synod.

Work of the Group. The first meeting began with presentations on the faith and life of the two communions, which disclosed a number of unexpected parallels between their two historical experiences in America. "Liturgy and Theology in the Modern World" had originally been scheduled as the subject of the second meeting, but instead, the group continued its discussion of Scripture and tradition. To permit a systematic analysis of the respective positions, the two delegations met part of the time in separate sessions to prepare questions for each other and to formulate responses. The meeting did not produce any statement, but the questions posed are indicative of the trend of the discussion.

Orthodox questions to the Lutherans:

(1) How do you understand the concept of the self-sufficiency and the superiority of Holy Scripture? (What does Sola Scriptura (the Word alone) mean today?)

(2) How do you evaluate the Fathers of the Church as authentic interpreters of the Scripture and as witnesses of the dogmatic and liturgical life of the Church?

(3) By what criteria does one discern the presence and guidance of the Holy Spirit in correctly understanding and properly teaching the truths of Holy Scripture?

Lutheran questions to the Orthodox:

(1) If tradition is viewed as the critical spirit of the Church, made acute by the Holy Spirit, and its validity is established by a consensus, how is the tradition known to be Orthodox without a new Ecumenical Council?

(2) In the light of your present understanding of Lutheran attitudes towards tradition, do you recognize any ecclesial reality within the Lutheran Church? If not, why not?

(3) If the Holy Spirit sustains all Christians obedient to their Bishop, what are the doctrinal implications of schism?

A third meeting on "The Nature of the Church" scheduled for March 1970 was cancelled. The dialogue was later resumed in the form of a joint Lutheran-Reformed dialogue with the Orthodox.

Publications

Press releases 67-102 and 69-39, News Bureau, Lutheran Council in the USA, 315 Park Avenue South, New York, N.Y. 10010

19. Lutheran-Orthodox-Reformed/North America................L-O-R/nam

"Lutheran-Orthodox-Reformed Theological Conversations" sponsored by the Division of Theological Studies of the Lutheran Council in the USA, the Standing Conference of Canonical Orthodox Bishops in the Americas, and the North American Area of the World Alliance of Reformed Churches.

Theme: The Christian Gospel and Social Responsibility

Meetings

I. Princeton, N.J., November 9-10, 1973
Biblical Aspects

II. New York, N.Y., November 1-2, 1974
The Respective Historical Approaches as They Illuminate the Confessional Principles Involved

III. November 7-8, 1975
The Christian Gospel in Contemporary North American Society

The Orthodox conversations in North America with the Lutherans were adjourned in 1969 and those with the Reformed in 1970. To avoid vasteful duplication, informal consultations were initiated on the possibility of replacing these parallel dialogues with a trialogue - or rather an enlarged bilateral in so much as, in Orthodox perspective, the Lutheran and Reformed appear as minor variations within the same Reformation tradition. The proposal was approved in 1973 by the bodies concerned.

The plan calls for a series of three annual consultations, eventually resulting in a joint report. In the forefront stands the perennially controversial question of the interrelationship of theology and social ethics. The third session will deal with "civil religion", the political structures of North American society, and specific ethical issues. The group is composed of six theologians from each side.

Members of the Steering Committee

Dr. Paul D. Opsahl, Division of Theological Studies of the Lutheran Council in the USA, New York, N.Y.

Prof. John Meyendorff, St. Vladimir's Orthodox Theological Seminary, Tuckahoe, N.Y.

Prof. Joseph C. McLelland, McGill University, Montreal, Canada

20. Lutheran-Reformed/Canada..................................L-R/can

"Canadian Lutheran-Reformed Conversations" sponsored by the Lutheran Council in Canada and the two Canadian members of the World Alliance of Reformed Churches

Meetings

I. Winnipeg, Manitoba, May 15-17, 1972
Review of Lutheran-Reformed Dialogues in Europe and the USA; Planning

II. Toronto, Ontario, November 13-15, 1972
Mutual Examination of Each Other's Traditions; Lessons from the United Church of CanadaUnion in 1925; Aims, Methods and Procedure of the Dialogue

III. Saskatoon, Saskatechewan, May 14-15, 1973
How Lutheran and Reformed View Their Confessions

IV. St. Norbert, Manitoba, November 4-5, 1973
Concepts of Authority in the Church

V. Toronto, Ontario, May 14-16, 1974
The Lutheran and the Reformed Self-Understanding

Background. The idea of a Lutheran-Reformed Dialogue in Canada originated with the North American Area of the World Alliance of Reformed Churches and the invitation issued by the Reformed Churches was accepted by the Lutheran Church of Canada in early 1971.

Terms of Reference. The general aim of the dialogue is to remove misconceptions and to explore areas where cooperation and fellowship might be mutually beneficial. Organic union is not envisioned. The group has defined its objectives as follows:

(1) To work toward a fuller realisation and expression of the unity that is God's gift to us in Jesus Christ.

(2) Remove false images of our churches and develop among our people an understanding both of what we have in common and of the obstacles to unity between us.

(3) Encourage our churches to explore areas where they can cooperate with each other and also with other men and women of good will in community enterprises.

Composition of the Group. Deliberately kept small, it consists of two representatives each from the Presbyterian Church in Canada and the United Church of Canada, and one representative from each of the three Lutheran bodies composing the Lutheran Council, plus an officer of the Council.

Work of the Group. Attempting to chart a distinctly Canadian course in its deliberations, the dialogue commenced with a frank re-examination of the relationship of the partners. The establishment of the United Church of Canda in 1925 was an ecumenical landmark in Canadian church history, but it caused a split in the Presbyterian Church, with part of it rejecting the merger. The Lutheran Churches, on the other hand, were seeking union among themselves - a process which might have the negative side-effect of tending to strengthen their apartness, the more so since they are less "indigenized" than the Reformed, two of them moreover being connected organisationally with church bodies in the USA. Both dialogue partners would therefore have much to learn from each other's experience and insights, both in jointly re-examining their attitudes to the historic confessions and in gaining a clearer perception of the extent to which their self-understandings and divisions were conditioned by non-religious factors in European and Canadian history. "We share a common concern" states the group. "While recognizing the historical validity of our confessions, we seek to be confessionally relevant to an ever changing contemporary situation."

It was in this perspective that the group then proceeded to discuss the question of authority in the Church, stressing the servanthood of authority. "The authority of Jesus Christ to which Scripture and creeds testify is the authority of one who serves, and is therefore redemptive in intent and pastoral in character."

Following the 1974 meeting a small sub-committee was appointed to sum up the results and to shape plans for the future.

Chairman

Dr. James D. Smart, Islington, Ontario

Secretary

The Rev. Norman J. Threinen, Executive Secretary of the Division of Theological Studies, Lutheran Council in Canada, 500-365 Hargrave Street, Winnipeg, Manitoba R3B 2K3, Canada

21. Lutheran-Reformed/USA.................. ....L-R/usa

"Lutheran-Reformed Conversations" sponsored by the USA National Committee of the Lutheran World Federation (since 1971 by the Lutheran Council in the USA) and the North American Area of the World Alliance of Reformed Churches

First Series

Meetings

I. Chicago, Ill., February 21-24, 1963
Gospel, Confession and Scripture

II. New York, N.Y., February 27-29, 1964
Christology, the Lord's Supper and its Observance in the Church

III. St. Louis, Mo., February 25-28, 1965
Justification and Sanctification; Liturgy and Ethics; Creation and Redemption; Law and Gospel

IV. Princeton, N.J., February 24-27, 1966
Ethics and Ethos; Summaries and Comments

Background. The transplantation of the Lutheran and Reformed traditions to American soil entailed also a transplantation of their divisions, but now modified by certain indigenous characteristics. On the one hand, the persistent association with particular ethnic and linguistic heritages, brought over by successive waves of immigrants, added fresh complications to the religious scene and oftentimes greater rigidity to the inherited differences. On the other hand, unlike their European counterparts, they had all been exposed to the pervasive influence of a common American culture with its bent towards religious voluntarism, pluralism and pragmatism. Another and more recent development, which inevitably affects their mutual relations in America, is the development of the Consultation on Church Union initiated in 1960; while the United Presbyterian Church in the USA and the Presbyterian Church in the U.S. are taking an active part in the venture to unite nine Churches into one body, the Lutheran Churches, though sending observers, have remained aside.

Apart from the general movement of convergence in Protestant theology and biblical scholarship, the Lutheran-Reformed conversations in North America were especially stimulated by the parallel efforts in various European countries, particularly since the Second World War. Originally proposed by the secretary of the North American Area of the World Alliance of Reformed Churches Holding the Presbyterian Order, Dr. James I. McCord, the plan for such conversations was officially approved in the spring of 1961 by that group and by the USA National Committee of the Lutheran World Federation.

Terms of Reference. The stated aim was "to explore the theological relations between the Lutheran and the Reformed churches to discover to what extent differences which have divided these communions in the past still constitute obstacles to mutual understanding" (Marburg Revisited, "Preface").

Composition of the Group. In addition to official representatives of the North American churches affiliated with the two sponsoring bodies, the group included participants from the Lutheran Church-Missouri Synod, the Orthodox Presbyterian Church, and the Christian Reformed Church. The total membership consisted of sixteen delegates, six alternates, and three officers of the sponsoring organisations as consultants. With the exception of two of the latter, all the participants were professors of theology.

Work of the Group. Following a preliminary meeting in New York, in February 1962, four annual consultations wereheld. The papers and discussion summaries prepared in connection with each consultation were published in booklet form and, finally, as a single volume with the suggestive title Marburg Revisited. The annual meetings were conceived as stages in a progressive journey of exploration; the summary statements emanating from the individual meetings were accordingly regarded as tentative and the final meeting was given over to a review of the whole process, resulting in supplementary statements which amplified the earlier agreements.

As was the case with its European counterpart, the North American series of conversations represented an attempt to penetrate behind the divisive positions of the 16th century struggles to the religious issues at stake, and to rethink both the issues and the answers in the light of present-day biblical and theological scholarship. The result was a reaffirmation, in part also a fresh discovery, of common foundations and a mutual recognition of evangelical concerns. At its final meeting the group adopted a statement which appraised its work in these terms:

> A number of differing views and emphases remain to be resolved, but we are encouraged to believe that further contacts will lead to further agreement between the churches here represented. We regard none of these remaining differences to be of sufficient consequence to prevent fellowship. We have recognized in each other's teachings a common understanding of the Gospel and have concluded that the issues

> which divided the two major branches of the Reformation can no longer be regarded as constituting obstacles to mutual understanding and fellowship. (Marburg Revisited, "Preface")

While it had been stressed at the beginning that pulpit and altar fellowship were not an immediate objective, but only the subject of theological exploration, the concluding report to the sponsoring confessional organisations culminates in the recommendation "that they encourage their constituent churches to enter into discussions looking forward to intercommunion and the fuller recognition of one another's ministries" (ibid., p. 191).

Publication

Marburg Revisited: A Re-examination of Lutheran and Reformed Traditions. Edited by Paul C. Empie and James I. McCord. Minneapolis: Augsburg Publishing House, 1966

Second Series

Meetings

I_2 Princeton, N.J., April 14-16, 1972
The Church in Dialogue in 1972; An American (Lutheran) (Reformed) Looks at Leuenberg; Marburg Revisited in Light of 1972

II_2 Chicago, Ill., November 10-12, 1972
Appraisal of the Leuenberg Agreement

III_2 New York, N.Y., March 9-10, 1973
Identity and Identification; Catholicity and Confessional Identity; Sociology of the Protestant Church in America

IV_2 Grand Rapids, Michigan, October 25-27, 1973
Official Positions of the Eight Participating Churches Regarding Requirements for Pulpit and Altar Fellowship; the Role of the Eucharist in the Life of the Church

V_2 New York, N.Y., March 15-16, 1974
Assessment of the Consensus and the Remaining Differences; Plans for Final Report

VI_2 Princeton, N.J., September 27-28, 1974
Drafting of Final Report

Background. The first series of the conversations, although bereft of any positive response on the part of church authorities, signaled a new era in Lutheran-Reformed relations in the United States, which called for a continued effort. The Leuenberg conversations in Europe were followed with close attention. Moreover, the previously mentioned Lutheran-Reformed Joint Committee at its meeting in January 1970 had commended the Leuenberg approach to the two world bodies as a possible modus operandi for all member churches engaged in similar conversations. In line with these developments, it was decided in July 1971 to launch a second round of conversations, with the Lutheran Council in the USA replacing the USA National Committee of the Lutheran World Federation as joint sponsor.

Terms of Reference. The stated purpose is "to assess the consensus and the remaining differences in the theology and life of the participating churches as they bear upon the teaching of the Gospel in the current situation".

Composition of the Group. The group is composed of twelve representatives and six alternates designated by the Presidents of the three Lutheran Church bodies participating in the Lutheran Council in the USA and by the North American Area of the WARC. The Churches represented are: American Lutheran Church, Lutheran Church in America, the Lutheran Church-Missouri Synod, the Presbyterian Church in the U.S., the United Presbyterian Church, the Christian Reformed Church, the Reformed Church in America, and the United Church of Christ.

Work of the Group. Having reviewed the previous conversations, the group undertook a critical analysis of the Leuenberg Agreement among Lutheran and Reformed Churches in Europe as a possible model for its own work. In view of the very different religious situation in the USA, however, it was decided rather to investigate "other resources for a possible consensus statement", exploring the meaning of the Gospel for a "fuller expression of church fellowship, witness and service" among the churches involved. As steps in such an enquiry, the group focused its attention on one of the most sensitive issues in current interconfessional debate - the problem of self-identity - and on the juridical and disciplinary aspects of altar and pulpit fellowship. A report with recommendations is expected to be submitted to the sponsoring organisations in 1975.

Co-Chairmen

Dr. William Weiblen, Wartburg Theological Seminary, Dubuque, Iowa (Lutheran)

Dr. M. Eugene Osterhaven, Western Theological Seminary, Holland, Michigan (Reformed)

Co-Secretaries

Dr. Paul D. Opsahl, Division of Theological Studies, Lutheran Council in the USA, 315 Park Avenue South, New York, N.Y. 10010

President James I. McCord, Princeton Theological Seminary, Princeton, N.J. 08540

22. Lutheran-Reformed-United/Europe..........................L-R-U/eur

Conversations sponsored by the Lutheran World Federation, the World Alliance of Reformed Churches and the Commission on Faith and Order of the World Council of Churches

First Series

Meetings

I. Bad Schauenburg, Switzerland, April 6-10, 1964

II. Bad Schauenburg, April 20-24, 1965

III. Bad Schauenburg, April 12-16, 1966

IV. Bad Schauenburg, March 28 - April 1, 1967
Report: "Lutheran and Reformed Churches in Europe on the Way to Each Other"

Second Series

I_2 Leuenberg, Switzerland, April 8-12, 1969
Church Fellowship and Church Divisions

II_2 Leuenberg, March 31 - April 4, 1970
Church Fellowship and Church Division

III_2 Leuenberg, September 19-24, 1971
First Official Draft of the Leuenberg Agreement

IV_2 Leuenberg, March 12-16, 1973
Final Text

Background. Since the 16th century repeated efforts have been undertaken to overcome the split between the Lutheran and Reformed traditions or to establish closer relationships between them. In the 19th century United Churches were created in Germany under the influence and pressure of the state. In other European countries, where the two churches formed a minority, as for example in Austria, France and Hungary, forms of practical Church fellowship emerged (including intercommunion) which, nevertheless, lacked the foundation of an official theological consensus. After the Second World War the endeavours to overcome the Lutheran-Reformed separation were intensified, especially in France, Germany, Holland and the USA. Since in all these endeavours the same basic theological problems were involved, it seemed appropriate to initiate Lutheran-Reformed conversations on a broader level.

History. A first initiative for Lutheran-Reformed conversations in Europe came from the Commission on Faith and Order of the World Council of Churches. Between 1955 and 1959 a number of meetings were held between leading Lutheran and Reformed theologians. In 1963 the Commission on Faith and Order, in cooperation with the Lutheran World Federation and the World Alliance of Reformed Churches, created a working group of Lutheran and Reformed theologians. This group, which was not officially appointed by the churches, held four meetings - the "Schauenburg Conversations" - between 1964 and 1967. As a result of these conversations three series of theses on "The Word of God", "The Law" and "The Confession" were published.

A Joint Study Committee of Lutheran and Reformed theologians, appointed by the Executive Committees of the LWF and the WARC, and a Consultation of participants of the Schauenburg Conversations, the LWF, the WARC and the Commission on Faith and Order, evaluated in Spring 1968 the results of the Schauenburg conversations. Both meetings proposed a continuation of the dialogue. Accordingly a new group was formed with a wider representation of European Lutheran and Reformed churches and including also delegates from United churches. After two meetings in Leuenberg in 1969 and 1970 the group completed its work. Its report closed with the proposal that church fellowship between the two Churches should be achieved by way of a "concord". A draft of such a "concord" was worked out by a sub-committee, subsequently revised and accepted by a larger group of official delegates in September 1971, and submitted to the European Reformation churches. The Agreement was again revised and finalised at a further Leuenberg conference in 1973 and sent out for the churches for ratification by September 30, 1974. The proposal generated intense and in part highly controversial debates. But by the date of ratification, sixty churches had declared their assent and of the remaining twenty-eight eligible to vote, many had informally indicated their intention to do likewise.

Terms of Reference. The aim of the Schauenburg conversations was to examine whether the historic split between the two traditions was still justified today. The theses which were worked out showed that the doctrinal differences had ceased to be of divisive import. The aim of the Leuenberg conversations consisted consequently in taking the next and decisive step of defining the necessary theological foundations for full church fellowship and projecting ways of implementation.

Appointment and Composition of the Group. The participants in the Leuenberg conversations were officially appointed by their respective churches. The 1973 conference comprised 45 delegates from 16 countries, a high proportion of whom were church leaders and officials, including legal experts. The group further included executive staff from the Faith and Order Secretariat, the LWF and the WARC.

The Leuenberg Agreement. The distinctive feature of the Agreement is the nature of the interchurch fellowship which it envisions. "Church fellowship means that, on the basis of the consensus they have reached in their understanding of the Gospel, churches with different confessional positions accord each other fellowship in word and sacrament and strive for the fullest possible cooperation in witness and service to the world." As here indicated, the fellowship does not imply a union with a new doctrinal basis, replacing the confessional identities of the participating churches. These are, on the contrary, affirmed. But on the other hand, the Agreement is based on the conviction that, despite their historic differences, the Reformation churches are essentially at one in their understanding of the Gospel as the message of God's free grace in Jesus Christ, imparted to men through the proclamation of the word and the administration of the sacraments. From this basic consensus there follow two further characteristics of the fellowship. The mutual condemnations expressed in the confessional documents no longer apply to the assenting churches. And positively, these churches acknowledge one another as part of the Church of Jesus Christ by according each other table and pulpit fellowship, which includes mutual recognition of ordination and the freedom to provide for intercelebration.

By creating this fellowship, the churches involved are inaugurating a new era in European Protestantism which will have far-reaching consequences for their life and witness, both individually and jointly. Provision has been made for a continuing process of conversation and cooperation. A constituting assembly, planned for March 1976 in Sweden on the theme "The Fellowship of Churches as a Fellowship of Witness and Service", will consider the ethical and political implications of Christian witness in the European context and the ministry of the Church.

Co-Chairmen of the Continuation Committee

Prof. Dr. Marc Lienhard, Strasbourg, France (Lutheran)
Prof. Dr. Max Geiger, Basle, Switzerland (Reformed)

Secretariat

Secretariat on Faith and Order, WCC
Secretariat for Interconfessional Research, LWF
Department of Theology, WARC

Publications

Report of the Schauenburg conversations: Auf dem Weg. Lutherisch-reformierte Kirchengemeinschaft. Zürich: Theologischer Verlag, 1967; English translation in Lutheran World XIV,3, 1967, 53-67

Report of the Leuenberg conversations: Auf dem Weg II. Gemeinschaft der reformatorischen Kirchen. Zürich: Theologischer Verlag, 1971

Marc Lienhard, Lutherisch-reformierte Kirchengemeinschaft heute. Der Leuenberger Konkordienentwurf im Kontext der bisherigen lutherisch-reformierten Dialoge. (Okumenische Perspektiven 2) Frankfurt/Main: Otto Lembeck Verlag, 1972

"Agreement ("Konkordie") among Reformation Churches in Europe", The Ecumenical Review XXV, 3, 1973, 355-359

A symposium of articles appearing simultaneously in Lutheran World XXI, 4, 1974; Lutherische Rundschau XXIV, 4, 1974; and Reformed World XXXIII, 4, 1974

23. Lutheran-Roman Catholic/Philippines.....................L-RC/phil

"LCP-RCCP Dialogue" sponsored by the Lutheran Church in the Philippines and the Roman Catholic Church in the Philippines

Following a Roman Catholic suggestion, it was decided in 1967 to launch a joint study of the doctrines and practices of baptism, looking toward a doctrinal consensus and a mutual recognition of the validity of each other's baptism. The committee, consisting of three representatives from each side and meeting once a month, drew up an "Agreement on Baptism" which was widely circulated for study and comment and subsequently, in 1971, formally signed by dignitaries of both Churches in a solemn service of worship.

In the second series of meetings, 1970-1972, the dialogue focused on the eucharist which was studied in three stages: interpretation of principal New Testament passages; presentation of the respective eucharistic liturgies; the historical and dogmatic positions held. Agreement was reached on essential points, such as the meaning of the eucharist, the nature of Christ's sacramental presence and of the anamnesis. While unable to reach a common mind on the concept of sacrifice, the group removed a nest of mutual misunderstandings by each side explaining to the other how the term is understood within the religious context of its own tradition.

The group then proceeded to a study of the valid minister of the eucharist. In an orderly progression, it is examining the early Church Fathers, 16th century confessional sources, and present-day rites and doctrines of ordination. The outcome hoped for is that "the two panels mutually recognize the eucharistic ministry of the two Churches as valid, at least in emergency situations".

As a major resource, the group is using volumes IV and V of the United States series Lutherans and Catholics in Dialogue and the parallel statements of the Anglican-Roman Catholic International Commission, and its own findings take the same general line.

Publications

"Agreement on Baptism between the Lutheran Church in the Philippines and the Roman Catholic Church in the Philippines", 1971

"Progress Report to the Respective Churches on the Current LCP-RCCP Dialogue on the Holy Eucharist", 1972

24. Lutheran-Roman Catholic/USA..........................L-RC/usa

"Lutheran-Roman Catholic Theological Consultation" sponsored by the USA National Committee of the Lutheran World Federation and the Bishops' Committee for Ecumenical and Interreligious Affairs

Meetings

I. Baltimore, Md., July 6-7, 1965
The Status of the Nicene Creed as Dogma of the Church

II. Chicago, Ill., February 10-13, 1966
One Baptism for the Remission of Sins

III. Washington, D.C., September 23-25, 1966

IV. New York, N.Y., April 7-9, 1967

V. St. Louis, Mo., September 29 - October 1, 1967
III-V: The Eucharist as Sacrifice

VI. New York, N.Y., March 8-9, 1968
Intercommunion

VII. Williamsburg, Va., September 26-29, 1968

VIII. San Francisco, Calif., February 21-23, 1969

IX. Baltimore, Md., September 26-29, 1969

X. Bermuda, February 19-22, 1970

XI. New York, N.Y., October 30 - November 1, 1970
VII-XI: Eucharist and Ministry

XII. Miami, Fla., February 19-22, 1971

XIII. Greenwich, Conn., September 24-26, 1971

XIV. New Orleans, La., February 18-21, 1972

XV. Minneapolis, Minn., September 22-25, 1972

XVI. San Antonio, Texas, February 16-19, 1973

XVII. Allentown, Pa., September 21-24, 1973
XII-XVII: Ministry and the Church Universal: Differing Attitudes toward Papal Primacy

XVIII. Mariattsville, Md., February 15-17, 1974

XIX. Princeton, N.J., September 20-22, 1974

XX. January 30 - February 2, 1975

XXI. September 1975
XVIII-XXI: Different Views of Infallibility in Relation to the Church, Councils, Creeds, Papacy

<u>History</u>. The origin of this consultation can be traced back to an informal discussion in 1963 between Bishop (now Cardinal) John J. Wright and Dr. Paul C. Empie, the then Executive Director of the National Lutheran Council, New York. After nearly two years of negotiations, the idea was unanimously approved by the National Lutheran Council acting in its capacity as the USA National Committee of the Lutheran World Federation, and with the concurrence of the Executive Committee of the Lutheran World Federation. Shortly afterwards the newly-formed Roman Catholic Bishops' Commission for Ecumenical Affairs likewise gave its approval and established a subcommission "for dialogue with the National Lutheran Council" which met in March 1965 with a corresponding committee of the National Lutheran Council to do the ground-work for the conversations.

<u>Composition of the Group</u>. The two groups named seven theologians each, augmented by church officials and co-opted consultants on particular subjects. The Lutheran Church-Missouri Synod, although not a member of the Lutheran World Federation, was invited to send two representatives. Thus for example, one of the 1970 meetings comprised a total of 24 participants, including 18 professors in various theological disciplines, two bishops, one diocesan official, and three denominational ecumenical executives.

<u>Work of the Group</u>. The concerns and issues of the consultation, and the advances made, are reflected in the joint statements or press releases issued from the meetings and, chiefly, in five volumes entitled <u>Lutherans and Catholics in Dialogue I-V</u>. Instead of launching a frontal attack on the controversial issues that had led to the tragic split in the 16th century, the group decided to begin with the role of the Nicene Creed as a dogma in the Church, on the grounds that the Creed is acknowledged as a basic statement of faith common to both traditions, and that its examination would significantly illumine the role and development of dogmas in the respective traditions. The group found substantial agreement in confessing the Nicene Faith, and made some tentative exploration of the broader problem of the nature and role of dogma. It was recognised "that the problem of development of doctrine is crucial today and is in the forefront of our commen concern".[1]

[1] <u>The Status of the Nicene Creed as Dogma of the Church</u>, p. 32.

The exploration of the Nicene Creed was continued at the second meeting, this time with particular emphasis on the affirmation, "One baptism for the remission of sins". The parallel Catholic and Lutheran presentations of the New Testament material, interpreting baptism essentially as a rite of initiation into the community of faith, demonstrated a concordance of views which continued to prevail in the historical and doctrinal discussion. "We were reasonably certain that the teachings of our respective traditions regarding baptism are in substantial agreement, and this opinion has been confirmed at this meeting."[2]

The group then turned to two questions which "have been especially divisive in the past and are involved in most of our historical disagreements on eucharistic doctrine and practice"[3] - the eucharist as sacrifice, and the mode of Christ's presence in the sacrament. In a mutual reinterpretation of meanings and intentions, the group made "immense progress" in rooting out ingrained misconceptions, in uncovering large areas of common belief and narrowing down unresolved differences, such as the conceptual inadequacy of the doctrine of transubstantiation. The concluding statement declares: "Despite all remaining differences in the ways we speak and think of the eucharistic sacrifice and our Lord's presence in his supper, we are no longer able to regard ourselves as divided in the one holy catholic and apostolic faith on these two points."[4]

The next logical step appeared to be a re-examination of the possibilities of intercommunion. It became clear, however, that no advance would be possible without first considering the key question of what constitutes a valid ministry in eucharistic celebrations. An important step forward in the ensuing studies on "Eucharist and Ministry" was the acknowledgement "That there was no demonstrable normative pattern of the ministry during the period covered by the New Testament" but rather "a great richness and variety ... The implications of these findings offer hopeful possibilities in efforts to harmonize the existing differences in the Lutheran and Roman

---

[2] "Joint Statement", One Baptism for the Remission of Sins, p. 85

[3] The Eucharist as Sacrifice, pp. 187f.

[4] Ibid., p. 198

Catholic traditions of ministerial service". The study resulted in a unanimously adopted joint statement, followed by parallel commentaries by both partners, which together "represent a forward step of immense significance".[5] The latter statements culminate in reciprocal recommendations that the authorities of the participating churches recognize the validity of the ministry and the eucharistic administration of the other communion.[6]

On the consenus foundations thus laid, the group turned its attention to another aspect of the subject, usually ignored or rejected as a taboo in Protestant discussions of ministry, namely papal primacy. The outcome of several years of deliberation was a joint statement which appeared in March 1974, followed by parallel Lutheran and Roman Catholic reflections and questions for their respective authorities. Which form of ministry, it is asked, can best nurture and serve the universal Church in its global mission? The report here develops the key notion of a "Petrine function" describing "a particular form of ministry exercised by a person, office-holder, or local church with reference to the Church as a whole". The Petrine function is implied in the New Testament, but its various forms are subject to continuous evolution and renewal. Placing the papacy in this broader setting, the report formulates guiding principles for a renewal of its structures: adaptability and legitimate diversity, collegial responsibility, subsidiarity.

Alongside the new agreements, the critical divergences are also noted. Thus the Roman Catholics continue to regard papacy as a divinely-willed institution, whereas the Lutherans take a functional view regarding it as a possible symbol and centre of unity. "The one thing necessary, from the Lutheran point of view, is that papal primacy be so structured and interpreted that it clearly serve the Gospel and the unity of the Church of Christ and its exercise of power not subvert Christian freedom." In conclusion the statement addresses a series of searching questions to both sides. The Lutheran churches are asked to consider "the possibility and desirability of the papal ministry, renewed under the gospel and committed to Christian freedom,

---

5 "Foreword", Eucharist and Ministry, p. 4

6 Ibid., pp. 22 and 32

in a larger communion which would include the Lutheran churches". The Roman Catholic Church in turn is asked to consider "the possibility of a reconciliation which would recognize the self-government of Lutheran Churches within a communion" and the acknowledgement of the "Lutheran churches represented in our dialogue as sister churches which are already entitled to some measure of ecclesiastical communion".

To undergird the enquiry, two task forces were appointed to undertake separate studies, one on "Peter in the New Testament" and the other on "Peter in Patristic Literature". The former task force included biblical scholars also from other churches, with the hope that the results might serve other interconfessional dialogues as well.

The commission is currently grappling with a more intractable problem, dogmatised by the Roman Catholic Church and universally rejected by all other churches - papal infallibility. Applying its proven broad-based approach, it is investigating a range of related issues, such as the indefectibility of the teaching office, counterparts to infallibility, the authority of councils and creeds, and the incidence of psycho-social factors in the evolution of doctrine.

<u>Co-Chairmen</u>

Dr. Paul C. Empie, Retired General Secretary, USA National Committee of the Lutheran World Federation, New York, N.Y. (Lutheran)

The Most Rev. T. Austin Murphy, Auxiliary Bishop of Baltimore, Md. (Roman Catholic)

<u>Co-Secretaries</u>

Dr. Virgil R. Westlund, Director for Studies and International Exchange, USA National Committee,LWF, New York, N.Y.

The Rev. Dr. John F. Hotchkin, Executive Director, Bishops' Committee for Ecumenical and Interreligious Affairs, Washington, D.C.

<u>Publications</u>

<u>Lutherans and Catholics in Dialogue</u>, I-V, ed. by Paul C. Empie and T. Austin Murphy

Vol. I. <u>The Status of the Nicene Creed as Dogma of the Church</u>, 1965

II. <u>One Baptism for the Remission of Sins</u>, 1966

III. <u>The Eucharist as Sacrifice</u>, 1967

IV. <u>Eucharist and Ministry</u>, 1970

V. <u>Papal Primacy and the Universal Church</u>, 1974

The volumes include, besides the agreed findings, a number of individual papers produced in the course of the study of each subject.

Vols. I-III (in a combined reprint at $ 2.95) and vol. V (at $ 1.95) are published in paperback form by Augsburg Publishing House, Minneapolis, 1974. Vol. V contains also the material from the task force on "Peter in Patristic Literature". Vol. IV is available from the Publications Office, United States Catholic Conference, 1312 Massachusetts Avenue, N.W., Washington, D.C. 20005; USA National Committee of the Lutheran World Federation, 315 Park Avenue South, New York, N.Y. 10010; or the Augsburg Publishing House (price $ 1.00)

<u>Peter in the New Testament</u>. A Collaborative Assessment by Protestant and Roman Catholic Scholars. Edited by Raymond E. Brown, Karl P. Donfried and John Reumann. Minneapolis: Augsburg Publishing House; New York/Paramus/Toronto: Paulist Press, 1973. $ 1.95

25. <u>Methodist-Roman Catholic/Australia</u>........................<u>M-RC/aus</u>

Joint Working Group sponsored by the Methodist General Conference and the Episcopal Conference of the Roman Catholic Church

<u>Meetings</u>

I. May 11-12, 1973
   Baptism: Joint Statement

II. September 7-8, 1973
   Christian Marriage

III. March 1-2, 1974
   Christian Marriage (cont'd.): Joint Statement

The Joint Working Group was set up at the suggestion of the Roman Catholic Episcopal Conference which nominated the Roman Catholic members, while the Methodist were appointed by the President-General. The group began with a study of the sacraments. A statement, recommending mutual recognition of each other's baptismal practice and the use of a common baptismal certificate, was approved by the Episcopal Conference of the Roman Catholic Church in 1973 and the Methodist General Conference in 1974. The ecumenical significance of baptism is underscored. "Since all Christians are baptized into the one Christ, we recognize this union in Christ as the starting point of all ecumenical endeavours." The group has recently completed a similar document on the meaning of Christian marriage and the pastoral care of mixed marriages, which will be presented to the church authorities and released for publication in 1975.

Co-Secretaries

The Rev. R.W. Hartley, c/o Methodist Connexional Office, 139 Castlereagh Street, Sydney, NSW 2000, Australia

The Rev. Fr. F.X. Roberts, 2 Wooley Street, Forest Lodge, NSW 2037, Australia

26. Methodist-Roman Catholic/England........................M-RC/eng

"The Catholic-Methodist Committee" sponsored by the Roman Catholic and Methodist Ecumenical Commissions

Meetings

I. London, (all meetings), April 14, 1972
Re-organisation

II. October 13, 1972
Planning

III. February 2, 1973
The Nature of the Church: Church and World

IV. October 12, 1973
How Do We Use the New Testament?

V. February 21, 1974
Theme Continued

VI. October 10-11, 1974
Authority

At the invitation of Cardinal Heenan, a group of Methodists and Roman Catholics met in December 1967 to consider ways of achieving better understanding between the two Churches. An unofficial steering committee was formed for the purpose. The meetings have chiefly been devoted to mutual exchange on current questions. It has also sought to promote consultation and cooperation at local levels. A small working party, numbering four persons from each side, was set up to prepare a statement for wide distribution on the common beliefs held by the two communions and their relation to the world of today. The result was a pamphlet, Christian Belief, discussing matters of shared faith.

The committee was re-organised in 1972, with its membership being appointed by the authorities of the two Churches, and given a more definite theological orientation. At the request of the International Methodist-Roman Catholic Commission, a sub-group has undertaken a study of eucharistic doctrine and of the ministry, with special reference to the corresponding Anglican-Roman Catholic statements. A report will be submitted in 1975. Paralleling the Anglican-Roman Catholic Commission also in this respect, the committee began in 1974 a study of the problem of authority, based on the relevant section of the international Methodist-Roman Catholic report of 1971.

Co-Chairmen

The Rev. Dr. Harold Roberts, Turnbridge Wells, Kent (Methodist)

The Rt. Rev. Mervyn Alexander, Auxiliary Bishop of Clifton, Bath (Roman Catholic)

Secretary

The Very Rev. Canon Richard L. Stewart, Secretary, Roman Catholic Ecumenical Commission of England and Wales, 44 Gray's Inn Road, London WC1X 8LR

Publication

Christian Belief: A Catholic-Methodist Statement. London: Epworth Press and Living Parish Pamphlets, 1970

27. United Methodist-Roman Catholic Dialogue/USA..............M-RC/usa

Sponsored by the General Commission on Ecumenical Affairs of the United Methodist Church and the Bishops' Committee for Ecumenical and Interreligious Affairs

First Series

Meetings

I. Chicago, Ill., June 28, 1966
Planning Meeting

II. Chicago, Ill., December 18-20, 1966
Salvation, Faith and Good Works

III. Lake Junaluska, N.C., June 28-30, 1967
Presence of the Holy Spirit in Individuals and in the Corporate Church

IV. New York, N.Y., December 17-19, 1967
Government Aid for Church Related Elementary and Secondary Schools

V. San Antonio, Texas, September 30 - October 2, 1968
Shared Convictions on Education

VI. Delaware, Ohio. October 9-11, 1969
Mutual Examination of Ecumenical Documents from Both Churches

VII. Chicago, Ill., January 30, 1970
Review and Planning Session

Second Series

I_2 Cincinnati, Ohio, February 25-26, 1972
Spirituality of the Ordained Ministry

II_2 Dayton, Ohio, October 13-14, 1972
The Holiness of the Church

III_2 Washington, D.C., March 9-10, 1973
Holiness in the New Testament; Holiness of the Church and Ministerial Holiness

IV_2 Washington, D.C., November 1-2, 1973
Spiritual Renewal of the American Priesthood

Initiated in 1965, the conversations have been marked by the discovery of larger areas of agreement than had been expected on the nature of saving grace, the growing trend of both communions to "combine the Loaf and the Word into one center of the Holy Spirit in the Church", and educational philosophy. In 1970 the dialogue was limited to the bishops on the original team. Two task forces were set up for a substantive exploration of "Religious Responsibility for Education in a Contemporary Society" and "Mutual Recognition of the Ministry of Word and Sacrament".

In 1971 it was decided to reorganise the group and develop a structured study on "Spirituality in the Ministry". The decision was prompted by several considerations. It directed attention to a matter deeply rooted in the ethos of both traditions - the concern for holiness. Focusing on the vocational and personal life of the clergy, the study would be of immediate benefit to both Churches and it would also helpfully complement other bilateral discussions on different aspects of the ministry. The group is expected to publish a report on its findings in 1975.

<u>Co-Chairmen</u>

The Rt. Rev. James K. Mathews, Washington, D.C. (United Methodist)
The Most Rev. James W. Malone, Youngstown, Ohio (Roman Catholic)

<u>Co- Secretaries</u>

The Rev. Dr. Robert W. Huston, General Secretary, Division on Ecumenical and Interreligious Concerns, The United Methodist Church, 475 Riverside Drive, New York, N.Y. 10027

The Rev. Dr. John F. Hotchkin, Executive Director, Bishops' Committee for Ecumenical and Interreligious Affairs, 1312 Massachusetts Avenue, N.W., Washington, D.C. 20005

28. Old Catholic-Roman Catholic/Europe .... OC-RC/eur

History. Since the break-away following the First Vatican Council, relations between the two Churches have continued to be marked by opposition and controversy. The rise of the ecumenical movement, the new signals of the Second Vatican Council, and not least the friendly personal contacts established between Old Catholic observers and Roman Catholic churchmen during the Council, have produced a definite change of climate from disputation to dialogue.

With the approval of the Vatican authorities and the International Conference of Old Catholic Bishops, the bishops of both Churches in the Netherlands, Switzerland, Germany and Austria appointed theological commissions which, while functioning on a national basis, are cooperating closely with one another. The work of the German commission may be singled out here by way of illustration; the others follow a similar pattern (see P. Bläser's article listed below).

Composition and Focus of the Group. The joint commission is composed of three scholars from each side. It has focused its investigations on a specific issue, namely, whether and on what conditions the Roman Catholic Church could extend the rules concerning limited intercommunion, set forth in the Decree on Eastern Catholic Churches of the Second Vatican Council, to apply also to the Old Catholic Church.

Results. As such an act of mutual recognition would of necessity presuppose sufficient consensus in the essentials of the faith, the group examined relevant themes, notably the doctrines of sacraments, Scripture and the Church, the teaching office, and papal primacy and infallibility. A basic accord was found on all points except the last. With respect to the controversial doctrine of transubstantiation, for example, the group noted that "the reservations sometimes voiced on the Old Catholic side against the expression 'transubstantiation' do not mean a rejection of the affirmation intended by the Council of Trent in accord with the entire tradition of the ancient Church, namely, the affirmation of a 'conversio' (metabole)". Similarly, both parties acknowledged Sacred Scripture as "norm for the faith and teaching of the Church". In regard to Scripture the Church has an "interpretative function". This function is exercised primarily by the apostolic office, represented by the community of bishops as successors of the Apostles, but the whole people of God participates in the prophetic office of Christ. After its delineation of a broad range of agreements, the commission is forced to admit, however, that "there exists as yet no consensus with respect to the juridictional primacy and the supreme teaching authority of the Pope" (quotation from "Protokolle" mentioned below).

Having shown the analogy between the Orthodox and the Old Catholic Churches, the German commission, following an initiative of the Swiss commission, recommended a limited eucharistic communion. The Roman Catholic Bishops' Conference in the countries concerned endorsed the recommendations in differing ways in 1970, and submitted them to Rome for approval. In concurrent actions in 1972, the Vatican Secretariat for Promoting Christian Unity, the Congregation of the Doctrine of the Faith, and the International Conference of Old Catholic Bishops authorised the Roman Catholic and Old Catholic bishops in Germany, the Netherlands and Switzerland to study appropriate ways of implementing the said recommendations.

Co-Chairmen

Prof. Dr. Werner Küppers, Bonn, Germany (Old Catholic)
Prof. Dr. Peter Bläser, Paderborn, Germany (Roman Catholic)

Publications

"Protokolle der bisherigen Sitzungen der römisch-katholisch/altkatholischen Gesprächskommission in Deutschland", Internationale Kirchliche Zeitschrift 61, 2, 1971, 75-78
Peter Bläser, "Das altkatholisch/römisch-katholische Gespräch", ibid. 60, 1970, 347-360

29. Orthodox-Reformed/North America ....O-R/nam

"Orthodox-Reformed Consultation" sponsored by the Standing Conference of Canonical Orthodox Bishops in the Americas and the North American Area of the World Alliance of Reformed Churches

Meetings

I. Princeton, N.J., May 3-4, 1968
The Role of Creeds and Confessions in the Life of the Church

II. Brookline, Mass., April 18-19, 1969
God's Revelation and History

III. Princeton, N.J., May 13-14, 1970
The Christian Community and the Second Century; Theosis and Sanctification

Background. The Consultation was initiated in 1968 under the joint auspices of the Standing Conference of Canonical Orthodox Bishops in the Americas and the North American Area of the World Alliance of Reformed Churches. The first of its kind on the North American continent, it was prompted by the belief that the two communions might well have more in common than their distance over the centuries would seem to indicate, and that the American situation provided an exceptional opportunity for probing essentials, "because many of the historical and cultural obstacles to mutual understanding between our churches have been removed". As in other conversations with Orthodox participation, it was also felt that the predominant Protestant-Roman Catholic dialogue needed to be corrected and enriched by the voice of Orthodoxy. The participants comprised five representatives from each side, the majority being professors of theology.

Work of the Group. In order to preserve openness and informality of debate, the group abstained from seeking formal agreements. Instead the main trends of the discussion were summed up in brief statements for general release. The debate on the basic problem of "Revelation and History" shed light on characteristic differences and affinities in perceiving the nature of tradition both as a historical reality and as a theological concept, the significance of credal guideposts, and the ways in which differing historical experiences have shaped religious self-understanding. Orthodoxy looks back on an unbroken continuity with the apostolic age, relatively unaffected by events which have profoundly impressed the Reformation tradition, such as the Augustinian-Pelagian controversies in the West around original sin and the nature of man, the ferment of the Renaissance and the 16th century Reformation. A study of the second century Church, with its crucial role in setting later directions, proved a fruitful approach by pursuing a re-examination of the origins of shared concerns. A genuine consensus was noted "concerning the ultimate authority of the Holy Spirit in the Church, as witnessed by such signs as scripture, order and sacraments". In considering the consequences for the Christian community of the presence and authority of the Holy Spirit, however, a difference of interpretation became evident in the opposing views of intercommunion. An ecclesiological contrast, though by no means an opposition, appeared between the emphasis on the community of "hearing and obedience" and the insistence on the Church as "the locus of sacramental participation in the Body of Christ".

The comparison of the Orthodox teaching on divinisation and the Reformed teaching on sanctification turned out to be a high point of the encounters by sweeping away a host of misconceptions on both sides. It produced "extensive preliminary agreement, particularly on the primacy of God's initiative in man's salvation, the role of the life and teaching of Jesus Christ, and the necessity for a proper appreciation of divinisation - sanctification". The Orthodox concept of synergy ceased to be unacceptable to the Reformed once it was seen that its meaning must be dissociated from the Western controversies of Pelaganism and predestinationism and especially the doctrine of merit. "Divinisation - sanctification means the fulfilment of man's potentiality and calling by grace."

<u>Co-Chairmen</u>

Prof. John Meyendorff, St. Vladimir's Orthodox Theological Seminary, Tuckahoe, N.Y. (Orthodox)

Prof. Joseph C. McLelland, McGill University, Montreal, Canada, (Presbyterian)

<u>Publication</u>

<u>The New Man: An Orthodox and Reformed Dialogue</u>. Edited by J. Meyendorff and J.C. McLelland. New Brunswick, N.J.: Standard Press, 1973. (The volume contains the papers from the consultation together with interpretative essays by the editors, discussion summaries and a bibliography.)

30. <u>Russian Orthodox-Roman Catholic</u> ....<u>O-RC/rus</u>

"Theological Conversations between Representatives of the Roman Catholic Church and the Russian Orthodox Church"

<u>Meetings</u>

I. Leningrad, USSR, December 9-13, 1967
The Social Thought of the Roman Catholic Church

II. Bari, Italy, December 6-10, 1970

The Role of the Christian in the Developing Society

III. Zagorsk, USSR, June 4-7, 1973

The Church in a World of Transformation

The presence of Orthodox observers at the Second Vatican Council, the proliferation of unofficial and official visits, and above all, the historic meetings between the Ecumenical Patriarch Athenagoras I and Pope Paul VI, resulting in the formal removal of the mutual excommunication of 1054, were signs of a new era in the relations between these two Catholic traditions. On the other hand, the divergent developments during a millenial separation, aggravated by the Roman claims of papal infallibility and jurisdictional supremacy, have erected formidable hindrances - religious, ecclesiastical, psychological - on the road to full communion. Hence the seemingly paradoxical situation that, whereas Pan-Orthodox commissions are entertaining dialogues on the world level with the Anglican and Old Catholic communions, this is not yet the case with the Roman Catholic Church. The present dialogue represents therefore an interim stage, illustrated by its asymmetrical sponsorship: on the one hand, an individual Orthodox Church and, on the other, the Roman Catholic Church.

The dialogue had its origin in an exchange between Bishop (later Cardinal) Willebrands and Metropolitan Nikodim, following an address which the latter had delivered on the subject of "Dialogue with Roman Catholics on Contemporary Christian Social Thought" at the Geneva World Conference on "Church and Society"in 1966. The discussions have ranged from the most fundamental issues of Church-world relations to the concrete problems of Christian service in contemporary society. Thus the Bari meeting focused on the three topics of the Christian's personal formation and his contribution to the building of a human society, Christian involvement in development, and the perennial nature of the Word of God and the relativity of its incarnations in changing civilisations. The Zagorsk meeting in turn directed attention to the religious and pastoral tasks of the Church in an increasingly secularised and technicised world, under the threefold aspect of the Church and salvation in a changing world, pastoral preoccupations today, and the people of God and contemporary crises.

No formal consensus statements are published, but the discussions have disclosed broad areas of agreement, especially as regards basic principles governing the Christian approach to society. Thus at Zagorsk, the participants agreed on certain "general observations", including (a) the need for a deeper understanding of the role of the liturgy in the life of the Church, (b) the possibility and necessity of the cooperation of Christians with non-Christians in the humanisation of society, (c) the acceptance of the legitimate efforts of man, created in the image of God, to dominate and transform the world, and (d) the recognition of the fact that there is a strong tendency towards some forms of "socialism" in many parts of the world. Among particularly pressing questions for further study were noted the significance of the Incarnation of Christ for the world and for the Christian living in the world, liberation and salvation, and the implications of a legitimate variety for Christian ethical attitudes in a pluralistic society.

Co-Chairmen (at the 1973 meeting)

The Most Rev. Juvenaly, Metropolitan of Tula and Belev (Orthodox)

The Most Rev. Angelo Fernandes, Archbishop of New Delhi, India (Roman Catholic)

Publications

Joint communiqués from the conferences are published in Orthodox and Roman Catholic journals. For the 1973 meeting see The Journal of the Moscow Patriarchate 1973, 7, 51-53 and 8, 56-66; Secretariat for Promoting Chr.‑tian Unity, Information Service 22, October 1973/IV, 10-13

31. Orthodox-Roman Catholic/USA ....O-RC/usa

"Orthodox-Roman Catholic Consultation" sponsored by the Standing Conference of Canonical Orthodox Bishops in the Americas and the Bishops' Committee for Ecumenical and Interreligious Affairs

Meetings

I. New York, N.Y., September 9, 1966
Planning meeting

II. Worcester, Mass., May 5, 1967
Theological Diversity and Unity; Intercommunion; Common Witness in Theological Education

III. Maryknoll, N.Y., December 7, 1968
The Eucharist; Indissolubility of Marriage; Cooperation in Theological Education

IV. Worcester, Mass., December 12, 1969
The Eucharist; Membership in the Church

V. New York, N.Y., May 19, 1970
Membership of Schismatics and Heretics in the Ancient Church; Current Practices Concerning Common Worship; Mixed Marriages

VI. Brookline, Mass., December 4, 1970
Doctrine and Practice of Marriage

VII. Boylston, Mass., November 3, 1971
Ethical Issues Relating to Marriage

VIII. New York, N.Y., December 6, 1973
Review and Planning for Future Meetings; Sanctity of Marriage

IX. Washington, D.C., May 23-24, 1974
The Process of Ecumenical Dialogue; The Church's Role in and Expectations from American Society; Where Do We Stand vis-à-vis Each Other as Churches?; Agreed Statement on Respect for Life

X. New York, N.Y., December 9-10, 1974
Continuity of the Church according to Catholic and Orthodox Understanding; Agreed Statement on the Church

Initiated in 1966 by the Bishops' Committee for Ecumenical and Interreligious Affairs and the Standing Conference of Canonical Orthodox Bishops in the Americas, the consultation is the first official dialogue between the two communions and can therefore be seen also as a pilot project for the international dialogue forecast at the time of the Second Vatican Council.

Initially, the group numbered fifteen Orthodox and fifteen Roman Catholic members appointed by the respective sponsoring bodies. The membership has now been reduced on both sides to seven participants with active voice. The participants are church leaders, theologians biblical scholars and historians.

The consultation has issued an agreed statement on the nature of the eucharist, and has recommended that in mixed marriages the Roman Catholic partner be permitted to be married in an Orthodox ceremony, since this is canonically required for Orthodox believers. After several years of discussion on the theology and ethics of marriage, the consultation issued a statement scoring abortion and affirming the right of the unborn, the mentally retarded, the aging, and the under-privileged to "a decent life and to full human development".

At the same meeting in May 1974, the consultation began to move towards the crucial issue in Orthodox-Roman Catholic relations: the question of mutual recognition as Churches. The resulting statement does not attack the problem frontally, but probes instead the common foundations by interpreting the nature of the Church in the light of its "origin and prototype in the Trinity". The local church is seen as independent in its corporate existence (expressed best in its eucharistic celebration), and at the same time interdependent in relation to other churches. It is in this interplay of independence and communality on the local, territorial and patriarchal levels that the Church mirrors its prototype: the Trinity. The recognition of "the fundamental equality of all local churches" is thus part of the far-reaching consensus revealed in the statement. But on the controversial matter of primacy, it must confine itself to stating the two opposing claims: the Roman Catholic belief in a primacy exercised by the Bishop of Rome and the Orthodox belief in a primacy depending on the consent of the Church and "at present exercised by the Patriarch of Constantinople". Nonetheless the statement ends on a note of hope - the shared conviction that "the Spirit is ever active to show us the way by which we can live together as one and many. We have the hope that we will be open to his promptings wherever they may lead".

<u>Co-Chairmen</u>

The Most Rev. Iakovos, Archbishop of the Greek Orthodox Archdiocese of North and South America, New York, N.Y. (Orthodox)

The Most Rev. William W. Baum, Archbishop of Washington, Washington, D.C. (Roman Catholic)

<u>Co-Secretaries</u>

The Rev. Prof. Maximos A. Agiourgousis, Holy Cross School of Theology, Hellenic College, Brookline, Mass. 02146

The Rev. Prof. Edward J. Kilmartin, SJ, School of Theology, Weston College, Cambridge, Mass. 02138

Publications

"An Agreed Statement on the Eucharist" (December 1969)
"An Agreed Statement on Mixed Marriages" (May 1970)
"An Agreed Statement on Respect for Life" (May 1974)
"An Agreed Statement on the Church" (December 1974)
Can be obtained from the Bishops' Committee for Ecumenical and Interreligious Affairs, 1312 Massachusetts Avenue, N.W., Washington, D.C. 20005, or the General Secretariat of S.C.O.B.A., 10 East 79th Street, New York, N.Y. 10021. 25¢ each.

32. Reformed-Roman Catholic/USA..............................R-RC/usa

"The Reformed-Presbyterian and Roman Catholic Consultation" sponsored by the North American Area of the World Alliance of Reformed Churches and the Bishops' Committee for Ecumenical and Interreligious Affairs

First Series

Meetings

I. Washington, D.C., July 27, 1965
Organisational Meeting
II. Philadelphia, Pa., November 26-27, 1965
The Role of the Holy Spirit in the Renewal and Reform of the Church
III. The Bronx, N.Y., May 12-13, 1966
Revelation, Scripture and Tradition
IV. Chicago, Ill., October 27-29, 1966
The Development of Doctrine
V. Collegeville, Minn., April 26-29, 1967
VI. Lancaster, Pa., October 26-28, 1967
VII. Bristow, Va., May 9-11, 1968
VIII. Detroit, Mich., October 24-26, 1968
IX. Charleston, S.C., May 21-24, 1969
X. Macatawa, Mich., October 29-November 1, 1969
XI. Morristown, N.J., May 13-15, 1970
XII. Princeton, N.J., October 28-31, 1970
XIII. Columbus, Ohio, May 12-15, 1971
XIV. Richmond, Va., October 27-30, 1971
V-XIV: Theology Section: Ministry and Order
Worship and Mission Section: Mixed Marriages; Women in the Church

In 1963 the General Assembly of the United Presbyterian Church urged Presbyterians to foster fraternal relations with Roman Catholics. This action and the stimulus afforded by the ecumenical reorientation of the Second Vatican Council opened new doors for conversation and cooperation. Two years later, the 1965 General Assembly issued another statement on relations with Roman Catholics, which went further in detailing opportunities for cooperation and outlined a study guide on the two Council documents De Ecclesia and De Oecumenismo.

The North American Area of the World Alliance of Reformed Churches and the Bishops' Committee for Ecumenical and Interreligious Affairs set up an official Presbyterian and Reformed-Roman Catholic Conversation Group, which adopted as its main theme "The Renewal and Reform of the Church as a Continuing Process". The group was divided into two working sub-groups: the Theology Section and the Worship and Mission Section.

From 1967 on, the Theology Section has been engaged in a wide-ranging exploration of the ministry of the Church to the world, the plurality of ministries and forms of rule in the Church, the representative ministry, and intercommunion. Joint statements have been issued on "The Ministry of the Church" (1967) and "Ministry in the Church" (1970 and 1971) which spell out a wide "meeting of minds on many matters of faith and ministry". The group holds that "ordination of women must be part of the Church's life". It also recommends to the ecclesiastical authorities to designate specific occasions for limited eucharistic sharing.

The Worship and Mission Section, in its parallel sessions, has undertaken an inquiry into the question of mixed marriages, pastoral and canonical aspects of the marriage ceremony, and the religious education of children of a mixed marriage. In 1969 the section presented to the sponsoring bodies a series of unanimous recommendations, proposing joint pastoral counselling before and after the marriage, solemnisation of the marriage by the clergy of both partner, "the clergy acting equally and with true parity", and elimination of pre-nuptial promises regarding the bringing up of children. In 1970 the group began a study of the role of women in the Church, and in October 1971 it issued a joint report with recommendations to the parent bodies entitled "Women in the Church".

Co-Chairmen

Dr. James H. Nichols, Princeton Theological Seminary, Princeton, N.J. (Section on Theology) (Presbyterian)

The Rev. William B. Ward, Eastminster Presbyterian Church, Columbia, S.C. (Section on Worship and Mission) (Presbyterian)

The Most Rev. Ernest L. Unterkoefler, Charleston, S.C. (Roman Catholic)

Publications

Reconsiderations. Roman Catholic-Presbyterian and Reformed Theological Conversations, 1966-67. New York: World Horizons, 1967 (The booklet contains the six position papers from meetings III-V together with discussion summaries.)

"The Ministry of the Church" (joint statement), Journal of Ecumenical Studies V, 2, Spring 1968, 462-65

"Ministry in the Church" (joint statement), ibid., VII, 3, Summer 1970, 686-90

"Women in Church and Society" (joint statement), ibid., VII, 3, Summer 1970, 690-91

"Ministry in the Church: A Statement by the Theology Section of the Roman Catholic-Presbyterian-Reformed Consultation, Richmond, Va., October 30, 1971", ibid., IX, 3, 1972, 589-612

"Women in the Church: A Statement by the Worship and Mission Section of the Roman Catholic-Presbyterian-Reformed Consultation, Richmond, Va., October 31, 1971", ibid., IX, 1, 1972, 235-41

The final statements of the two sections on "Ministry in the Church" and "Women in the Church", adopted by the October 1971 meeting of the consultation, are obtainable from the Presbyterian and Reformed Office, Mrs. E.A. Rowles, Princeton Theological Seminary, Princeton, N.J. 08540, or from the Publications Office, United States Catholic Conference, 1312 Massachusetts Avenue, N.W., Washington, D.C. 20005. 25¢ each.

Second Series

Meetings

I_2 Cincinnati, Ohio, October 26-29, 1972
The Task Ahead; the Shape of the Unity We Seek; What Is Happening Locally and Regionally

II_2 Columbus, Ohio, May 31-June 2, 1973
The Columbus Study: Theological Considerations; Community and Industrial Factors Involved

III_2 Cincinnati, Ohio, October 24-27, 1973

IV_2 Columbus, Ohio, May 8-11, 1974

V_2 Cincinnati, Ohio, October 23-26, 1974

II-V: The Columbus Study

The first series of meetings was terminated in 1961 and it was decided to restructure the consultation, adopting a new, more empirical approach and relating the study directly to the lives and concerns of local communities. The two sections were merged into a single group including twelve Reformed and Presbyterians and fifteen Roman Catholics, and working through task forces and assisted by outside experts for specific assignments.

Under the theme "The Shape of the Unity We Seek", the consultation is focusing its work on "The concrete goal of the Christian unity of our Churches". Three interlocking steps are projected: (a) a thorough sociological investigation of a local ecumenical situation, with an evaluation of the data thus collected; (b) delineation of the shape of unity in the light of Christian experience and theology and the data of the enquiry; and (c) projections of new possibilities of realising unity and the concrete steps to be taken. The city of Columbus, Ohio, was chosen as reseach model for this interdisciplinary study of what the experiences of people engaged in local activities have to contribute to the search for unity.

The statements of the groups, completed in the fall of 1974, will be circulated to other bilaterals and other agencies for comment. A final report, with recommendations for action and supporting background papers, is scheduled to appear in late 1975.

<u>Chairman</u>

The Most Rev. Ernest L. Unterkoefler, Charleston, S.C. (Roman Catholic)

<u>Vice-Chairman</u>

Dr. Andrew Harsanyi, Dean, Hungarian Reformed Church in America, Eastern Classis, Carteret, N.J. (Reformed)

<u>Co-Secretaries</u>

Dr. Raymond V. Kearns, Jr., Louisville Presbyterian Theological Seminary, 1044 Alta Vista Road, Louisville, Ky. 40205

The Rev. Peter Sheehan, Associate Executive Director, Bishops' Committee for Ecumenical and Interreligious Affairs, 1312 Massachusetts Avenue, N.W., Washington, D.C. 20005

The Rev. N. Robert Quirin, 811 Cathedral Place, Richmond, Va. 23220

III
AIMS OF THE CONVERSATIONS

Like the ecumenical movement at large, these conversations display a great diversity of aims and goals, as the preceding accounts have shown. In certain instances it is clear that the group deliberately abstained from an explicit determination of aims, letting this be part of the dialogue experience itself. In most instances, however, the group operates within given terms of reference; and the set aims of the conversations are consistently pursued all through, or re-examined and modified in response to new insights. The varying conceptions of aims range from promoting mutual understanding to achieving full communion.

(1) An immediate object of almost all conversations is to assess the common situation in which the participating churches find themselves today and to give a mutual presentation of their history and characteristics. They seek to clarify existing difficulties as well as new possibilities in interchurch relations.

(2) Some bilaterals have so far restricted themselves to a discussion of selected topics and problems, aiming at a deeper mutual understanding and a possible convergence - or a recognition of existing convergences - in doctrinal, ecclesiastical, and pastoral matters. The question of unity in one form or the other is not yet taken up (e.g. conversations with Orthodox churches; M-RC; R-RC).

(3) Attempts to solve the specific problem of mixed marriages are made in a number of conversations with the Roman Catholic Church. In this area the new joint commission of the Lutheran World Federation, the World Alliance of Reformed Churches and the Roman Catholic Church constitutes a new form of bilateral approach.

(4) A number of conversations have taken up the task of coordinating the relations between two groups of churches or confessional families and to initiate or encourage all kinds of practical cooperation and exchange on different levels. These include convenant relationships between parishes for mutual support, clergy cooperation, common prayer and witness, social action projects, joint recommendations to church authorities concerning the pastoral care of mixed marriages, etc. (e.g. A-RC; A-RC/usa; M-RC).

(5) An important development can be seen in an increasing number of conversations. They were inaugurated as a theological dialogue with a similar intention as mentioned above in (2). But the dynamics of the dialogue, the emerging agreements and convergences inevitably raised the question of concrete steps towards unity. This resulted in a number of recommendations or proposals concerning:
(a) mutual recognition of ministries and sacraments (L-RC; L-RC/usa); (b) intercommunion on special occasions (L-RC; R-RC/usa); (c) mutual recognition as churches (including recognition of ministries) and some form of full communion (A-L/usa; EO-OO).[1]

(6) Some conversations are already looking toward some form of union from the very outset. An example of this is the "Common Declaration", signed by the Pope and the Archbishop of Canterbury in Rome, March 1966. Both church leaders declared their intention of inaugurating "a serious dialogue which, founded on the Gospels and on the ancient common traditions, may lead to that unity in truth for which Christ prayed". Consequently, the Anglican-Roman Catholic International Commission expressed its desire to come to some form of organic unity between the two communions. Yet in the course of the conversations, because of certain difficulties, this aim was modified in such a way that the more immediate goal of the conversations was defined as "partial" communion.

Similarly, the Lutheran-Reformed-United conversations in Europe were started with the final goal of full "church fellowship" in mind. This dialogue has worked out the most definitive scheme thus far by drafting a "concord" as a basis of full fellowship and submitting it to the churches, which ratified it in 1974.

These conversations generally differ from church union negotiations in that they do not seek to forecast the concrete form of unity to be achieved and leave the decision about organic unity, in the sense of a unification of hitherto separated churches, to the individual churches in their particular situations.

Experience of bilateral conversations so far prompts the suggestion that those involved in ongoing dialogues or preparing new ones should pay more attention to the precise aims to be achieved. It is not enough for them to consider the specific tasks and possibilities

---

1. For further references, see pp. 239f.

of worldwide dialogues as distinct from those at a national or regional level. They must also consider the possibilities <u>and</u> the limitations of theological dialogue as distinct from other forms of ecumenical rapprochement, and assess realistically the relationship between possible advances within a small group and the far more complex situation of the churches and their interrelationships. Such a careful target analysis would not only bring out more clearly the rationale for bilateral conversations, which many people are questioning; it would also ensure that these conversations contributed more constructively to the whole concert of ecumenical endeavours.

IV
METHODS AND PROCEDURES

A. Planning and Organisation

A study of bilateral conversations points up the familiar truth that, while careful planning and organisation afford no guarantee of success, they are nevertheless an important enabling factor and therefore deserve reflective attention here. This applies, of course, in even higher degree to the dynamics of the dialogue process itself, in which new understandings and convergences are laboriously hammered out or unexpectedly discovered.

Preparations. The preparations usually involve a long series of successive or concurrent steps. (a) In various reports it is expressly mentioned that the official meetings were preceded by a protracted period, sometimes extending over years, of informal approaches, conferences with and between denominational leaders on both sides, consultations with ecumenical officials and with participants in other dialogues, proposals to the appropriate ecclesiastical authorities, their policy decisions, and the like. Because of the particular nature and sponsorship of the bilaterals, it is natural that officers of the world confessional families concerned figure prominently as initiators, organisers and consultants. Some of these bodies - the Vatican Secretariat for Promoting Christian Unity, the Lutheran World Federation, the Roman Catholic Bishops' Committee for Ecumenical and Interreligious Affairs in the USA - even have staff members who devote most, if not all, of their time just to the field of bilateral conversations alone. (b) The official authorisation will indicate the terms of reference of the commission and instruct the appropriate denominational officials to appoint, or sometimes itself appoint, the participants. (c) Once a project has been authorised, denominational ecumenical officers or a preliminary ad hoc committee or the officers of the bilateral commission, if already appointed, engage in a new round of consultations on topics and procedures. Sometimes it is left to the commission itself to decide on matters of agenda. (d) Not infrequently it is reported that the members of one or both of the confessional groups involved meet separately, prior to the inaugural meeting, to clarify their own confessional positions, to identify - in a kind of simulated dialogue - probable areas of agreement and divergence with the prospective partner, and to consider topics and speakers (e.g. A-L; A-O, Jerusalem 1969; the Inter-Orthodox Commissions on Dialogue with the Anglicans and the Old Catholics). (e) In order to reap maximum benefit from the personal encounter, some of the groups have arranged for position papers and other preparatory documents to be circulated and studied prior to the meeting.

Timetable and Agenda. If the bilaterals are ranged on a scale from unstructured to highly structured, the overwhelming majority are to be found on the latter half of the scale. This is not surprising if one considers the potential importance attached to them and the investment of resources which they represent. There is also an observable correlation between the proposed aims of a project and, on the other hand, its degree of structural articulation. If a project serves the general purpose of furthering mutual understanding, the agenda, changing from meeting to meeting, may touch on a variety of subjects of common interest, without an attempt to follow through in the form of joint declarations or recommendations for action. By contrast, if a project is designed to serve some concrete purpose - as, for example, to resolve a particular doctrinal controversy or to seek agreement on a pastoral problem like that of mixed marriages - there is a natural tendency to shape the whole undertaking as functionally as possible towards this end. In other words, a project directly oriented towards change usually prompts a more purposeful and efficient structuring.

Turning now from these general observations, one can observe different patterns of organisation. (a) Conversations extending over a lengthy period of years, meeting at intervals of one or several years covering a broad range of subjects, and showing considerable changes in membership (e.g. A-O/usa). (b) Conversations extending over a period of three to five years, but focused throughout on one or two fixed subjects or clusters of subjects and conceived as a continuing process of inquiry, involving a planned alternation of official meetings, informal consultations of officers and commission members, individual research, and sometimes circulation of documents inbetween meetings (A-RC/usa; L-RC; L-RC/usa). Occasionally, a commission may be divided into parallel sub-commissions for different areas of concern (e.g. A-RC; R-RC/usa, which had one section on theology and one on worship and mission). (c) Short-term conversations involving a series of four to five meetings, in some instances held twice a year, and pursuing a more narrowly defined objective (A-L; L-R-U/eur, Leuenberg). (d) Supplementing these organisational patterns is a more recent development, representing a second stage: the appointment of joint review committees which examine the responses of the churches to the findings of a dialogue, revising the initial statements accordingly, and submitting recommendations to the respective authorities (e.g. A-L; L-RC).

The meetings vary in length from one to ten days, with the average length being three to five days.

The bilateral nature of the meetings is usually reflected also in their leadership: two co-chairmen, one from each side; two presenters of position papers; two writers of - joint or parallel - discussion summaries. This strict observance of parity, as a matter of principle and politeness, is more noticeable, however, in the earlier phases. As the two parties begin to coalesce in a fellowship of friendship and trust, the concern for representative equality is transformed into mutuality. As a result, the question of whether a meeting should have one or two secretaries, or of the composition of a drafting committee, ceases to be a sensitive matter of interconfessional balance; it becomes a matter to be settled on grounds of competence and efficiency.

Recording. The recording of meetings takes the usual variety of forms: tapes, minutes of discussions, joint statements, discussion summaries, press releases. Because of the potential importance of such bilateral encounters for the communions concerned and no less for others engaged in similar pursuits, and in order to facilitate continuity of discourse between successive meetings in a series, one would expect them to establish adequate records of problems and tendencies in the discussions. This is by no means uniformly the case, however. In particular, there is a marked difference in the way in which the end-product of a meeting and the preceding discussion process are recorded. Major attention is focused on registering and formalising the accomplishments of the group. In certain conversations, a cumulative record is established in preliminary statements which then are revised or amplified at a final meeting (A-RC; L-RC; R-RC). In some other cases, however, no trace can be found of the outcome of a meeting.

With regard to the group discussions themselves, the situation is less satisfactory. Only in rare cases are tapes or notes available, allowing a re-presentation of the dynamics of such an encounter. One of the reports avows,somewhat euphemistically, that "it is not always easy to relate the summary statements to the papers discussed prior to their formulation" since "all the discussions were 'off the record'" (L-RC/usa, Marburg Revisited, "Preface"). In many instances, it is therefore virtually impossible to grasp the precise meanings, the discoveries and compromises, which the final statements with their compacted and ambiguous formulations seek to convey - not to speak of the fact that many times the dialogue itself may be a more realistic and powerful contribution to ecumenical advance than is an agreed summary.

B. The Dialogue Process

The movement of reflection and dialogue, by which new insights come to birth, is a mystery not only in the profound sense that, however well prepared and organised it may be, its success always remains a gift of the Spirit, but also in the sense that little is revealed of its inner dynamics in the available records. Yet there exists sufficient direct and indirect evidence to allow some general observations.

The bilateral dialogue process is an instance of Christian theologising in general and of ecumenical theologising in particular. The assumptions and criteria, the modes and techniques of investigation and construction are basically the same as those found elsewhere. Similarly, the multiplicity of theological stances and methodologies is reflected in the bilaterals. Yet at the same time, because of their specific purpose and field of inquiry, they show certain characteristics which are also reflected in the manner in which problems are penetrated and resolved.

The bilaterals employ a number of approaches which from different angles seek to identify, to reduce and, if possible, to overcome existing divisions. (a) Mutual presentations of the shape of the confessional families concerned: what they believe and how they function. (b) Parallel expositions of the stance of the two confessions regarding the subject under debate, coupled with some exploratory bridge-building in the form of occasional side glances at the (presumed) stance of the dialogue partner. (c) A direct point-by-point comparison of similarities and unresolved divergences in the matter at hand, presented in the form of either parallel or joint statements.

(d) A mutual interrogation by means of questions and answers, in which each confessional group probes the position of the other and in turn sets forth its own beliefs and suggests areas of concord. (e) A subject-oriented approach, exploring shared beliefs, and referring only incidentally to confessional peculiarities and differences.

In these several modes of approach, the systematic discussion is usually undergirded by biblical and historical considerations. Despite all the problems inherent in biblical interpretation, there is a truly remarkable consensus in accepting the biblical witness as a common bond and court of appeal, and in seeking to correct distorted and lopsided later developments by recourse to the inexhaustible richness of the Gospel itself. While the numerous discussions of the problem of Scripture and tradition are the most conspicuous sign of this concern for a recentering of Christian traditions, it is a motif recurring throughout the conversations.

Linked with this is a persistent awareness of historical perspectives and developments. The appeal to history is used to overcome the stereotypes and absolutisms of sacralised history, whether ancient or modern. Several groups have effectively used the method of comparing the historical context in which the partners once grew to selfhood and the context in which they find themselves today - a comparison resulting in better mutual understanding and new solidarity. Thus, to take a prominent example, the Leuenberg Agreement among the Reformation Churches in Europe would hardly have been possible without the careful studies preceding it of the interaction of religious, cultural and societal factors which once shaped the nascent Reformation tradition, the transformations these have undergone in the intervening centuries, and the present-day constellation. Basic to this approach is an acceptance of the historicity of the Gospel and of all its interpretations. And the conclusion is compellingly drawn that the Reformation Churches, precisely in order to be faithful to their origins, cannot merely repeat the 16th century formulae but must labour to express the one Gospel in the thought categories and structures of today. The conversations abound in such object lessons of the truth that theological convergence often stems from, and in turn leads to, historical reinterpretation.

However varied the specific definitions of the purposes of

bilateral dialogues may be,[1] they share the general assumption that dialogue is directed towards reaching a consensus. What is meant by consensus, however, the ways by which it is attained, its varying degrees of relevance and necessity in different areas such as biblical interpretation, witness, dogma, doctrine, theology, ecclesiastical polity, and the role of consensus statements in the interplay of unitive and divisive forces in Christendom - all this is still not clarified. The current emphases on plurality in religious expression and on historical particularity, in the sense that confessional traditions may be seen as varied responses of faith in differing circumstances and hence partially complementary, seem to question the very notion of consensus. To this comes a further complication: the recognition of deep diversities within the New Testament itself, which immensely increase the difficulty of framing a normative concept of the purpose of bilateral dialogue. In this fluid state of reconsideration, it would be illusory to seek to substantiate any consensus about the nature of ecumenical consensus. But some recurring assumptions may be noted.

Although "consensus" is frequently used interchangeably with "theological agreement", the bilaterals operate in fact with several distinctions which, while still ill-defined, shed light on the matter. Thus it is recognised that consensus denotes in the first place a consensus with the Gospel of Christ, and only in the second place a common mind among consentient believers. It is an accepted truism that a consensus in the faith can and does embrace vigorous theological disagreements, while on the other hand an agreed statement may well cover unresolved tensions. In a refinement of the analysis, the notion of consensus is related to the continuum kerygma-dogma-doctrine-theology, pictured as a series of concentric circles; for each step, the meaning of consensus becomes gradually transformed into a widening plurality of options. Sometimes there appears an explicit reflection on the dialectical relationships of consensus and conflict. A consensus, it is suggested, is not a peaceful harmony of minds beyond controversy; it is hammered out and asserted in a constant confrontation with opposing views. And even though a controversy many times does not eventuate in a consensus, it may nevertheless afford an im-

1. See above pp. 124ff.

portant positive contribution to the renewal and unity of the Church by forcing the contestants to probe deeper into the truth and thereby to stimulate and enrich one another. It further belongs to the ambiguities of consensus that it, in turn, engenders counter-reactions and new conflicts. Thus when representatives of two communions reach a significant agreement - as has been the case in several of the bilaterals - it is virtually inevitable that this will induce new tensions along the edges of the agreement between those who support it and those who oppose it.

It goes without saying that such an analysis is a conceptual abstraction detached from the larger ecclesial reality of which dogmatic, doctrinal, and theological consensus or dissensus form but one aspect. It is therefore not without reason that the dialogues increasingly focus attention also on other ways of manifesting and deepening Christian unity, such as common worship, missionary witness, and cooperation in public affairs.

In short, the notion of consensus which plays such an important regulative role in bilateral discussions does by no means constitute an univocal measurement of ecumenical advance. In actual practice, the bilaterals tend to use the notion operationally, that is, the meaning of consensus and dissensus is conceived in each case in function of the specific purpose of the dialogue group. And this may range from the concrete question as to whether the Roman Catholic rules for limited eucharistic sharing with the Orthodox can be applied also to the Old Catholics, to the pastoral proprieties in celebrating mixed marriages, to mutual recognition of ministries, to conditions for union. Common to these diverse usages, however, is a formal criterion of prime importance, often expressed in this negative form: Is a particular divergence or conflict of such a grievous nature that it prevents ecclesial fellowship or not? [1] Is it "church dividing"? This is the controlling issue in bilateral deliberations. Accordingly, the purpose of the inquiry becomes to show that on closer analysis the divergences do not justify maintaining ecclesial separation, or to seek to overcome their divisiveness by a fresh approach to the matter. This "negative consensus" is something more than just an exclusion of

---

1. Cf. the A-RC/usa statement of January 1972 on "Doctrinal Agreement and Christian Unity:Methodological Considerations" with its six "operative principles" for assessing whether particular divergent doctrinal formulations constitute an essential obstacle to full communion.

onesided and divisive extremes. Although appearing in the form of a negation of a negation, it would not have been possible without a positive awareness of an underlying fellowship - perhaps still too inchoate and elusive to permit conceptual articulation.

The related question of how consensus formation and dialogue interact likewise deserves mention. To put the issue in the form of a (false) antithesis: Does dialogue presuppose or produce consensus? When two confessional bodies initiate a series of official conversations, they do so because of changed or new conditions, which permit a hope for some positive results. "The time is ripe." Thus already before the conversations begin, the participants are aware of affinities waiting to be identified. It is this anticipatory mood of informal mutual recognition which, for example, makes its possible for a group to commence its deliberations, as sometimes occurs, with a joint paper instead of separate position papers, or with paired papers in which the presenters, after previous agreement, explore common grounds. The function of a dialogue group is therefore largely a matter of discernment - discovering and formulating convergences which are already beginning to crystallise in the Christian community, and presenting them for public debate and approval. This reception of diffuse pre-existing convergences is of no mean significance however. Explorations by individual theologians, having up to now the character of private research, are lifted up to another level and receive a more representative recognition in the search for unity. On the other hand, many bilateral conversations have also been able to press forward, beyond a mere reception, to unexpected discoveries and creative syntheses.

The question of consensus is intimately linked with that of representativeness. In what sense are the members of a dialogue group, its discussions and its consensus statements representative? And representative of whom and what? The problem arises at several levels. In interconfessional dialogues, the participants - besides possessing the general qualities and competences of an ecumenical dialogist - are expected to meet two requirements: to be "at home" in their own communion, which includes being able to present and to represent it; and secondly, to be in sympathy with the goals of the conversation, which includes being knowledgeable about and favourably disposed towards the dialogue partner. But with the increasing multiformity and intermingling of confessional traditions, criteria of representativeness elude precise definition. Further, if all important groupings within a confessional family or even within a single national church were to be included, the group would become unmanageable. A selection is therefore inescapable; and a prime responsibility falls here on the appointing executive or committee, with the attendant risk of arbitrariness and the bureaucratic propensity to appoint "safe" and "reliable" spokesmen.

The two most serious defects in the overall composition of dialogue groups are without doubt the negligible representation of persons from the 99.99 per cent of the Christian community who are not professional theologians, and, on a different level, from the Third World. Among the theologians, the process of natural selection favours those with specialised competence in the field of confessional characteristics and problems, which tends to exclude those for whom the inherited divisions are of minor importance. As for the churches of the Third World, it might possibly be argued that the bilateral conversations present little interest insomuch as these deal with obstacles originating in European and American church history. But the Third World churches are the inheritors - and victims - of these transplanted divisions; moreover, because of their different experience, they can offer challenging perspectives on the developments also in the West. And as the bilaterals increasingly move on to explore concrete goals of church fellowship, a full participation of Third World churchmen becomes even more imperative.

At the same time, however, there is a genuine effort to reach out for representativeness, within the limits set by the accepted nature of interconfessional dialogue. This concern is apparent, for instance, in the sometimes extensive consultation process which customarily precedes appointments. In the actual conversations, it manifests itself in the tendency to refer back to classic standards or symbols such as the ancient Creeds, the Augsburg Confession, the Book of Common Prayer, Wesley's Hymns, the Second Vatican Council, and the like.

Yet the quest for representativeness, however defined, includes an ineluctable tension. Confessional identity, whether corporate or personal, is not a fixed and static thing; the separated confessional traditions are acknowledged to be provisional formations constrained to move forward to fuller manifestations of the one Church.

Hence the principle of confessional representativeness implies also, and above all, a commitment to that eschatological self-transcendence which reaches out beyond the present divisions. This awareness that a bilateral group represents, ideally and intentionally, the whole oikoumene is also manifest in the conversations. It finds expression in the common appeal to the predenominational Bible, the self-evident recognition of the dialogue partners as brothers in Christ, and in such small but not unimportant signs as the frequent references to supportive ecumenical documents and the growing custom of inviting observer-participants from other confessions and dialogue groups.

Any joint statements or recommendations emanating from a bilateral group are initially only representative of that group, however official its status. It must be formally accepted by the sponsoring churches in order to become a recognised consensus and to serve as a basis for ecclesiastical decision-making. But before and besides such official actions, consensus statements may have a considerable formative influence on theological and public opinion in the churches, if effectively disseminated. They indicate that at the highest levels the communions involved recognise each other as Christian brethren and that the kind of fraternal dialogue and fellowship, exemplified in such joint statements, is regarded as legitimate and desirable. In this manner they also serve to stimulate useful local experimentation and to help build pressure for official action.

If one should seek to indicate a common denominator for the highly varied modes of inquiry, of reasoning and dialogical exchange, that characterise the bilateral conversations, this can perhaps be described by a term which found currency in connection with the Faith and Order World Conference in Montreal - "catholicity in method" (Preparatory Commission Report on Christ and the Church, 1963, pp. 10ff.) By this is meant a mode of thinking, which perceives the work of God and his world, man, the Church, the Bible, in categories of wholeness and plural fullness. It sees theologising not as a self-contained intellectual pursuit, but rooted in the soil of worship and ministry and mission. Instead of reiterating the sharp disjunctions and sometimes oppositions between, for example, Scripture and tradition, word and sacrament, freedom and authority, unity and diversity, with their disruptive repercussions in Christian history, it proceeds on the hypothesis that these may rather be complementary and interdependent.

Instead of describing confessional traditions in terms of polemical distinctives, it is intent on discovering transconfessional connectives and common determinants.

C. Communication

With its inconsistencies and restrictions, the diffusion of information about the bilaterals reflects a familiar conflict of interests: on the one hand, the concern for a broad and open dialogue and for continuing dissemination of new ideas among the churches; and on the other hand, the concern for preserving the freedom and spontaneity of debate and confidentiality of controversial explorations.

There is no bilateral conversation that has not been wrestling with this problem. Despite internal and external restraints, the groups would nevertheless in general tend to concur in the sentiment forcefully expressed in the report from an A-RC/usa meeting (VII).

> "The work in which we are engaged, however, is not secret by nature and from time to time may be of interest and concern to the people of God in general. They, too, are part of the process whereby the Church makes its decisions, and their reactions, whether favorable or unfavorable, are significant to the authoritative decision-making bodies .....
> We believe that a policy of openness, in spite of occasional confusion and mistakes, will result, in the long run, in more positive achievements than a policy of close control of the dissemination of information. This group itself must, of course, be sensitive to its responsibilities not to misrepresent either its own status or the actual state of ecumenical agreement between our two Communions." (ARC-DOC I, p. 22).

The communication of materials and findings takes several forms: (a) formal consensus statements, with recommendations, which are submitted to the respective authorities and subsequently released for publication; (b) press releases to the general public; (c) publication of papers and discussion summaries; (d) personal reports by members to their denominational executives, synods, etc. and by observers from other bilateral groups or the World Council of Churches; (e) multirelational exchanges within the confessional family concerned and, thus far only to a minor extent, with corresponding groups in other confessional families as well. This latter form of expanded participation deserves noticing, for it marks an attempt to break through the initial isolation and obscurity of bilateral conversations and place them more firmly in the midstream of ecumenical endeavour. Thus in several instances, conference reports have been widely distributed and studied especially among the clergy of the related church bodies, and the responses collated and taken account of in the continuing studies (cf. in particular A-RC; A-RC/usa; L-R-U/eur).

D. Review and Evaluation

In most dialogues, occasional review is a built-in element in the proceedings. But with the proliferation of bilateral groups and the completion of an initial series of meetings, the need has arisen for independent reviews which take a fresh look at a single or a group of bilaterals, assess their accomplishments, and point to future directions. The importance of this review stage for the dialogues themselves, as well as for their follow-through in the churches, needs hardly to be underlined. The reviewing takes different forms: (a) In some instances where a commission has completed its assignment, the sponsoring bodies have appointed a joint working group for the purpose of examining the responses from the churches, indicating problem areas which call for deeper probing, and proposing ways of implementation (A-L; L-R-U/eur; L-RC). (b) Other surveys have undertaken a comparative and evaluative study of the dialogues in which a particular tradition is engaged. The Lutheran World Federation and its agencies have sponsored three such consultations - one covering the international scene (Geneva, November 1971), another the American scene (Minneapolis, June 1973), and finally one surveying the Lutheran-Orthodox conversations (Liebfrauenberg, France, March 1974).[1] No other world body has as yet performed a similar assessment of its dialogues. On the Roman Catholic side, a committee of the Catholic Theological Society of America has carried out a "theological review and critique" of the bilateral consultations between the Roman Catholic and other churches in the United States.[2] A group of scholars is currently cooperating

1. The papers and findings of the consultations are on file in the offices of the Lutheran World Federation in Geneva and New York. A personal interpretation of the Lutheran dialogues in American perspective is offered in Warren A. Quanbeck, Search for Understanding: Lutheran Conversations with Reformed, Anglican, and Roman Catholic Churches. Minneapolis: Augsburg Publishing House, 1972.

2. Published in Proceedings of the Catholic Theological Society of America, 1972; available from CSR Executive Office, Wilfrid Laurier University, Waterloo, Ontario N2L 3C5, Canada. Price $7.50. Offprints of the survey may be ordered at a price of $1.00 from CTSA Proceedings, Darlington Seminary, Mahwah, New Jersey 07430, USA.

with the Faith and Order Secretariat in preparing a review and appraisal of the Orthodox-Protestant conversations, which is scheduled to appear in late 1975. (c) The present Survey, sponsored by the Conference of Secretaries of World Confessional Families in cooperation with the Faith and Order Secretariat, is the first attempt to present a global picture. On the occasion of its annual meeting in December 1974, the Conference also invited an international group of dialogue representatives to undertake a personal assessment of the bilateral movement; its report, reproduced below, represents the latest stage in this maturing process of self-evaluation.[1]

E. Implementation and Outreach

Bilaterals are undertaken for specific ends, and their results must consequently be judged in the first place in terms of that purpose (this does not, of course, exclude the possibility that the initial definition of the purpose itself may have been unresponsive to the real needs and opportunities of the situation). There is as yet comparatively little evidence of any tangible impact of bilaterals on the life and thought of the churches concerned. Several reasons are given for this. It is only in the last few years that bilaterals have begun to produce joint reports and concrete recommendations for implementation, and it is therefore too early to expect noticeable results. Many groups, because of their limited mandate, conceive of their assignments as completed with the production of a theological report and its submission to the sponsoring bodies. In other cases, a group may feel bound to defer the submission of concrete proposals on some particular issue until it has also reached agreement on other, related problems whose solution determines the issue. To illustrate, official agreements on intercommunion are conditional upon a consensus not merely on the nature of the eucharist but also on mutual recognition of ministries and ecclesial communities. A similar multiple conditioning prevails with reference to mixed marriages. Other groups again do include in their findings specific recommendations for action in various areas of church life. Usually such recommendations look towards programmes in the field of study and education, particularly among the clergy and in theological schools, and also in the field of social action. Some groups go a step further and include definite requests affecting ecclesiastical policy and politics.

1. See pp. 258ff.

The response of the receiving agencies likewise varies widely. The action of world confessional families is necessarily limited by their lack of executive and legislative power; but as opinion-forming bodies, they nevertheless exercise considerable influence in supporting bilateral conversations and extending their outreach. The critical locus of implementation, however, is, on the one hand, the decision-making process of individual church bodies, and, on the other hand, the common life of Christians in local communities. The two are, of course, interdependent. The last few years, however, have seen a marked shift of attention, also in the bilateral field, from institutional to local possibilities of implementation, or, more correctly, of active participation in a joint venture which ultimately concerns every parish member of the two communions involved. The following examples illustrate this multi-faceted approach.

On a world scale, the Anglican-Roman Catholic commission is probably ahead of others in its efforts to stimulate local participation and experimentation. National and regional groups are invited to contribute preparatory statements to the international commission and to comment on its findings in a continuing process of vertical interaction. As an indispensable element in the growing unity, the national and diocesan agencies of both churches in the USA are encouraging such ventures as "living room dialogues" on the local implications of the international consensus statements,prayer fellowships, inter-visitations and "convenanted" relationships among Episcopal and Roman Catholic parishes, etc. [1] The Lutheran World Federation is sponsoring a research project aiming at the development of suitable models for integrating bilateral conversations in the total life of the member churches. The Leuenberg Agreement of European churches, again, exemplifies another procedure with its alternation of deliberative meetings, official and unofficial discussions of the draft proposal among the churches, and subsequent review and revision. Once the goal had been defined as the achievement of full interchurch fellowship, the programme was structured accordingly: theological reflection was wedded to reflection on problems of ecclesiastical and legal implications, and to the preparatory con-

1. The news bulletins of the Ecumenical Office of the Executive Council of the Episcopal Church and of the Roman Catholic Bishops' Committee for Ecumenical and Interreligious Affairs bring frequent reports on such efforts.

ferences were appointed a high percentage of church leaders and administrators, ministers, educators, and also specialists in church law. In the Federal Republic of Germany, no church document has reportedly been discussed so extensively in local congregations, clergy meetings, etc. during the past few decades as the drafts of the Leuenberg Agreement. In the USA, the Reformed-Roman Catholic commission has gone still further in the direction of local participation. After several years of discussion of theological and pastoral matters, the commission in its present phase is reversing the order and enlisting Presbyterian and Roman Catholic congregations of a pilot area in an interdisciplinary study of their ecumenical relationships and of the implications which can be drawn for the unity to be sought from their experiences.

Yet, notwithstanding such ventures as these, there undoubtedly still exists a glaring hiatus between, on the one hand, the theological discoveries and agreements, sometimes of historic significance, which have been reached in bilateral conversations, and, on the other hand, the actual momentum of the life and thought of the churches involved. Part of this is explained by the fairly recent emergence of the bilaterals to which reference has already been made. The lack of effective implementation is rooted partly in the general failure of ecclesiastical bodies to combine theological inquiry with an equally professional analysis of targets, the ways of reaching them, and the supportive and counteracting forces in Church and society which must be taken into consideration. Nor can the stubborn resistance of ecclesiastical _faits accomplis_ to new insights be overlooked, which might upset venerated patterns of confessional self-understanding and self-determination. Sometimes the lack of implementation can be traced to quite specific and immediate causes. As a member of a dialogue group working in a denominational office once frankly avowed: "The resistance starts in the department next door." Like charity, the step from ecumenical conversation to ecumenical conversion must begin at home.

V
SUBJECT MATTERS

The following chapter contains (A) a table of topics which have been a main theme of a meeting or occupied a prominent place in discussions and reports, and (B) cross-conversational analyses of six prominent subjects in the bilaterals.

A. TABLE OF TOPIC FREQUENCIES

Gospel, Revelation, Scripture, Tradition	A-L; A-L/usa; A-RC; A-RC/can; A-RC/saf; Ev-O/frg-r; L-O/usa; L-R/usa; L-R-U/eur; L-RC; L-RC/usa; M-RC; M-RC/eng; OC-O; OC-RC/eur; O-R/nam; Pe-RC; R-RC; R-RC/usa
Creeds and Confessions	A-L; A-L/usa; A-O; A-RC; A-RC/usa; C-P; L-R/can; L-R/usa; L-R-U/eur; L-RC; L-RC/usa; M-RC; OC-RC/eur; EO-OO; O-R/nam
Ecumenical Councils	Ev-O/frg-c; Ev-O/frg-r; EO-OO
Development of Doctrine	A-L/usa; A-RC/usa; L-RC; L-R-U/eur; L-RC/usa; R-RC/usa
Holy Spirit	A-O; Ev-O/frg-c; Ev-O/frg-r; M-RC; M-RC/usa; Pe-RC; R-RC/usa
Christ	A-O; Ev-O/frg-c; Ev-O/frg-r; L-R/usa; L-R-U/eur; M-RC; OC-O; EO-OO; R-RC
Spirituality, Worship	A-L; A-L/usa; Ev-O/frg-r; M-RC; M-RC/usa; Pe-RC
Salvation, Faith, Sanctification	A-Ev/e-frg; AB-RC/usa; Ev-O/frg-c; Ev-O/frg-r L-O/f-r; L-R/usa; L-R-U/eur; L-RC; M-RC; M-RC/usa; O-R/nam; Pe-RC
Church - World	A-L; A-O/usa; A-RC; A-RC/eng; A-RC/usa; AB-RC/usa; Ev-O/frg-c; Ev-O/frg-r; Ev-O/gdr-r L-R-U/eur; L-RC; M-RC; O-R/nam; Pe-RC; R-RC; R-RC/usa
Mary	A-RC/eng
Man	Ev-O/frg-c

Baptism	A-L; A-L/usa; A-RC/scot; B-R; AB-RC/usa; CC-RC/usa; Ev-O/frg-r; L-R-U/eur; L-RC/phil; L-RC/usa; M-RC/aus; O-RC/usa; Pe-RC
Eucharist, Intercommunion	A-Ev/e-g; A-L; A-L/aus; A-L/usa; A-O; A-O/usa; A-R; A-RC; A-RC/eng; A-RC/jap; A-RC/lam; A-RC/scot; A-RC/usa; CC-RC/usa; Ev-O/frg-r; Ev-O/gdr-r; L-O/f-r; L-R/usa; L-R-U/eur; L-RC; L-RC/phil; L-RC/usa; M-RC; OC-O; OC-RC/eur; O-RC/usa; R-RC; R-RC/usa
Preaching	Ev-O/gdr-r
Apostolic Succession	A-L; A-L/usa; A-RC; L-RC; L-RC/usa; R-RC/usa
Ministry, Priesthood	A-L; A-L/aus; A-L/usa; A-RC; A-RC/eng; A-RC/lam; A-RC/saf; A-RC/usa; AB-RC/usa; CC-RC/usa; L-O/f-r; L-R-U/eur; L-RC; L-RC/usa; M-RC; M-RC/usa; OC-RC/eur; R-RC; R-RC/usa
Women in the Church	R-RC/usa
Episcopacy	A-L; A-L/usa; A-RC; A-RC/usa; L-RC/usa; OC-O
Papacy	A-RC; A-RC/usa; L-RC; L-RC/usa; OC-RC/eur; R-RC; R-RC/usa
Teaching Authority of the Church	A-Ev/e-g; A-RC; A-RC/eng; A-RC/saf; A-RC/usa; AB-RC/usa; L-R/can; L-RC; L-RC/usa; M-RC; OC-RC/eur; EO-OO; R-RC; R-RC/usa
Authority and Freedom in the Church	A-Ev/e-g; A-L; A-RC; A-RC/usa; AB-RC/usa; L-RC; L-RC/usa; M-RC; M-RC/eng; R-RC
Mixed Marriages	A-RC; A-RC/eng; A-RC/jap; A-RC/lam; A-RC/saf; CC-RC/usa; M-RC; M-RC/aus; O-RC/usa; L-R-RC; R-RC; R-RC/usa
Church and Society	A-O/usa; A-RC; Ev-O/frg-r; Ev-O/gdr-r; L-O/f-r; L-O-R/nam; L-R; L-R/usa; L-RC; M-RC; M-RC/usa; O-RC/rus; O-RC/usa
Unity, Union	A-L; A-L/usa; A-OC; A-O; A-O/usa; A-RC; A-RC/usa; AB-RC/usa; C-P; CC-RC/usa; Ev-O/frg-r; L-R; L-R-U/eur; L-RC; L-RC/usa; OC-O; EO-OO

B. SYNOPTIC PRESENTATION OF PROMINENT SUBJECTS

1. Gospel, Scripture and Tradition

Sources

A-L	Anglican-Lutheran International Conversations, Report ... 1970-1972; Lutheran World XIX, 4, 1972, 387-99
A-L/usa	Lutheran-Episcopal Dialogue: A Progress Report, 1972
A-RC	Venice, September 1970, "Church and Authority", Theology (SPCK) LXXIV, 608, 1971, 49-67; The Catholic Mind (USA), April 1971; One in Christ VII, 2-3, 1971, 256-76
L-O/usa	New York, 1967 and 1969, "Scripture and Tradition"
L-R/usa	Chicago, 1963, "Gospel, Confession and Scripture", Marburg Revisited, Part I, pp. 1-38, 180f.
L-R-U/eur	Bad Schauenburg, 1967, "Lutheran and Reformed Churches on the Way to One Another", Lutheran World XIV, 3, 1967, 53-67; Lutherische Rundschau XVII, 3, 1967, 380-97; Auf dem Weg, Lutherisch-reformierte Kirchengemeinschaft, 1967
	Leuenberg, 1969-70, "Church Fellowship and Church Division", Gemeinschaft der reformatorischen Kirchen, Auf dem Weg II, 1971
	Leuenberg, 1973, "Agreement ("Konkordie") among Reformation Churches in Europe", The Ecumenical Review XXV, 3, 1973, 355-59
L-RC	Zurich, 1967, Nemi, 1969 and Cartigny, 1970, Lutheran World XVI, 4, 1969, 363-79 and XVIII, 2, 1971, 161-87
	Malta, 1971, Final Report, "The Gospel and the Church", Lutheran World XIX, 3, 1972, 259-73
L-RC/usa	Baltimore, 1965, The Status of the Nicene Creed as Dogma of the Church, 1965
	Peter in the New Testament, 1973
	Papal Primacy and the Universal Church, 1974, pp. 13-19, 38-42
M-RC	"Report of the Joint Commission between the Roman Catholic Church and the World Methodist Council, 1967-70", Book of Proceedings of the Twelfth World Methodist Conference, 1972
OC-O	"Dokumente zum orthodox-altkatholischen Dialog", Internationale Kirchliche Zeitschrift 61, 2, 1971, 65-74

OC-RC/eur "Protokolle der bisherigen Sitzungen der römisch-katholisch/altkatholischen Gesprächskommission in Deutschland", ibid. 61, 2, 1971, 75-78

Pe-RC Horgen/Zurich, 1972 and Rome, 1973, Reports, One in Christ X, 2, 1974, 113-16

R-RC Cartigny/Geneva, 1971, "The Teaching Authority of the Church", Common Report

R-RC/usa New York, 1966, "Revelation, Scripture and Tradition", Reconsiderations, 1967

Chicago, 1966, "The Development of Doctrine", Reconsiderations, 1967

Morristown, 1970, "Ministry in the Church", Journal of Ecumenical Studies VI, 3, 1970, 686-90

Richmond, Va., 1971, "Ministry in the Church", Final Statement, ibid. IX, 3, 1972, 589-612

The problem indicated in the title has again emerged as a frontier issue in theological reflection as well as interconfessional dialogue - not only because of its intrinsic importance but also because of an awareness that the conventional positions need to be fundamentally rethought. It is symptomatic that "Tradition and Traditions" was one of the main themes of the Faith and Order World Conference at Montreal in 1963. Some of the most significant debates at the Second Vatican Council turned around the same subject; its weight is apparent already in the fact that the statement on "Divine Revelation" was one of the (merely two) documents promulgated as dogmatic constitutions. Similarly the subject of the Holy Tradition figures prominently on the proposed agenda for the forthcoming Orthodox synod.

A number of factors have combined to spur this centripetal movement. In the encounter of the great confessional families of Christendom, these are inevitably challenged not only to expound their faith but also to explain it. "On what grounds and by what authority do you believe what you believe?" They are forced, individually and jointly, to reexamine the legitimacy of their diverse interpretations of Scripture and of tradition. And today this internal reexamination of Christian foundations is even more necessary and urgent than before because of the recognition that it cannot be separated from the external dialogue with other religions, world views, modes of thought, and their claims to truth.

However great the need for a reexamination of the problem, the conventional antithesis of sola scriptura versus Scripture and tradition might well have presented an insuperable impasse had it not been for new developments in some related fields such as research into the formation of the Bible and the canon, as well as into the complexities of historic continuity and change. The awareness that the Bible itself, in one aspect, is an outgrowth of a long and cumulative history of traditions has opened up new horizons of mutual understanding, from which the bilateral conversations have benefited.

The discussion of the matter has been obfuscated by the oscillating meanings attached to the term tradition. It is being variously used to denote such disparate things as: the content of the Gospel, the process of its interpretation and transmission, the continuing stream of Trinitarian life in the community of the Church, oral as contrasted with written tradition, revealed truth as distinct from other manifestations of church life, a medium of revelation and source of faith independent of Scripture, ecclesiastical customs and ceremonies, confessional or denominational families.

In an effort to bring some clarity into the prevailing confusion, the Faith and Order World Conference in Montreal in 1963 adopted a language which is worth recalling since it usefully seeks to establish a common terminological and conceptual framework, without prejudging substantive differences still unresolved. The statement is significant also for the reason that it reflects an unusually broad-based consideration of the subject in that the discussion included not only Protestant and Orthodox conference members but also Roman Catholic consultants.

> "Our starting point" - states the Montreal Report - "is that we are all living in a tradition which goes back to our Lord and has its roots in the Old Testament, and are all indebted to that tradition in so much as we have received the revealed truth, the Gospel, through its being transmitted from one generation to another. Thus we can say that we exist as Christians by the Tradition of the Gospel (the paradosis of the kerygma) testified in Scripture, transmitted in and by the Church through the power of the Holy Spirit. Tradition taken in this sense is actualized in the preaching of the Word, in the administration of the Sacraments and worship, in Christian teaching and theology,

> in mission and witness to Christ in the lives of the members of the Church.
>
> ... We can speak of the Christian Tradition (with a capital T), whose content is God's revelation and self-giving in Christ, present in the life of the Church. But this Tradition which is the work of the Holy Spirit is embodied in traditions (in the two senses of the word, both as referring to diversity in forms of expression, and in the sense of separate communions). The traditions in Christian history are distinct from, and yet connected with, the Tradition. They are the expressions and manifestations of the one truth and reality which is Christ."[1]

The Montreal reformulation has exercised a noticeable influence on several bilateral dialogues, and it can provide a useful heuristic frame when assessing the ongoing discussions. It should be noted that similar emphases appear in the dogmatic constitution on "Divine Revelation" from the Second Vatican Council.

The Supremacy of the Gospel. The problem of Scripture and tradition (to use the conventional formulation of the subject) has sometimes been conceived as that of finding the proper relationship between two separate entities, with the answer depending on the variable meanings attached to each term. In the bilateral conversations, as in contemporary theology generally, the problem is advisedly set in a wider, multidimensional frame of reference. The main issue is not the interrelation of Scripture and tradition as such, but the relationship of both to a prior reality: the Gospel, revelation, the Word of God, the saving act of God in Jesus Christ. In this transcendent perspective, it is furthermore necessary to discern their connections with other data of the faith such as the Holy Spirit, conscience, the corporate experience of the Christian community, and the teaching office of the Church. A L-R/usa statement speaks, for instance, of receiving the Gospel "as it is revealed in the prophetic and apostolic Scriptures, attested through the witness of the Holy Spirit, and preserved in the tradition of the catholic faith as expressed in the commonly accepted creeds of the ancient church" (Marburg Revisited, p.37; M-RC, Report, nos. 102ff.).

---

1. The Fourth World Conference on Faith and Order, Montreal 1963, ed. P.C. Rodger and L. Vischer. New York: Association Press, 1964, pp. 51f. For recent developments in ecumenical biblical study, cf. the Faith and Order study on "The Authority of the Bible", Faith and Order, Louvain 1971, pp. 9-23.

In accord with the biblical understanding of the act-character of the Word of God, the Gospel is seen not as a mere cognitive message, and even less as a doctrinal system, but as the good news of God's saving act in Jesus Christ, or as that act itself. "What God has done for the salvation of the world in Jesus Christ is transmitted in the gospel and made present in the Holy Spirit. The gospel as proclamation of God's saving action is therefore itself a salvation event" (L-RC, Report, 1971, nos. 16, 24). "... that Jesus is the only mediator of salvation ... is the centre of the Gospel and the only ground and canon of the teaching life of the Church" (L-R-U/eur, Leuenberg, 1969/70). The R-RC/usa group, in considering the ministry in the Church, declares that "In all that we say about church and ministry, we begin with the gospel, the word about what God has done in the cross of Christ and in raising him from the dead" (Morristown, 1970, 687).

It is this Gospel "to which both the Scriptures and the confessions bear witness" (L-R/usa, Marburg Revisited, p. 180). It holds priority and superiority over the Scriptures as well as the traditions of the Church. "We agree that the Church as Creatura Verbi with her traditions stands under the Word" (R-RC, Report, 1971; A-RC, Venice, op.cit., no. 15; L-RC, Report, 1971, no. 17).

The (Derived) Supremacy of Scripture. As already suggested, the terms Word of God, Scripture, Gospel are used in these documents as familiar codewords, and therefore mostly left undefined and with oscillating overtones of meaning.[1] It would be superficial to ascribe this imprecision only to the muddleheadedness of theologians. Rather, it reflects the complex dialectic of the actual relationship of Gospel and Scripture, and in part also differing ways of conceiving this "distinction in unity". On the one hand, it is maintained that the Scripture is not to be identified with the Gospel; it "proclaims" the Word of God; it is "the sufficient, inspired, and authoritative record and witness, prophetic and apostolic, to God's revelation in Jesus Christ" (A-L, no. 17; L-R-U/eur, Leuenberg, 1973, no. 13; M-RC, Report, no. 105). But precisely because Scripture is the unique and authorita-

1. A conspicuous example of the ambiguities in the use of the term "Word of God" can be found in the L-R/eur, Schauenburg Report, Lutheran World XIV, 3, 1967, 62.

tive witness, it shares - though distinct - in the revelatory authority and power of the Gospel itself. A L-R-U/eur report states it explicitly: "Because of its witness to Christ, the whole Scripture of the Old and New Testaments is the origin and norm of the entire service with which the Church is commissioned" (Leuenberg, 1971; similarly A-L, nos. 17-22; L-RC, Report 1971, no. 17). The A-RC group states in a similar vein: "Believers know the Word of God to be mediated to them in the Bible, because its focus is found in him" (Venice, 1970, no. 1; cf. OC-RC/eur, 78).

According to a R-RC/usa report, "For both Churches, the apostolic preaching as recorded in the New Testament is normative". But it adds a realistic remark, recurring in several other dialogues as well: "There is however a difference in the way Scripture is conceived of as being normative, as well as in the way this norm is applied. This varies also within each Church" (Reconsiderations, p. 103). The remark is a reminder that the convergent emphasis on biblical authority, which undoubtedly characterises bilateral conversations, cannot be taken as an accomplished consensus.

Diversity and Unity in the Bible. In seeking biblical guidance in its quest for consensus and unity, ecumenical thinking has long tended to accentuate the great unifying centralities that characterise biblical faith. This assumption has of late been subjected to serious criticism, and this shift is reflected in the preoccupation of some bilaterals with the diversities within the New Testament itself and the possible implications for legitimising the later diversity of Christian traditions. The existence in the New Testament of very diverse forms of worship and belief, of ministry and organisation, is not minimised or denied; it is on the contrary accepted as an enriching asset, which must not be suppressed by doctrinaire attempts at standardisation. But with equal emphasis it is affirmed that "in or behind the diverse theological conceptions of the New Testament there is a unifying center which one must draw out" (L-RC, Zurich, 1967, 370f. and Report 1971, no. 24; R-RC, Cartigny, 1971).

The acceptance of a diversity of images, concepts, and forms in expressing the mystery of Christ has obviously a direct bearing on the disputed question of the hermeneutical key to the Scripture. Lutherans, and to a lesser degree the Reformed, have singled out the Pauline idea of justification, making it the central article of faith and the clue of biblical interpretation. This position is in evidence when it is claimed, for instance, that "the message of justification as the message of God's free grace is the measure of all the church's preaching" (L-R-U/eur, Leuenberg, 1973, no.12). For churches of the Catholic tradition, such an emphasis on the concept of justification appears as an unwarranted reduction of the rich biblical salvation imagery to a single aspect - all the more questionable since it also perpetuates the polemical battle-fronts of the 16th century, particularly when linked with the exclusive formula "by faith alone". In the consensus statements any monopoly of the concept is abandoned. A L-R/usa report avows that "The scriptures also present the same gospel in other concepts, such as reconciliation, regeneration, and redemption. An evangelical confession accordingly may be, and has been, framed in terms of one or more of these" (Marburg Revisited, p. 37; similarly L-RC, Report 1971, no. 27). Sometimes care is taken to preclude a misleading, purely forensic interpretation by explicitly conjoining justification with adoption and sanctification in describing the fulness of the Gospel (L-R-U/eur, Leuenberg, 1969/70 and 1973, nos. 10f.).

The Relationship of Scripture and Tradition. These affirmations about the supremacy of Scripture would give an erroneous impression, if taken in isolation; they are to be seen in the context of changing and more differentiated understandings of tradition, which at important points transcend former misconceptions and dichotomies. Of basic importance in this reorientation are four recurring emphases. (1) Scripture and tradition, if properly understood, are not antithetical but joined together in a relationship of mutual inherence - and this not only in the history of the Church but in the Bible itself. (2) Tradition - in the double sense of that which is transmitted, the Gospel of Jesus Christ, and the process of traditioning - existed prior to the formation of the scriptural canon. (3) Although Scripture is a result and record of tradition, it nonetheless possesses normative priority and functions as the criterion of all subsequent traditions, at least in the negative sense that nothing can be held as true tradition which contradicts Scripture. The exact meaning, however, of this dialectic and the role of the Church as the interpreter of both remain a matter of dispute. (4) The notion of tradition cannot be reduced to doctrine alone; it embraces spirituality, liturgy, ethos, and all other manifestations of the life of the Church.

In the A-RC conversations this intricate co-inherence is described in these terms: "The tradition of the community in Bible, ministry, catechesis, and liturgy is both witness to and preserver of the authentic doctrine and fellowship of the apostles" (Venice, 1970, nos. 1, 5, 15). The phrase is qualified by the common recognition of the supremacy of Scripture, and it bypasses any views of tradition as a second, extrabiblical source or vehicle of revealed knowledge. The Anglicans and Lutherans in turn agree "that all traditions are secondary to tradition [i.e. the transmission of the apostolic witness] and that they, therefore, have to be tested by that tradition. If they are in accordance with and expressions of this ultimate standard they are to be regarded as important means of continuity ... At all times, however, there has been a sharply critical attitude to tradition if this implied an additional source for historical data supplementing the history given in the gospels or a source for a 'secret' doctrine additional to that given in the scriptural witness" (A-L , Report, 1972, nos. 34 and 38).

The L-RC/usa study of the nexus of Peter and papacy concretely illustrates the complex interaction between apostolic Tradition and post-apostolic traditions. In Roman Catholic teaching it has been axiomatic to claim that Christ's commission to Peter constituted the sure foundation for the papal office. The other churches have as categorically rejected such an interpretation as an illegitimate introjection of later historical models into the scriptural material. A related instance is the divergent assessments of the roles of Peter and Paul, which can be found among Roman Catholic and Protestant biblical scholars since the 16th century. While the former show a steadily growing tendency to exalt the role of Peter as the head of the apostolic college, the latter inversely have tended to exalt Paul (a Lutheranised Paul) as the foremost apostle.

The study <u>Peter in the New Testament</u> seeks to overcome the impasse by focusing attention on the images of Peter and the roles attributed to him in New Testament thought. In comparing the different strata, it traces a mounting "trajectory" of images - a trajectory which must be regarded as theologically significant also by non-Roman Catholics since it forms part of the New Testament witness itself. The question therefore is not whether Christ founded the papacy but rather whether the subsequent use of the images of Peter in reference to the papacy is consistent with the trajectory discernible in the New Testament texts (op.cit., p. 168). The group gives an affirmative answer, but the answer is immediately qualified by a further question: to what extent is that trajectory of Petrine images also in its turn influenced by later history? In sum, while a historical-critical biblical inquiry is able to trace New Testament pointers and paradigms for Petrine roles in the Church, it cannot settle the relationship between Peter and papacy; this is rather a matter of theological reflection and spiritual discernment of the providential workings of God in history. But by thus redefining the problems, the American study moves out beyond many entrenched positions and paves the way for more open-minded and flexible investigations of a common concern - the need for a ministry symbolising and serving the unity of all of Christendom.

The Orthodox bilaterals under review have not yet resulted in any definite consensus statements which would indicate its stance in current rethinking of scripture and tradition, showing the patterns of convergence and difference. Its doctrine of Holy Tradition is likely to adduce new perspectives. In earlier conversations,[1] Orthodox spokesmen have presented concepts of tradition which - with their organic connection of Spirit, Tradition, Scripture, Church - express a position independent of the classic Roman Catholic-Reformation controversies in the matter.

Criteria of Traditions. In interconfessional conversations the existence of a plurality of Christian traditions is accepted both as a factual premise and as a dilemma to be resolved. If there is one apostolic Tradition which is appropriated and transmitted in the life of the Church, where is it to be found among the multitude of divergent and partly conflicting traditions? Two facile answers are discarded whether expressly or by implication. No single tradition is identifiable with the Tradition; nor can the Tradition be equated with the totality of traditions or be assumed to be equally present in each and all of them.

1. See, for example, the report of the Joint Anglican-Orthodox Doctrinal Commission, London, 1931, which states that "everything necessary for salvation can be found in Holy Scripture as completed, expounded, interpreted, and understood in the Holy Tradition, by the guidance of the Holy Spirit residing in the Church ..." and that "nothing contained in Tradition is contrary to the Scriptures. Though these two may be logically defined and distinguished, yet they cannot be separated from each other nor from the Church".

It is within these demarcation lines that the discussion is groping forward to establish common principles of discrimination.

These explorations have perhaps been pushed farthest in the L-RC conversations in a discussion of tests for distinguishing between legitimate and illegitimate doctrinal and ecclesiastical developments (Zurich, 1967; Cartigny, 1970; Report 1971, nos. 18ff.). The centre of the Gospel, God's saving deed in Jesus Christ, is reaffirmed as the supreme criterion. An attempt is then made to spell this out in more specific terms by suggesting a series of secondary criteria such as (1) the enhanced significance of the _sensus fidelium_ as a direction-finder at a time when conventional references to the principle of _sola scriptura_ or to the binding authority of the _magisterium_ no longer suffice; (2) the tradition of the Church ("as the history of the Gospel lived by sinful men") projecting critical orientations into a new future; (3) the mutuality of orthopraxis and orthodoxy; and (4) the responsible exercise of Christian freedom.

The generality of such considerations reveals how difficult and tentative this search for _common_ criteria still is. A direction has been agreed upon: the supremacy of the Gospel over Scripture, tradition and the Church. But the question of the respective roles of the latter three and the ways in which they interact in manifesting the originating Christ-event receives differing answers.

Comment

The documents under review contain frequent, though mostly rather perfunctory and conventional, references to the Holy Spirit as _the_ Traditioner of the Gospel of Jesus Christ. Here runs, it would appear, one of the principal divides in contemporary thinking on the subject - a divide characterised by different understandings of the presence of the Spirit in the Church. There are those who, mindful of the fallibility of the Church, see the work of the Spirit as strictly correlative with the saving word of Scripture. Their nascent reappraisal of tradition is linked with an almost instinctual apprehension for the perils of unevangelical traditions. The implications of the truth that Scripture, as a word _to_ the Church, is transmitted and interpreted only _in_ the Church, have not yet been fully digested. By contrast there are others, mindful of the abiding presence and power of the Spirit in the continuing life of the Church, who rather see the apostolic truth safeguarded in the concordance of Scripture and tradition, manifested in the teaching and worship and witness of the whole Church. Here an opposite peril is lurking: that the sovereignty of the Gospel appears beclouded by an insistence on the preordained harmony between Scripture and tradition and on the indefectibility of the Church. It is likely that a more serious and systematic exploration of the extraordinary Christian belief in the Holy Spirit would bring the debate around Scripture and tradition a great deal further towards clarity and unity.

2. Creeds and Confessions

Sources

A-L Anglican-Lutheran International Conversations, Report ... 1970-1972, nos. 17ff.

A-L/usa Lutheran-Episcopal Dialogue: A Progress Report, 1972, pp. 14ff., 23

A-RC Venice, September 1970, "Church and Authority", Theology LXXIV, 608, February 1971, 49-67; The Catholic Mind (USA), April 1971; One in Christ VII, 2-3, 1971, 256-76

A-RC/usa New York, January 1972, "Doctrinal Agreement and Christian Unity: Methodological Considerations", Joint Statement, ARC-DOC II, 1973, pp. 49-53; Journal of Ecumenical Studies IX, 2, 1972, 445-48; One in Christ VIII, 3, 1972, 299-303

EO-OO Aarhus, 1964, The Greek Orthodox Theological Review X, 2, Winter 1964-1965; Bristol, 1967, ibid. XIII, Fall 1968; Geneva, 1970 and Addis Ababa, 1971, ibid. XVI, 1 and 2, Spring and Fall 1971

L-R/usa Chicago, 1973, "Gospel, Confessions and Scripture", Marburg Revisited, Part I, pp. 1-38, 180f.

L-R-U/eur Bad Schauenburg, 1967, "Lutheran and Reformed Churches in Europe on the Way to One Another", Lutheran World XIV, 3, 1967, 53-67; Auf dem Weg, Lutherisch-reformierte Kirchengemeinschaft, 1967

Leuenberg, 1969-70, "Church Fellowship and Church Division", Gemeinschaft der reformatorischen Kirchen, Auf dem Weg II, 1971

Leuenberg, 1973 "Agreement ("Konkordie") among Reformation Churches in Europe", The Ecumenical Review XXV, 3, 1973, 355-59

L-RC Zurich, 1967; Båstad, 1968; Cartigny, 1970, Lutheran World XVI, 4, 1969, 363-79 and XVIII, 2, 1971, 161-87

Malta, 1971, Final Report, "The Gospel and the Church", Lutheran World XIX, 3, 1972, 259-73

L-RC/usa Baltimore, 1965, The Status of the Nicene Creed as Dogma of the Church

Chicago, 1966, One Baptism for the Remission of Sins

M-RC "Report of the Joint Commission between the Roman Catholic Church and the World Methodist Council, 1967-1970", 1971, Book of Proceedings of the Twelfth World Methodist Conference, 1972

OC-RC/eur "Protokolle der bisherigen Sitzungen der römisch-katholisch/altkatholischen Gesprächskommission in Deutschland", Internationale Kirchliche Zeitschrift 61, 2, 1971, 75-78

R-RC Cartigny, 1971, "The Teaching Authority of the Church", Common Report

R-RC/usa Chicago, 1966, "The Development of Doctrine", Reconsiderations, pp. 47-104

The very existence of a Conference of Secretaries of World Confessional Families, and the increasing cooperation between these families and the World Council of Churches within the larger ecumenical movement, are telling indications of the significance of the realities called "confessional". This is not to suggest that the relations between the confessional and the ecumenical have been clarified either in theory or in practice. Because of the varied and changing meanings attached to both these adjectives, the equation contains too many variables to allow a single and commonly acceptable answer.

In terms of facts, the history of the past few decades, and particularly of the 1960s, has been a history of tensions and adjustments.[1] The criticisms, for example, levelled by Asian Christian leaders against world confessionalism, are still fresh in memory. Yet at the same time both parties - or rather the several parties, since the world confessional families by no means constitute a common front among themselves - have gradually attained a status of mutual recognition at least pragmatically. This process of tension and rapprochement has not only produced a more realistic understanding of what the individual confessional families are and aspire to be within the Christian oikoumene. It has also of necessity given fresh impetus to theological reflection upon deeper and cognate questions such as: What is confession? A confession? A credal or confessional statement? And what is their role in the life of particular churches and in the

1. Harold E. Fey, "Confessional Families and the Ecumenical Movement" The Ecumenical Advance: A History of the Ecumenical Movement, Vol.2, 1948-1968, pp. 115-42

universal Church? Although the general relationships of confessional and other organised forms of ecumenical endeavour are beyond the scope of the present study, this glancing introductory reference is not out of place. For it calls to mind the factual context within which the bilateral conversations approach the confessional problem in its various aspects.

Considering the august claims implied in titling oneself a confessional family or tradition, it is a matter of some surprise that the subject of confession has not, thus far, received far more thematic attention than it actually has in the bilaterals. One of the reasons for this may be the difficulty of finding common denominators for comparing the widely differing understandings of doctrine and dogma, creed and confession, that inform the various traditions. The difficulty is compounded by emotional inhibitions: it sometimes appears, strangely enough, as if a church were more sensitive to challenging questions regarding its dogmatic or confessional self-image than regarding its interpretation of the Bible.

Prominent issues in the discussion are the function of confessions and creeds in the life of the churches, their authority and range of validity, and the consequences of their being recognised as historical documents.

Confession, Confessions, and Confessional Formulae. In the Faith and Order movement the so-called "Lund approach" represented an attempt to go beyond the level of comparative ecclesiology by seeking to penetrate behind the existing differences to a common understanding of the New Testament testimony about the one Christ and his one Church, thereby obtaining a critical perspective on subsequent divisions and deviations. In the bilateral conversations on confessions and creeds, a similar approach can be noticed in the desire to break open exclusive and narrowly intellectualistic or juridical definitions by a recourse to the pre-denominational fulness of such notions as homologia, martyria and correlates in the worship and teaching of the early Church. The basic question - states the L-R/eur Schauenburg Report - is "what the confession in the confessions is", and it replies by pointing to the confessions of faith in the New Testament, responding in praise and thanksgiving and witness to the glory of God in Jesus the Messiah and the Lord. There is but one confession; but already in New Testament times it expresses itself in a variety of formulations corresponding to the diverse needs of the community - later amplified and codified in rules of truth, creeds, and conciliar definitions. The confession of the Church, therefore, cannot be identified with any single or all of the doctrinal formulae used; on the contrary, the whole life of the Church is to be a confession of the lordship of Christ.

In contrast to the sometimes propounded theory that credal and confessional formulae primarily serve to defend the faith against threatening errors, the bilateral documents exhibit a more discriminating view. Several types, meeting different functions, are distinguished; among them the doxological one is seen as primary. According to the L-R/usa group, "The history of the Church exhibits such types as the doxological confession which celebrates the glory of the gospel, the kerygmatic which identifies and declares the gospel, the catechetical which serves for the instruction of believers, and the critical which distinguishes the gospel from errors and misunderstandings" (p. 37). Other statements, while taking the same general line, point up specific implications of these functions when they speak, for instance, of the confession as a hermeneutical key, a bond of unity and continuity, and an instrument of renewal and reform (A-L).

Authority. Despite the wide diversity of religious authority structures exhibited among the confessional families, efforts are made, here too, to identify and extend the areas of agreement.

In the hierarchy of authorities, the creeds and conciliar definitions of the ancient Church are ascribed a special place of prominence, because of their substantive congruity with Scripture. They are pointed summaries or expositions of central tenets of the scriptural witness and provide "authoritative guidance and direction in the interpretation of this normative scripture" (L-R/usa, p. 38; A-L, nos. 23ff; A-RC, nos. 5f.). Thus, for example, "The Nicene Faith possesses a unique status in the hierarchy of dogmas .../for it/ gathers up and articulates the biblical testimony concerning the Son and His relationship to the Father" (L-RC/usa, The Nicene Creed, p. 31f.). The acceptance of the ancient creeds "implies agreement ... on the fundamental trinitarian and christological dogmas" (A-L, no. 25). These conciliar decisions must be regarded as irreversible (A-RC, no.6).

Yet the authoritative claim does not inhere in the formulations as such, but in the intention. The current Eastern Orthodox-Oriental Orthodox consultations offer an illuminating illustration of historic significance. They call to mind the fact that the formation and reception of the ancient creeds, notably the christological definition of the Council of Chalcedon, was by no means an unambiguous process. And they clearly demonstrate that divergent formulations, once held to be irreconciliable, may in fact express the same intentions - and thus no longer provide a cause for separation. The principal outcome of these consultations thus far is the acknowledgement that the two traditions are in full agreement "on the essence of the Christological dogma ... as expressed by St. Cyril". "Through the different terminologies used by each side, we saw the same truth expressed" (Aarhus, 1964, 14; Geneva, 1970, 3).

But does not such a reinterpretation of past controversies undermine the authority of the creeds? The group has not shunned this question, but answers it in a manner which parallels similar explorations in other dialogues. "Distinction is to be made not only between the doctrinal definitions and canonical legislations of a Council, but also between the true intention of the dogmatic definition of a Council and the particular terminology in which it is expressed, which latter has less authority than the intention" (<u>ibid</u>.,5). Neither are the christological anathemas of the time irreversible. "We are agreed that the lifting of the anathemas is fully within the authority of the Church and does not compromise her infallibility in essential matters of the faith" (Addis Ababa, 1971, 212). In these consultations the Orthodox theologians are grappling with common ecumenical problems, such as the historicity of creeds, the legitimacy and limits of pluralistic variability not only in liturgical and canonical but also in dogmatic expression, the distinction between universal and local creeds, and the like.

The confessional formularies of the 16th and 17th centuries are no less caught up in the current movement of historical reexamination. This is true not only of the various Reformed confessions of faith and the Anglican Thirty-Nine Articles. It is true also of Lutheranism which, singling out <u>pura doctrina</u> as criterion of the true Church, has tended to elevate the Augsburg Confession to the status of a timeless norm.

In the bilateral conversations the historical differences in conceiving the nature and authority of confessional formularies are not smoothed over, but an effort is made to overcome their sectarian and polemical features by seeking to unravel their common thrusts and by acknowledging the legitimacy of different emphases in response to differing situations. In the Leuenberg Agreement, the assenting European churches declare after having explained their common understanding of the Gospel: "In this understanding of the Gospel we take our stand on the basis of the ancient creeds of the church and reaffirm the common conviction of the Reformation confessions ... "(L-R-U/eur, 1973, no. 12). The A-L report asserts: "Since confessional formularies are not a mark of the Church their significance lies in their expression of the living confession to the living Lord. Different approaches to the authority of these formularies are possible between Communions as long as they share a living confession which is a faithful response to the living Word of God as proclaimed in Holy Scripture" (op. cit., no. 31). Consistent with the historical approach, the point is also variously made that continuity of apostolic tradition does not preclude but, on the contrary, demands situational flexibility. Thus Roman Catholics and Lutherans join in affirming that "the structures and formulations in which the gospel is concretized share in the historical conditionedness of the world in its social and cultural transformations .../they/are simultaneously transitory and anticipatory. Their role is to open up the future and not be closed to it. Thus the continuity of the gospel - a gift of the Holy Spirit - is to be seen, not only in fixed structures and formulations, but also in its ability to make itself known in ever new forms by constant reflections on Holy Scripture and on its interpretation in the church's history" (L-RC, Report 1971, no. 44; R-RC, Cartigny, 1971, "Confessions").

As the authority of a confession and the nature of subscription are correlative, the latter is seen in the same historical perspective. In a report dealing explicitly with this question, the L-R/usa group states that a confession is seen as binding "because it is acknowledged as a responsible and effective way of interpreting the gospel ... One who subscribes to a confession affirms that it faithfully interpreted scripture with reference to the issues in question at the time the confession was framed. Insofar as the issues are the same ... the confessional position is still affirmed ..." (L-R/usa, Marburg

Revisited, p. 181). But because of its subordinate and historical nature, no confession can be accepted as a final and exhaustive interpretation. It must be open to the testimony of other churches and the problems of new generations (ibid; A-RC; L-RC/usa).

There is one point, in particular, where the endeavour to work out historical and ecumenical reinterpretations runs into a painful stumbling-block, and that is the existence of anathemas in credal and confessional formularies, especially when used in liturgical practice. Two solutions are advanced: either applying a historical interpretation consistently, including the anathemas, or choosing to rephrase or rescind them altogether because of their obtrusive incompatibility with the new-found spirit of reconciliation. In the Eastern Orthodox-Oriental Orthodox consultations referred to earlier, "the lifting of the anathemas pronounced by one side against those regarded as saints and teachers by the other side" is held to be "an indispensable step" on the way to unity between the two traditions (Addis Ababa, 211). The L-R-U/eur conversations, in turn, have wrestled with the vexing question of how to come to terms with the mutual doctrinal condemnations contained in the formularies of the Reformation period. The solution proposed in the Leuenberg Agreement is to declare that these condemnations "no longer apply to the contemporary doctrinal position of the assenting churches" and consequently "are no longer an obstacle to church fellowship" (nos. 27,32).

Authorisation. As the religious authorities in and for the Church are multiple, so are the modes of authorising or legitimising credal and confessional formularies. The test of agreement with Scripture, though primary, is not an exclusive one. In the view of the A-L group, "Their [the ancient creeds'] authority is established in the first place by their faithful witness and interpretation of the biblical message, and in the second place, by their acceptance and use in the early church. They, therefore, hold a unique place among all confessional documents" (A-L, no. 24). The A-RC, Venice Report states in a similar vein: "The authority of the creeds and definitions of Councils is recognized partly through their consonance with Scripture and partly through their reception by the people of God. They have also an inherent authority as the work of assemblies of men who, though fallible, meet under the inspiration of the Spirit, and are exercising together the charisma of discerning the truth among the conflicting voices of debate" (no. 5).

The latter quotation points inferentially to one of the most difficult problems in interconfessional relations - the role of the magisterium in defining and promulgating the faith of the Church. It is symptomatic that the A-RC, Venice Report, when it proceeds to discuss the teaching authority of bishops and popes, no longer presents a joint, but two parallel statements. There are intimations in several bilateral documents, however, that new answers are being explored, suggesting at least a growing mutuality in the recognition of common concerns. The fresh emphases on collegiality and on the importance of the sensus fidelium, the hypertrophy of doctrinal definitions, the felt need for a rethinking of the decision-making processes of the Church, are notable examples (cf. A-RC; A-RC/usa; L-RC/usa).[1]

The Development of Doctrine. In several statements referred to above, a general problem has been surfacing which in fact is inherent in all the bilaterals. That is the dialectic of continuity and change in the life of the Church, and here more particularly, the question of doctrinal development. The influence of modern historical consciousness in the past two centuries and the acknowledgement of the historicity of the Church have affected all the Christian traditions, albeit in very differing degrees and at different points. The outstanding example from recent years is of course the Roman Catholic Church, which is undergoing greater transformations also in the realm of doctrine than probably any other communion in this century.

While implicit everywhere, the subject is rarely dealt with thematically in the bilaterals since they focus on specific divisive issues, but there are a few instances which should be noticed. The Presbyterian and Reformed-Roman Catholic dialogue in the United States devoted one of its early meetings to a comparison of various theories, but the matter was not pursued to the point of a formulated consensus (Reconsiderations, pp. 49ff.). The L-RC/usa consultation likewise discussed the problem in its first two meetings, concluding in a "Summary Statement" that "We together acknowledge that the problem of the development of doctrine is crucial today and is in the forefront of our common concern" (The Status of the Nicene Creed, p. 32; One Baptism, especially pp. 75ff.). More recently, the A-L/usa dialogue

1. The Faith and Order Commission also has recently decided to undertake a study of "How the Church Teaches Authoritatively Today"; cf. Minutes, Accra 1974, pp. 91ff.

touched on the subject in a discussion of apostolic continuity with its interwoven strands of scripture, creed, sacrament, ministry - a continuity which is qualified by the insistence that "this substance of apostolic succession must take different forms in differing places and times, if the Gospel is indeed to be heard and received" (A Progress Report, p. 21). Doctrinal development, in continuity as well as change, is thus a necessary aspect of the apostolic mission.

The A-RC/usa consultation has thus far gone farthest in probing the methodological implications of the matter, by projecting common criteria for assessing whether divergent doctrinal formulations, adopted in the course of separated histories, are still "church-dividing", that is, constitute an essential obstacle to full communion. The document enumerates and explains six "operative principles" (ARC-DOC II, 1973, pp. 49-53): paradoxical tension; contextual transfer; relative emphasis; doctrinal pluralism; empathetic evaluation; responsive listening.

Comment

The preceding synopsis suggests a number of fresh understandings, indicating an evolving consensus in certain areas. On the other hand, it hardly needs to be stressed that the subject embraces issues of agelong controversy, which touch the very nature of confessional traditions and to which no satisfactory solution is still in sight. Two of the critical ones may be mentioned.

The remark sometimes made that the Anglican Communion consists of credal and not of confessional churches points to one of the problems. In the bilateral discussions of the ancient creeds, their acceptability to virtually all the churches of Christendom is assumed, and accordingly the theological effort is directed to the purpose of explicating this common bond of unity. Not so with the confessional decisions and formularies of the Reformation period. Although usually presented with universal claims, at least in their central tenets, they express only a limited consensus and are in fact rejected, in whole or in part, by other churches as unacceptable. An analogous situation obtains with respect to the doctrinal definitions of the Roman Catholic Church, especially the Marian and papal dogmas, and also to some of the religious practices with "confessional" implications of the Orthodox Church, such as the veneration of icons. As has been suggested above, certain advances have been made in a common understanding of the function of confession and creed in the life of the Church, and, more specifically, in the recognition of the ancient creeds. The question therefore arises: Will this nascent consensus be solid and dynamic enough to prompt a similar united and unifying approach to the doctrinal decisions which individual churches have taken later in their state of separation? The investigations into the teaching office of the Church, which have been initiated by several dialogue groups, will provide a critical test. They should help to shed more light on the complex hierarchies of authorities that guide the thought and practice of the churches, the range of validity of confessional and dogmatic utterances, and the mysterious processes by which new expressions of the truth of Christ are wrought out and certified.

This rescrutiny of confessional identities can be illumined also from another angle. Bilateral conversations have a multiple relationship to confessions and creeds. They examine them as an object of theological inquiry. They are themselves carried out or sponsored by confessional families, which appear as distinct individualities on the ecumenical scene. But at the same time the bilaterals display transconfessional features which clearly challenge any particularistic and self-absolutising assumptions surviving from the past. A telling illustration are the frequent references to the fact that the agreements and divergences cut across confessional boundaries. As an R-RC/usa report strikingly puts it: "In argument after argument, Reformed theologians presented insights in support of a position expressed by a Roman Catholic, and Roman Catholic theologians presented insights in support of a position expressed by one of the Reformed tradition" (Reconsiderations, p. 9). These transconfessional alignments are significant in more than one respect. They indicate that the ecumenical dialogue has not been without fruit: it has strengthened the awareness that the inherited confessional patterns are not fixed and self-contained but in a state of flux. They sharply point up the discrepancy that exists between the new insights arising through the bilateral movement and, on the other hand, the persistent momentum of ecclesiastical separation and self-sufficiency. In so doing, the bilaterals are pressing the churches to search more earnestly for their common confession of faith amidst the diversity, and in part disunity, of their credal and confessional statements.

3. Eucharist and Intercommunion

Sources

A-L	Anglican-Lutheran International Conversations, Report ... 1970-1972, nos. 61ff.
A-L/aus	"Combined Anglican-Lutheran Statement on the Eucharist", 1973
A-L/usa	Lutheran-Episcopal Dialogue: A Progress Report, 1972
A-RC	Windsor, September 1971, Agreed Statement on Eucharistic Doctrine. London: SPCK, 1972; ARC-DOC I, 1972, pp. 47-50
A-RC/scot	The Ecclesial Nature of the Eucharist, 1974
A-RC/usa	Joint Statements, ARC-DOC I and II
CC-RC/usa	St. Louis, April-May, 1968, "Responsible Theology for Eucharistic Communion in a Divided Church: Summary Memorandum", Mid-Stream II, 2, 1967-68, 90f; An Adventure in Understanding, pp. 3f.
Ev-O/frg-r	Die Eucharistie: Das Sagorsker Gespräch über das heilige Abendmahl, 1974
L-O/f-r	Turku, 1970 and Zagorsk, 1971 "Summary Report", Lutheran World XIX, 3, 1972, 288-92; Järvenpää, 1974, The Journal of the Moscow Patriarchate 1974, 10, 61-69
L-R/usa	Marburg Revisited, 1966, pp. 103f., 183 and 191
L-R-U/eur	Leuenberg, 1973, "Agreement ("Konkordie") among Reformation Churches in Europe", The Ecumenical Review XXV, 3, 1973, 355-59
L-RC	Malta, 1971, Final Report, "The Gospel and the Church", Lutheran World XIX, 3, 1972, 270f.
L-RC/phil	"Progress Report", 1972
L-RC/usa	The Eucharist as Sacrifice, 1967, pp. 187ff. Eucharist and Ministry, 1970, pp. 32f.
M-RC	"Report of the Joint Commission between the Roman Catholic Church and the World Methodist Council, 1967-1970", Book of Proceedings of the Twelfth World Methodist Conference, 1972
OC-RC/eur	"Protokolle der bisherigen Sitzungen der römisch-katholisch/altkatholischen Gesprächskommission in Deutschland", Internationale Kirchliche Zeitschrift 61, 2, 1971, 75-78
O-RC/usa	Worcester, Mass., December 1969, "An Agreed Statement on the Holy Eucharist", Diakonia 5, 1970, 72
R-RC	Woudschoten/Zeist, February 1974, "Common Report"

R-RC/usa Richmond, Va., October 1971, "Ministry in the Church, no.11: Shared Eucharist", Journal of Ecumenical Studies IX, 3, 1972, 589-612

Since the beginning of a theological dialogue on an ecumenical level the eucharist has for manifold reasons been one of the crucial and continuing topics. Yet even without the participation of the Roman Catholic Church, the discussions on this subject did not prove very successful up to Edinburgh 1937. The wide range of convictions, extending from non-sacramental communities to churches which made a particular form of ministry a condition of a valid eucharist or churches which asked for agreement on a particular doctrinal interpretation of the eucharist (especially of the real presence), made any convergence or wider agreement very difficult. New developments in biblical scholarship and sacramental thinking and practice during the years after World War II have created a new situation, which allowed a greater measure of agreement, especially within the work of Faith and Order. The documentation on ecumenical statements on the eucharist, published by Faith and Order, bears witness to the emerging convergence in ecumenical thinking on this subject.[1]

The entrance of the Roman Catholic Church into the ecumenical discussion carried with it new problems. These have increasingly been infused into the general ecumenical debate, and particularly in the bilateral dialogues. Because of the special position which the Roman Catholic Church occupies in this context, the conversations with this Church will here be dealt with separately.

The presentation of the discussions will concentrate on the divisive issues. All statements on the more general understanding of the nature and function of the eucharist are therefore left aside; they reflect very much the present state of eucharistic theology which exhibits many common lines cutting across diverse traditions.

1. Cf. the consensus reports in Faith and Order, Louvain 1971, pp. 54-57 and One Baptism, One Eucharist and a Mutually Recognized Ministry: Three Agreed Statements. Geneva: World Council of Churches, Publications Office 1974. This statement on the eucharist is noteworthy also for the reason that it represents a first attempt to take full account of bilateral findings in the formation of a multilateral consensus.

<u>Conversations with Roman Catholics</u>

<u>Presence</u>. The bilaterals are at one in affirming the real presence of the risen Lord in the eucharist. Whatever differences there may exist in emphasis and elaboration, these are embraced by that conviction. Negatively, the consensus is expressed in a discarding of two extreme positions usually attributed, with doubtful accuracy, to two Christian traditions: a Roman Catholic, or rather a particular philosophical, interpretation of transubstantiation, and on the opposite side, a supposedly Reformed reduction of the presence to a mere commemoration of a past event.

In accordance with common Christian tradition the bilaterals affirm the special connection of the presence with bread and wine. But while eucharistic reflection long was distorted by a narrow focusing on the presence in the elements, the bilaterals tend to take a more comprehensive view, interpreting Christ's presence in the eucharistic act in personal and corporate categories and relating it to other forms of his presence. The A-RC Windsor statement, for example, asserts that Christ's presence can "only be understood within the context of the redemptive activity whereby he gives himself, and in himself reconciliation, peace and life, to his own" (A-RC, no. 6). Similarly the Scottish report speaks of the New Testament image of the sacred banquet "as the source and context for our understanding of the real presence of Christ" (A-RC/scot, p.14).

The relationship between Christ's body and blood and bread and wine is generally described in "sign" language: "The term 'sign', once suspect, is again recognized as a positive term for speaking of Christ's presence in the sacrament. For, though symbols and symbolic actions are used, the Lord's supper is an effective sign: it communicates what it promises" (L-RC/usa, <u>The Eucharist as Sacrifice</u>, pp. 192f.). Accordingly it is stated that "Jesus Christ, true God and true man, is present wholly and entirely, in his body and blood, under the signs of bread and wine" (<u>ibid</u>., p. 192); or "Communion with Christ in the eucharist presupposes his true presence, effectually signified by the bread and wine which, in this mystery, become his Body and Blood" (A-RC, no. 6); or "Bread and wine do not mean the same outside the context of the Eucharistic celebration as they do within that context. Within the Eucharistic celebration they become the sign <u>par excellence</u> of Christ's redeeming presence to His people ... they are therefore efficacious signs of the Body and Blood of Christ" (M-RC, no.83).

These three quotations nevertheless indicate slight differences in formulation and possibly also in understanding. The strongest expression might be the A-RC one: bread and wine become his body and blood. Yet even in that statement the question of the "how" of a change and even the term "transform" or "transformation" were avoided. Exactly at this point the issue of "transubstantiation" was raised in all conversations. After lively debates, which take account of recent attempts at new understandings and formulations in Roman Catholic theology, this issue seems to be no longer an insuperable barrier (cf. OC-RC/eur, p. 76). In the A-RC conversations it was finally restricted to a footnote saying: "The term (i.e. transubstantiation) should be seen as affirming the <u>fact</u> of Christ's presence and of the mysterious and radical change which takes place. In contemporary Roman Catholic theology it is not understood as explaining <u>how</u> the change takes place." In the L-RC/usa conversations the agreement is expressed in exactly the same manner. Here Lutherans add only that "they continue to believe that the conceptuality associated with 'transubstantiation' is misleading and therefore prefer to avoid the term" (L-RC/usa, p. 196). In the M-RC report the Roman Catholic belief that in the eucharist bread and wine are transformed into another reality is still regarded as a point of difference (no. 84).

The R-RC commission shows a particular interest in overcoming misleading conceptions and antinomies of the past, by exploring other avenues of understanding such as the non-dualistic concepts of the Bible and patristic thought, and, on the other hand, current attempts to describe the paschal mystery in personalist-interpersonal categories. Like other bilaterals, the commission abstains from relating the reflection on the real presence exclusively to the elements, but rather to the whole act. Examining the New Testament narratives, the report points out that "The word 'is' is not understood primarily in the sense of transformation or changed significance, but as an answer to the question Why? The emphasis is ... on the event,i.e. on the eating and drinking and the memorial character of the paschal meal ... " (Report, 1974, no.I, 4). In contrast to the other dialogues referred to, the report does not use the term "sign" but employs a language drawing on the analogy of the two natures of Christ.

The Orthodox, with their insistence on the mystery-character of the eucharist, customarily avoid the theory of transubstantiation. In the O-RC conversations in the USA, the controversial term is omitted and the agreed statement declares: "In this eucharistic meal, according to the promise of Christ, the Father sends the Spirit to consecrate the elements to be the Body and Blood of Jesus Christ and to sanctify the faithful" (1969, no. 2).

Closely connected with the question of transubstantiation is the question of the extension of the presence beyond the eucharistic celebration (reservation and adoration of the elements). Some Roman Catholic participants in the conversations tended to make the acceptance or non-acceptance of this belief and devotional practice a test for the authenticity of their partner's affirmation of the real presence. In the A-RC conversations this was regarded as one of the remaining differences; however, the issue was not mentioned in the statement because it was apparently not regarded as being an essential part of eucharistic doctrine but rather belonging to the field of devotional practices. In the L-RC/usa statement the issue is taken up but not regarded as a dividing difference. Two "bridges" are mentioned: (1) Lutherans may distribute the elements to the sick in private communion (this practice is even more common among Anglicans); (2) according to the Roman Catholic "Instruction on Eucharistic Worship" (May 25, 1967) distribution of the host to the sick is the "primary and original purpose" of reservation. Roman Catholic members of the conversations add that "the adoration of Christ present in the reserved sacrament is of later origin and is a secondary end" (L-RC/usa, p. 194). In the M-RC report it is again stated as a factual point of difference that the worship of the blessed sacrament does not obtain in Methodism (no. 84). This applies of course also to the other partners of the Roman Catholic Church, but they regard this "point of difference" apparently not as dividing while the M-RC report abstains from any judgment here.

There is universal agreement that the presence of Jesus Christ does not come about through the faith of the believer or through any human power (A-RC, no. 8; L-RC/phil; L-RC/usa, p. 193; M-RC, no. 83); but it cannot be separated from faith either, since only if the gift is met by faith "a life-giving encounter results" (A-RC, no. 8; M-RC, no. 83). Similarly the gift of the presence and the act of sacramental eating cannot be dissociated (A-RC, no. 9; L-RC/usa, p. 193f; M-RC, no. 84). The positive affirmation with regard to the question of when and how the presence comes about is to point to the power of the Holy Spirit (O-RC/usa), associated either with the consecratory prayer (A-RC, no. 10; R-RC, no. III) or the words of the institution (M-RC, no. 83) or simply "the word" (L-RC/usa, p.193). There is a fresh emphasis on the epiclectic character of the whole act, which tends to neutralise earlier controversies about the role of the epiclesis in different eucharistic liturgies. A receptionist understanding is dismissed: "The true body and blood of Christ are present not only at the moment of reception but throughout the eucharistic action" (L-RC/usa, p. 193; A-RC/scot, p. 14; less explicitly in A-RC).

The reflection on the eucharistic presence is placed in the wider context of multiple modes of presence. Sometimes this is done without any explicit differentiation. Thus the L-RC/usa report speaks simply of a "manifold presence of Christ", e.g. in his Church, in baptism, in the reading of the Scripture, in the proclamation of the Gospel and in the eucharist (p. 192). Referring to the relationship of the word and sacrament, the reports generally reflect the current convergence manifest in the Catholic reaffirmation of the liturgy of the Word and the corresponding Protestant reappreciation of the liturgy of the Sacrament. Yet certain variations are noticeable, which may point to issues requiring further clarification. Sometimes the centrality of the eucharist is stressed in a manner which might suggest according merely a preparatory function to the Word, but this is counterbalanced by an emphasis on their interdependence. For the A-RC Windsor statement, "Christ is present and active, in various ways, in the entire eucharistic celebration. It is the same Lord who through the proclaimed word invites his people to his table, who through his minister presides at that table, and who gives himself sacramentally in the body and blood of his paschal sacrifice" (no. 7). The M-RC report speaks of "a distinctive mode or manifestation of the presence of Christ", but this is later qualified by a "point of difference" : "The presence in the eucharist for the Methodists is not fundamentally different from the presence of Christ in other means of grace, i.e. preaching" (nos. 83f.). A nuanced differentiation is made in the joint L-RC/phil report, but its exact meaning is not explained: "Christ is uniquely present in the Lord's Supper; he is also present in a special way in the reading or proclamation of the Word, in Baptism, and in the fellowship of Christians" (no. C, 1).

Sacrifice. The eucharist as sacrifice has been another highly controversial and church-dividing issue between Roman Catholics and other traditions. Here again the agreements (e.g. OC-RC/eur) and convergences reported in some of the conversations are remarkable. Two fundamental statements are not disputed and serve as a common basis for all other reflections: (1) "The Eucharist is the celebration of Christ's full, perfect and sufficient sacrifice, offered once and for all, for the whole world" (M-RC, no. 84; also A-RC, no. 5; L-RC/usa, p. 188; R-RC); (2) "There can be no repetition of or addition to what was then accomplished once for all by Christ" (A-RC, no. 5; L-RC/usa, p. 189).

In order to establish a nexus between the sacrifice of Christ on the cross and the eucharist, the notion of "memorial" (anamnesis) is taken up and revalorised. "The Holy Eucharist is the memorial of the history of salvation, especially, the life, death, resurrection and glorification of Jesus Christ" (O-RC/usa). In almost identical language it is explained that "memorial" is no mere recollection of a past event, but rather the making effective in the presence of an event in the past or, more strongly expressed in the M-RC report, "a re-enactment of Christ's triumphant sacrifice" (M-RC, no. 83; A-RC, no. 5; A-RC/scot, pp. 11ff; L-RC/usa, p. 189, there quoting from the Faith and Order Report, Montreal, 1963). Therefore, in the eucharistic memorial the Church proclaims effectually God's mighty acts, entreats the benefits of Christ's whole life and passion and participates in them and shares in Christ's self-offering in obedience to the Father's will (M-RC, no. 83; A-RC, no. 5; L-RC/usa, p. 189).

Here the Protestant partners, despite their reluctance to weaken in any way the once-for-all-ness of Calvary, join in speaking of the Church's sharing in Christ's self-offering. On the basis of the intimate connection between Christ and his body, the Church, the Lutheran participants in the L-RC/usa dialogue (quoting Luther himself in support) find positive meaning in the statement that the Church "offers Christ" in the mass: "Through this union between Christ and Christians, the eucharistic assembly 'offers Christ' by consenting in the power of the Holy Spirit to be offered by him to the Father" (The Eucharist as Sacrifice, p. 189). A different note is struck in a statement from the A-RC/usa conversations, linking this offering with the empowering action of the priest. Christian people, it says, participate in Christ's priesthood, becoming a living sacrifice to God, and it is in the eucharistic offering that this sacrifice finds its fullest expression. "Such sacramental offering of the whole people is made possible through the special action of the ministerial priest, who is empowered by his ordination to make present Christ's sacrifice for His people" (Milwaukee, 1967, ARC-DOC I, p. 4). Here apparently a more traditional Roman Catholic concept has become dominant.

Intercommunion. The far-reaching agreements on the doctrine of the eucharist have not immediately led to proposals for intercommunion. The reasons for this reluctance are obvious. If intercommunion is regarded as an expression of full fellowship, then agreement on one particular point, important as it may be, does not yet provide a sufficient basis. There are other controlling issues which likewise must be resolved before some form of eucharistic sharing can be initiated. That is why in dialogues with Roman Catholic, Orthodox or Anglican partners the consideration of eucharistic doctrine and sharing necessarily involves an examination of such questions as the credentials of a valid celebrant, the nature of the true Church, and eucharistic discipline. From Orthodox point of view, the unity between the bishop-celebrant and the communicant within the community of the one apostolic faith is the decisive matter (O-RC/usa, Diakonia 1967, 2, 183-86). And while the A-RC commission reached such a substantial agreement on the meaning of the eucharist that "this doctrine will no longer constitute an obstacle to the unity we seek" (Windsor statement, no. 12), it left the question of eucharistic sharing for later consideration. Similarly in the M-RC conversations. And even where the question of the ministry has been taken up in the eucharistic context and been solved to an amazing degree, as in the L-RC/usa conversations, the possibility of intercommunion has not been discussed. In a very careful way it is only stated by the Roman Catholic participants that the recognition of valid ministry has consequences for sharing at the eucharistic table, but that they are not in a position to affirm "that the one must or should lead to the other" (Eucharist and Ministry, no. 59). Another instance is the A-RC conversations in the USA. After issuing an agreed statement on eucharistic sacrifice and after reporting that with regard to the understanding of the ordained priesthood there is no basic difference, it is stated: "Whatever minor differences of understanding exist, they do not in themselves constitute the barrier to the two Churches celebrating and receiving communion together." Yet after that meeting (January 1968) the two chairmen agreed that there were other obstacles to intercommunion and that "precipitous action by this group at this time would not be to the advantage of the whole Church" (One in Christ IV, 3, 1968, 299f.). In a later statement (December 1969) other subjects are mentioned - episcopacy, papacy, authority and teaching office of the whole Church - where agreements should be sought before possible steps of partial eucharistic communion are considered (ARC-DOC I, p. 17).

On the other hand, the growing practice of informal eucharistic fellowship across denominational barriers, the pressures of pastoral needs, and the softening of theological and ecclesiological preconditions have all converged in making some qualified form of intercommunion at least a matter of serious consideration. The rigid insistence on intercommunion as the goal and not a means of unity, is gradually being superseded by a more dynamic question: What degrees and forms of unity are legitimately required for the initiation of partial communion? The L-RC report which registers wide agreements on many points, including the ministry, does recommend occasional acts of intercommunion (e.g. at ecumenical gatherings, and in the care for mixed marriages). On the basis of the already existing agreements in faith and sacrament and as sign and anticipation of that unity, which is promised and hoped for, the authorities of the churches should allow such occasional acts of intercommunion. Eucharistic fellowship should not exclusively be made dependent on full recognition of ministries. Pastoral responsibility must also play an important role in the efforts to solve this burning problem (L-RC, nos. 73 and 74). In a similar way, a report from the conversations between the Church of Christ (Disciples of Christ) and the US National Conference of Catholic Bishops makes the following plea: "In our respective beliefs and churchly self-understandings and even within the officially expressed statements of our churches at present, we have found sufficient theological justification in principle for some eucharistic sharing. Furthermore, we detect that urgent theological, ecumenical and especially pastoral reasons exist in our country to make some eucharistic sharing desirable. We urge our communions to explore as rapidly as possible the circumstances and procedures for responsible eucharistic sharing" (Mid-Stream VII, 2,

1967-68, 91; cf. An Adventure in Understanding, p. 4). Here again an agreement on different aspects of the faith and pastoral necessities are mentioned as justification for considering first steps towards intercommunion.

Conversations without Roman Catholics

Despite the fact that the eucharist has been one of the main dividing issues between the Lutheran and Reformed Churches, this question seems no longer of controversial importance. When the "Leuenberg Agreement" between the Lutheran, Reformed and United Churches of Europe mentions the eucharist merely in two brief paragraphs, this is not only an indication of the changed historical and theological situation which has led to a consensus at this point. It is at the same time a result of preceding or parallel conversations in several European countries like France, Germany and Holland, which have focused on this question and have led to agreements on which the conversations at the European level could draw. The Agreement asserts: "In the Lord's Supper the risen Jesus Christ imparts himself in his body and blood, given up for all, through his word of promise with bread and wine. He thus gives himself unreservedly to all who receive the bread and wine; faith receives the Lord's Supper for salvation, unfaith for judgement." The act of eating and drinking cannot be separated from the communion with Jesus Christ in his body and blood; any interest in the mode of presence which neglects this action is in danger of obscuring the meaning of the eucharist. And, the statement concludes, where such a consensus has been achieved, "the condemnations pronounced by the Reformation confessions are inapplicable to the doctrinal position of these churches" (nos. 19f.).

The Lutheran-Reformed conversations in North America are a little more explicit in their statement. It is significant that here certain aspects are mentioned which also play an important role in conversations with Roman Catholics. Through this approach the danger of arriving at completely diverging utterances in intra-Protestant dialogues and in dialogues with Roman Catholics on the same subject is avoided. The statement mentions the common conviction "that the same gift is offered in the preached word and in the administered sacrament", the sacrament being a form of visible, enacted word through which Christ and his saving benefits are effectively offered to men. The realisation of the presence of the total Christ, the divine-human person, which is stressed by quoting the words of institution, is effected by the Holy Spirit through the word. It is not effected by faith, but acknowledged by faith. The worthy participant receives in faith and repentance the Christ who offers himself. The unworthy participant, who receives judgment, denies the Lordship of Christ, his presence in the sacrament, and the fellowship of the brethren. And the reference to sacrifice states: "The perfect self-offering of the Son of God is the atoning sacrifice whereby our self-offering to God in worship and in loving gift to the neighbor is made possible and acceptable" (Marburg Revisited, pp. 103f.).

In the international Anglican-Lutheran conversations the eucharist was not discussed in detail, as it did not represent a major point of controversy. Both delegations saw in each other's communions a true celebration of the sacrament. "Both Communions affirm the real presence of Christ in this sacrament, but neither seeks to define precisely how this happens. In the eucharistic action, including consecration and reception, the bread and wine, while remaining bread and wine, become the means whereby Christ is truly present and gives himself to the communicants." Both traditions would also recognise that the eucharist "in some sense involves sacrifice. In it we offer our praise and thanksgiving, ourselves and all that we are, and make before God the memorial of Christ's sacrifice" (A-L, nos. 68f; similarly A-L/usa, p. 20). The eucharist constitutes a problem only insofar as its validity is denied by Anglo-Catholic theologians in cases where it is administered by non-episcopally ordained pastors.

The Russian Orthodox conversations with Lutherans in Europe, while not yet completed, have resulted in agreements which offer significant parallels to those mentioned above. The true celebrant is the risen Christ, who in the eucharistic meal gives himself under the form of bread and wine and unites the believers with him and with one another (Ev-O/frg-r, pp. 23ff; L-O/f-r, pp. 288ff.). The eucharist is not a repetition of the sacrifice of Calvary, but re-presents its saving significance and effect in the life of the Church and of each Christian. A particular note of these documents is the insistence on the ecclesial and socio-ethical aspects of the eucharist; an individualistic interpretation is explicitly rejected. As the body of Christ, the whole Church participates in each celebration. Moreover, "The unity in the eucharist is the deepest manifestation of the oneness of the Church".

From this conformity between eucharist and Church the implication is drawn that there can be no intercommunion among churches separated by weighty doctrinal, and especially ecclesiological, differences. For, "... the eucharist cannot be used as a tool to bring about unity" (L-O/f-r, 289).

On the other hand, there is likewise a strong emphasis on the organic connection of the gifts of foregiveness, sanctification, and social action. In a series of theses on "The Eucharist and the Transformation of the World", it is said: "The Lord's Supper ... is a powerful force for the transformation of every Christian, the Christian community, and through them the surrounding world, for good and holiness. Through the operation of his Holy Spirit, Christ present in the eucharist makes the Christian open to every truly good will towards reconciliation, peace, and justice, which he encounters in the world" (Ev-O/frg-r, p. 26).

The possibility of intercommunion between the Protestant and Anglican Churches here mentioned seems to be no longer a major problem (apart from the remaining hesitancy on the Anglican side with respect to reciprocity). It is already widely practised. The "Agreement among the Reformation Churches in Europe" includes an official declaration of pulpit and altar fellowship. Intercommunion is here understood as the expression of full church fellowship (or unity). The first series of the L-R/usa conversations did not yet reach that stage. The statement on the Lord's Supper concludes: "Our churches are not in full agreement on the practice of intercommunion because they hold different views of the relation of doctrine to the unity of the Church" (Marburg Revisited, p. 104). Over against this rather ambiguous sentence, one of the final statements of the conversations reveals a more open attitude when it says: "Intercommunion between churches, which may give a mobile population readier access to the Lord's Table, is not only permissible but demanded wherever there is agreement in the gospel. Such agreement means proclamation of the same gospel as the good news of God's reconciling work in Christ rather than uniformity in theological formulation" (ibid., p. 183). And in the "Report to the Sponsoring Confessional Organizations" the following conclusion is drawn: "As a result of our studies and discussions we see no insuperable obstacles to pulpit and altar fellowship and, therefore, we recommend to our parent bodies that they encourage their constituent churches to enter into discussions looking forward to intercommunion and the fuller recognition of one another's ministries" (*ibid.*, p. 191). As to the A-L conversations, the international and the USA commissions again concur in their recommendations, with the latter offering a farther-reaching proposal. Whereas the former favours intercommunion "where appropriate and subject to the claims of individual conscience and respect for the discipline of each Church" (no.96), the latter commends, subject to the consent of the appropriate local authorities, "... intercommunion between parishes or congregations which, by reason of proximity, joint community concerns, and/or activities, have developed such a degree of understanding and trust as would make intercommunion an appropriate response to the Gospel" (pp. 23f.).

In intra-Protestant conversations the question of the celebrant is usually left aside, since the divisive issues reside in other areas. On the other hand, in conversations where Roman Catholics, Orthodox or Anglicans are partners, the integral connection between eucharist and ministry inevitably makes the question a prominent point on the agenda, and this has in turn led the Protestant partners to pay increased attention to it. [1]

Comment

There is no doubt that bilateral conversations dealing with the eucharist have led to remarkable results. An agreement which is considered as overcoming the church-dividing differences at this point has been reached in the A-RC, A-RC/usa, L-RC/usa and OC-RC/eur conversations and in the dialogues between Anglican and Protestant churches. This historic breakthrough cannot be understood apart from the presuppositions created by the general ecumenical discussion and by new tendencies in Roman Catholic eucharistic thinking. The agreements have not been wrought out in isolation; they reflect a manifest movement of exchange not only among the bilaterals themselves but also between these and the multilateral inquiries. This becomes strikingly clear if one compares the substance of the above-mentioned reports with such documents as the reports on the eucharist issued by the Faith and Order Commission at Louvain (1971) and Accra (1974), the statement entitled "The Eucharist in the Life of the Church: An Ecumenical Consensus" [2]

1. See below the section on "The Ministry".
2. The Ecumenist VIII, 6, Sep.-Oct. 1970, 90-93.

emanating from the Faith and Order Department of the National Council of Churches of Christ in the USA, and further the French statement "Towards a Common Eucharistic Faith?", by the interconfessional Groupe des Dombes. [1]

The tension between the mounting pressure for an expanding practice of intercommunion and, on the other hand, the slow theological dialogue and the even slower implementation of its results by church authorities, is felt in all conversations. They aim at solutions which are theologically responsible. Yet the effectiveness, validity, and authenticity of bilateral conversations will certainly be judged by the measure in which they are able to keep pace with the actual pressures and developments within and between the churches, especially in this matter of intercommunion. A basic problem in this field is the unresolved question of how much agreement must be achieved and acknowledged before intercommunion can be recommended. As an intermediate step, the possibilities of finding mutually acceptable forms of what now sometimes is called "eucharistic hospitality" are receiving increasing attention. But here too, the question of the necessary conditions has not yet been adequately clarified.

There are certain other features of current eucharistic thought - not discussed above since they are not separative - which should at least be mentioned because of their relevance for a broader, dynamic consensus. The not infrequent references to the actual practices and liturgical forms of eucharistic worship are significant. For they suggest an awareness that the actual experiences of local churches are an as important, and sometimes perhaps more illuminating, source for grasping the authentic convictions of a communion than are its official doctrines and formularies. The use of the motif of sacrifice in the new Roman Catholic liturgy, as compared with earlier ones, is a case in point. It is not by accident, therefore, that several of the dialogues, in seeking a common understanding of the eucharist and of intercommunion, begin their explorations by familiarising themselves with the liturgical texts and prevailing practices of the churches involved. Another motif is the current emphasis on

1. Vers une même foi eucharistique? 71460 Taizé-Communauté, France: Les Presses de Taizé, 1972; Eng. tr. in Modern Eucharistic Agreement (London: SPCK, 1973) pp. 51-79. The introduction to this booklet by H.R. McAdoo traces the similarity in the conclusions of these multilateral documents.

the missionary and social implications of the eucharist. Its celebration is not merely a source of inspiration and strength in the ministry to the world; it is itself an act of mission. If this perspective were taken seriously, this may well open the doors more boldly and freely for opportunities where Christians "in each place", who are engaged in common witness and service, can join together also at the Lord's Table.

4. Ministry

Sources

A-L	Anglican-Lutheran International Conversations, Report ... 1970-1972, nos. 73ff.
A-L/usa	Lutheran-Episcopal Dialogue: A Progress Report, 1972, pp. 20ff
A-RC	Venice, September 1970, "Church and Authority" and "Church and Ministry", Theology LXXIV, 608, February 1971, 49-67; The Catholic Mind (USA), April 1971; One in Christ VII, 2-3, 1971, 256-87 Canterbury, 1973, Ministry and Ordination
A-RC/usa	Joint Statements, III, October 1966; V, January 1968; VII, December 1969; in ARC-DOC I, 1972, pp. 9-22
CC-RC/usa	An Adventure in Understanding, pp. 5f.
L-R-U/eur	Leuenberg, 1973, "Agreement ("Konkordie") among Reformation Churches in Europe", The Ecumenical Review XXV, 3, 1973, 355-59
L-RC	Malta, 1971, Final Report, "The Gospel and the Church", Lutheran World XIX, 3, 1972, 266-70
L-RC/usa	Eucharist and Ministry, 1970, pp. 7-33 Papal Primacy and the Universal Church, 1974
M-RC	"Report of the Joint Commission between the Roman Catholic Church and the World Methodist Council, 1967-1970", Book of Proceedings of the Twelfth World Methodist Conference, 1972
OC-RC/eur	"Protokolle der bisherigen Sitzungen der römisch-katholisch/altkatholischen Gesprächskommission in Deutschland", Internationale Kirchliche Zeitschrift 61, 2, 1971, 75-78
R-RC/usa	Reconsiderations, 1967, p. 157 Richmond, Va., 1971, "Ministry in the Church", Journal of Ecumenical Studies IX, 3, 1972, 589-612 Richmond, Va., 1971, "Women in the Church", ibid. IX, 1, 1972, 235-41

The question of the ministry has been one of the principal topics in ecumenical discussions since the beginning of this century. This was mainly due to the fourth point of the Anglican Lambeth Quadrilateral requiring the acceptance of the historic episcopate as one of the basic structures of church unity. The strong Anglican involvement both in the work of Faith and Order and in church union negotiations has kept this question continuously on the agenda of ecumenical conversations. The entry of the Roman Catholic Church into the ecumenical dialogue has revitalised the long discussion on the ministry and introduced additional aspects and problems.

One of the main results of the debate in Faith and Order and of newer developments within Roman Catholic and Anglican thinking was the recognition that the special ministry of the Church cannot be treated in isolation. It is the concept of the Church and the ministry of the whole people of God which has to be taken as the context in which the special ministry can be understood properly. In addition, the ecumenical discussions on Scripture and tradition, the charismatic structure and the diversity and unity of the primitive church, historical studies, the hermeneutics of doctrinal decisions, and the debate on the task of the Church in the world of today have shed new light on the ministry.

This general background is naturally influencing the bilateral discussions on the ministry. They do not start _ab ovo_ and are not conducted in a vacuum. They are taking up what has already been said or proposed in other places. There are implicit and explicit references to this general discussion. This influence can also be seen in the fact that usually the question of the ministry is taken up only after a discussion of broader or related subjects (e.g. Gospel, Scripture and tradition, Church, sacraments).

A basic feature of these conversations is their unreserved acceptance of the historical character of the Church and the ministry. Specific conditions and presuppositions, particular situations, changes, different terminologies and thought forms, and openness for further change are stressed and are used as keys for the interpretation of past developments, decisions, and confessional documents (New Testament, the patristic period, Reformation documents, Trent, Vatican I, _Apostolicae Curae_, etc.).

The Ministry in Bilateral Conversations

The problem of the ministry as a special subject has been taken up so far in conversations between churches which (a) have either declared the ministry of the other church as invalid, or (b) do not in fact recognise this ministry as valid, or (c) see the goal of their conversations in the establishment of full intercommunion or even organic union, which presupposes, among other things, full mutual recognition of ministries.

Consequently, as the above list of documents indicates, the ministry appears chiefly on the agenda of conversations with a Roman Catholic or Anglican partner. The subject is more or less absent in Lutheran-Reformed conversations and thus far, for other reasons, in the conversations with Orthodox Churches. The national conversations in the USA, in particular, have devoted much time to the subject. In some cases, several meetings were devoted to this issue either wholly (e.g. L-RC/usa) or in part, in connection with related topics such as the eucharist (thus A-RC/usa; R-RC/usa). On the world level we find either one single meeting devoted wholly to the subject in a series (e.g. A-L; L-RC), or a number of meetings dealing with it in one working group alongside other groups having other assigned topics (e.g. A-RC, Venice).

Particular Aspects in the Discussions and Statements

Which particular aspects are dealt with depends, of course, on the individual dialogue partners. Since in most cases the Roman Catholic Church is involved, a relatively fixed pattern appears. This recurring set of aspects, however, may be modified in various ways depending upon the particular stance of the dialogue partners of the Roman Catholic Church or on whether a conversation is conducted at the world level or at a regional or national level.

The General and the Special Ministry. In tune with general thinking on the subject today, the bilateral conversations usually interpret the ordained ministry within a multiple sequential context: the ministry of Jesus Christ, the ministry of the apostles, the Church as a ministering community with its multiplicity of services and functions, participating in and continuing the ministry of Christ to the world and being equipped for this service (diakonia) through a great variety of gifts of the Holy Spirit (charismata), the special or ordained ministry. Rethought in this framework, several of the issues which have long been points of dissension among the churches have lost their divisiveness.

A programmatic sentence in the R-RC/usa report is characteristic: "In all that we say about Church and ministry we start with Christ himself and his own ministry" (1971, no. 2). The L-RC/usa report spells out the Trinitarian ground of the ministry more explicitly: "Just as the Church ... so also the Ministry is to be seen in light of the love of God, his saving act in Jesus Christ, and the ongoing activity of the Holy Spirit" (no. 12). And the A-RC international commission, expounding the ministry in terms of reconciliation, makes the same point when it says that the reconciliation between God and men, accomplished by the death and resurrection of Jesus Christ, is being realised and offered to men in and through the reconciled and reconciling community of the servant Church (nos. 3ff.). This Church is apostolic, not only in the sense that it is founded on the witness of the apostles to Jesus Christ and is called to reflect this witness in its own faith and life, but also in the sense that it is charged to carry forward the apostolic mission to the ends of the earth. The multiplicity of ministries, in which the common priesthood of all believers is articulated, is uniformly linked - following St. Paul - with the calling and empowerment of the Holy Spirit.

In describing the functions of the special ministry, the various statements naturally focus on its specific responsibility for proclamation of the word and administration of the sacraments. But in contrast to the traditional contraposition of a Catholic sacramental priesthood and a Protestant ministry of the word, the two functions are here held closely together, not in an artificial compromise, but in a reinterpretation of their mutuality. Behind this convergence lies undoubtedly the growing recovery of the sacramental life in Protestant devotion and theology and, on the other hand, the renewed Roman Catholic emphasis, authoritatively confirmed by Vatican II, on the proclamation of the Word of God. The A-RC, Canterbury report states the matter clearly: "The part of the ministers in the celebration of the sacraments is one with their responsibility for ministry of the word. In both word and sacrament Christians meet the living Word of God"(no. 11; similarly, e.g., A-L, nos. 63, 75ff. and R-RC/usa, no. 4).

Ministry through word and sacrament is the manner in which the ordained minister performs his function of building up the community of faith. This function of leadership service is presented in varying ways. Sometimes it appears as a third function alongside proclamation of the word and celebration of the sacrament, sometimes as an implementation of that ministry, sometimes again as the inclusive purpose of a minister's work. That these variations do not as such reflect necessarily any ecclesial divisions is evidenced by the fact that they can be found promiscuously in varying kinds of consensus statements. According to the A-RC statement, the Holy Spirit provides in the ordained ministry "a focus of leadership and unity" and it is the task of the minister "to co-ordinate the activities of the Church's fellowship and to promote what is necessary and useful for the Church's life and mission" (no. 7). For the R-RC/usa group, the special ministry is called "to unite and order the Church for the ministry of the whole people of God ... to nourish, heal and build up the household of faith through the ministry of word and sacraments" (no. 4; cf. A-L, no. 78; A-RC/usa, no. 12; L-RC/usa, nos. 11ff.).

A point where unresolved cleavages of opinion appear is the attempts to define the peculiar status of the ordained ministry within the community of believers. Its representative character is commonly acknowledged, notably in contexts where the mission of the whole Church as well as that of the ordained ministry is described as a priestly service, representing the concerns of God to men and those of men to God (L-RC/usa, no. 10). Special ministers are "called and ordained to represent Christ to the community and the community before Christ" (R-RC/usa, no. 4). "Christian ministers are ... representative of the whole Church in the fulfilment of its priestly vocation of self-offering to God as a living sacrifice" (A-RC, no. 13). That such statements are not to be understood in the sense of attributing to the ministry a mediatory character is clearly expressed, for instance, in the L-RC report: "Both agree that the office of the ministry stands over against the community as well as within the community. Further they agree that the ministerial office represents Christ and his over-againstness to the community only insofar as it gives expression to the gospel" (Malta report, no. 50). The same mode of thinking can be found in the Methodist-Roman Catholic dialogue, expressed with an explicit evangelistic emphasis. Here the ministry is understood "as,in some mysterious ways, an extension of the incarnational and sacramental principle, whereby human beings ... become, by the power of the Holy Spirit, agents of Christ for bringing God into the lives and conditions of men. (This means also, of course, that they are agents for enabling men to find their way toward God.)" (M-RC, no. 92).

But alongside the convergences there also appear certain ambivalences in the definitions of the status of the special ministry.

Historically and still today, Protestants speak of a difference of function but not of status, whereas Roman Catholics either maintain the historic doctrine of a difference in essence and not only in degree (so also Vatican II's Lumen Gentium, no. 10), or are groping for new language. It is interesting to note that whereas the R-RC/usa group insisted in its 1970 statement that the ordained ministry is not "distinguished from the rest of the people by superiority of status or function, but by difference of service", its 1971 version declares that "This ordained ministry does not constitute a self-sustaining body ... but there is an essential distinction of function and service ..." (no. 4). The A-RC conversations display further variations. The international commission, having spoken of the membership of Christian ministers in the priesthood of the people of God, adds by way of qualification: "Nevertheless their ministry is not an extension of the common Christian priesthood but belongs to another [underlined here] realm of the gifts of the Spirit" (no. 13). The classic Catholic two-level distinction is here retained but in a mitigated form, employing a deliberately open-ended phrase instead of ontological precisions. Commenting on this phrase, the A-RC consultation in the United States, on the other hand, intimates its preference for a formulation which would more clearly affirm "a generic relationship among the various special ministries, both ordained and unordained ... which exist within the common Christian priesthood and serve to build it up" (News Letter of the Bishops' Committee for Ecumenical and Interreligious Affairs, April 1974). The theological determination of the relationship between clergy and laity remains a problem because it implicates ultimate beliefs about the very nature of the Church.

Apostolic Succession and Apostolic Ministry. The convergences observable in the understanding of apostolic succession have an immediate carry-over in fresh approaches to the divisive question of what constitutes a valid apostolic ministry. These convergences are chiefly the result of a broadened vision of the apostolicity of the Church: once it is acknowledged that apostolicity embraces a variety of elements, which are interdependent and mutually supportive, it becomes difficult to maintain exclusive claims for any single line of ministerial validation, whether doctrinal or episcopal or charismatic. The dialogues on the ministry express this awareness in similar ways. The A-L report offers a particularly comprehensive description: "The succession of apostolicity through time is guarded and given contemporary expression in and through a wide variety of means, activities, and institutions: the canon of scripture, creeds, confessional writings, liturgies, the activities of preaching, teaching, celebrating the sacraments and ordaining and using a ministry of Word and Sacrament, the exercising of pastoral care and oversight, the common life of the Church, and the engagement in mission to and for the world" (no. 74; similarly A-L/usa, p. 21). In more summary fashion, the R-RC/usa statement affirms that "However much they may still differ on the methods of maintaining them, both traditions agree on the necessity of continuity and succession in the apostolic life, doctrine, and ministry of the Church" (no. 6). All converge in seeing the ultimate ground and safeguard of the apostolic continuity of the Church through the ages in God's own faithfulness in Jesus Christ and the abiding presence of the Holy Spirit.

Within the common framework of agreement, the various traditions naturally continue to stress what they each regard as necessary elements - though no longer in absolutising terms but tempered by a reappropriation of the signs of apostolicity stressed by the other partner. This reconception takes different forms.

In Anglican-Roman Catholic relations - with both parties upholding the necessity of episcopal succession - the problem is how to square two opposing views of the doctrine and fact of such succession. The impasse of the disputed Anglican succession (Apostolicae Curae) has been eschewed by abandoning any narrow "genealogical" idea of an uninterrupted transmission from one bishop to another (cf. R-RC/usa, no. 6) and instead recovering the older conception of an unbroken succession of apostolic teachings and teachers in the episcopal sees. As the Canterbury statement puts it, speaking of the participation of other bishops in the ordination of a new bishop: their participation signifies that the new bishop and his church are within the communion of churches. "Moreover, because they are representative of their churches in fidelity to the teaching and mission of the apostles and are members of the episcopal college, their participation also ensures the historical continuity of this church with the apostolic church and of its bishop with the original apostolic ministry. The communion of the churches in mission, faith, and holiness, through time and space, is thus symbolized and maintained in the bishop." A final sentence underscores the consensus: "Here are comprised the essential features of what is meant in our two traditions by ordination in the apostolic succession" (A-RC, no. 16).

As between episcopal and non-episcopal communions, the problem of recomposition is evidently far more difficult. Nonetheless, Anglicans and Lutherans have come to an agreement, recognising the validity and complementarity of each other's claims to apostolic succession and declaring that the ordained ministries of both communions are true apostolic ministries (A-L, nos. 75ff. and 85ff; A-L/usa, pp. 20ff.). The R-RC/usa report forthrightly admits the difference between the two traditions in the way they conceive continuity with the apostolic church, but at the same time they acknowledge its preservation on both sides, thus revising the mutual disavowals in the past: "Both of us believe that the Christian faith, Church and ministry were preserved by God through the polemic theologies of ministry on both sides of the Reform of the 16th century, despite their inadequacies" (1971, no. 6). A similar stance is apparent in the L-RC conversations. The 1971 Malta report states as a matter of agreement that "In the New Testament and the early fathers, the emphasis was obviously placed more on the substance of apostolicity, i.e. on succession in apostolic teaching. In this sense the entire church as the _ecclesia apostolica_ stands in the apostolic succession. Within this general sense of succession, there is a more specific meaning: the succession of the uninterrupted line of the transmission of office". In the early Church, this succession was not seen as an independent guarantee of continuity, but as a sign of the unimpaired transmission of the gospel and a sign of unity, particularly in the defence against heresies (L-RC, no. 57; L-RC/usa, no. 14). With such an approach, a mutual recognition, however qualified, becomes a genuine possibility.

Structures of Apostolic Ministry. Contemporary biblical and historical studies have also furnished a more realistic picture than previously available of the fluid and multiform development of forms and structures of ministry in the early Church, and this is part of the theological climate shared by the bilaterals. The relationship between the apostolic ministry, the variety of ministerial forms in the early Church and the later institutionalised forms is generally treated as an open question. The threefold ministry, it is asserted, participates in various ways in the apostolic ministry, but the exact relationship is beyond historical verification (A-RC, nos.5ff.). There are pointers in the New Testament to the threefold ministry of bishop, presbyter and deacon but it did not fully emerge until the second half of the second century (<u>ibid</u>., no. 6). Along the same line, it is recognised that the ordained ministry has gathered up various services mentioned in the New Testament, but there exists no direct correspondence (L-RC/usa, no. 11).

Similarly there is broad agreement that the concrete structures of the Church's ministry have not been instituted by God, but are the results of historical developments (e.g. L-RC, nos. 55ff.). Such affirmations are not to be misconstrued as historical relativism, however. For "the basic reality of the apostolic ministry can be preserved amid variations in structure and implementation, in rites of ordination and in theological explanation" (L-RC/usa, no. 22). It may be noted in passing that occasionally an attempt is made to illumine this distinction between a basic reality and its contingent embodiments by referring to the classic categories of <u>de iure divino</u> and <u>de iure humano</u>; but their exact meaning and applicability is a matter of debate.

In the discussions of the threefold ministry, the question of the role and the necessity or desirability of the episcopal office is of course a cardinal problem, increasingly so also for the non-episcopal communions, impelled as they are in these conversations to reflect critically on their own position. The historic episcopate belongs, the A-RC report insists, to the essential structure of the Church (no. 16), and a statement of the American commission speaks of "the necessity of an ordained ministry in which are included the three orders of bishops, priests (presbyters) and deacons" (A-RC/usa, <u>ARC-DOC</u> I, p. 10). However, in other contexts where non-episcopal churches are involved, the claim is qualified in ways which indicate a positive appreciation of non-episcopal traditions more in line with the new insights advanced at Vatican II and in contemporary Anglican thought. A statement by the Roman Catholic participants in the L-RC/usa conversations, in which they explain their recommendation of a recognition of the Lutheran ministry, illustrates the point: "... we affirm explicitly that the apostolic Ministry is retained in a preeminent way in the episcopate, the presbyterate, and the diaconate. We would rejoice if episcopacy in apostolic succession, functioning as the effective sign of church unity, were acceptable to all; but we have envisaged a practical and immediate solution in a de facto situation where episcopacy is not yet seen in this light" (no. 57). This qualified recognition of non-episcopal ministries is undergirded by references to historic precedents of ordination by priests, which were accepted as valid (L-RC, no. 58; L-RC/usa, nos. 20f; R-RC/usa, 1971, nos. 5f.). Hence the L-RC/usa commission is prepared to state that the divergent ways "in which the Ministry has been structured and implemented in our two traditions appear to us to be consonant with apostolic teaching and practice" (no. 22).

As would be expected, the Anglican recognition of non-episcopal orders is stronger, but it follows the same pattern of distinguishing between "full" and "partial", or "regular" and "exceptional". For example, the Anglican members of the A-L commission recognise in the Lutheran churches " a true communion of Christ's Body, possessing a truly apostolic ministry" and favour increasing intercommunion, but they "cannot foresee full integration of ministries (full communion) apart from the historic episcopate" (A-L, nos. 85ff.).

Yet these differing concerns form part of an enveloping convergence: (1) all the participating churches recognise the need for a transparochial corporate and/or personal episcopè; and (2) churches, possessing the historic episcopate and believing they hold it in trust for the united church of the future, nonetheless show an increasing readiness to acknowledge the gifts of the Spirit in other modes of succession and oversight, while, on the other hand, several non-episcopal churches show a similar readiness to consider the benefits of the historic episcopate as a valuable symbol of continuity and unity, provided a particular restrictive interpretation is not imposed.

Papacy. Not without reason, Paul VI once termed the papacy "the most serious obstacle on the path of ecumenism". Several among the bilaterals are probing fresh approaches to this obstacle, attempting a critical-constructive reformulation of the problem in the wider setting of ecumenical understandings of the Church and its apostolic ministry. The prime question is no longer whether Christ instituted the papal office, but rather whether the worldwide Church in this global age does not need a visible symbol and servant of its universality, and, if so, whether a renewed papacy would be the appropriate embodiment of this universal ministry.

In an interim report of the A-RC international commission, the Anglican members state their conviction that all the apostles and indeed the whole Church (and from there all the bishops) participate in the Petrine office. It may be possible "to envisage a papal primacy of honour and service, but such a primacy can ultimately be justified only as a useful historical development" (Venice, 1970, loc.cit., 65). Some Anglicans would go further and ask whether the New Testament does not witness to a personal Petrine office and whether the Roman primacy, exercised as a primacy of responsibility and service in patristic times, may not have a providential role to play also today (ibid., 66). In another report from the same meeting, the papacy is seen as " a visible focus not only of unity but also of final authority. Such a focal point could protect legitimate and enriching diversity from the tyranny of sectarianism" (ibid., 57).

Noting the pressing need to strengthen worldwide Christian unity, the R-RC/usa consultation on the ministry maintains that "the Church needs, in a spirit of pastoral service, to blend the unifying drive which a papacy of the future might provide, with the vitalizing growth which can come from the 'collegial' or representative spirit inherent in the Reformed tradition" ("Ministry in the Church", op.cit., 597). For Lutherans the understanding of the papal office as a visible sign of unity is by reinterpretation and restructuring subordinated to the primacy of the Gospel and seen as of human right (L-RC, no. 66). Developing this line of thought further, the L-RC/usa commission (which thus far is the only one to produce a major report on the subject) declares explicitly that papal primacy, renewed in the light of the Gospel, "need not be a barrier to reconciliation" (Report 1974, no. 32). This conclusion is based on a number of striking agreements (ibid., no. 29). The remaining disagreements - among them the issue of whether papal primacy is to be seen as an essential, or possible, or desirable feature of the universal Church of the future - are forthrightly recognised, but the cleft has been considerably narrowed. In Old Catholic-Roman Catholic conversations, the dogma of the jurisdictional supremacy and the infallibility of the pope continues to be the chief stumbling-block (OC-RC/eur, op.cit., 78).

The problem of infallibility has hardly yet surfaced in the published statements. When the doctrine is referred to, it is interpreted ecclesiologically, and preference is given to the term "indefectibility" which is interpreted as a gift of the Holy Spirit to the whole Church, preserving it against complete error and sustaining it in its battle against error and sin (A-RC, Venice, 56; R-RC/usa, op.cit., no. 8).

Ordination. With regard to the understanding and practice of ordination a marked similarity can be observed. The following elements are generally mentioned: a call by Christ in and through the Church, invocation of the Holy Spirit to bestow the gifts of ministry, commissioning for special service in the Church and for the world, and the quality of unrepeatability and permanence. A point of dissension has been the Roman Catholic and Anglican designation of ordination as a sacramental act (e.g. A-RC, Canterbury statement, no. 15). In the conversations, it has been agreed that this is chiefly a matter of terminology, as a closer analysis of the underlying intentions have made it plain that the Roman Catholic and Lutheran understandings of what is meant are in fact very close (L-RC, no. 59; L-RC/usa, nos. 16, 50; also R-RC/usa, no. 4).

The "indelible character" of the ordained ministry is taken up in some instances, especially in connection with ordination. While it is agreed that ordination is for a lifetime of service and irrevocable, Lutherans have objected to the term because of its metaphysical implications. But the new emphasis in contemporary Roman Catholic thought upon"the functional aspect of character and upon the gift of the Spirit" is held to open the way to an understanding also in this matter (L-RC, no. 60; L-RC/usa, no. 17).

The Roman Catholic/Presbyterian-Reformed consultation in the United States is thus far the only one to undertake a serious study of the role of women in Church and society, including the ordination of women. Four facts in the contemporary world demand a reexamination of the question: (1) the injustice imposed upon women in both Church and society; (2) the challenge of the women's liberation movement; (3) the conclusions of an ever growing number of theological investigations concerning the ministerial role of women; and (4) the joint ecumenical responsibilities of the churches for mission and service (R-RC/usa, "Women in the Church", loc. cit., 235ff.). Because of the growing consensus among Reformed and Roman Catholic theologians that there is "no insurmountable Biblical or dogmatic obstacle to the ordination of women", and because of the needs of the people of God, the consultation declares: "... we conclude that ordination of women must be part of the Church's life" ("Ministry in the Church", 1971, no. 4). It is consequently recommended that qualified women be admitted to ordination and that they be given "full and equal participation in policy- and decision-making, and voice in places of power, in the Churches on local, regional, national and world levels" ("Women in the Church", p. 239).

Mutual Recognition. The question of recognition of ministries has already been repeatedly touched upon, but it requires a fuller systematic presentation because of its pivotal position. For such recognition in some form is an indispensable ingredient in the growth of fellowship among divided churches, just as the attainment of a reunited church would be inconceivable without full mutual recognition and conflation of ministries. As the previous discussions have illustrated, the recognition of ministries cannot be reduced to a simple or even a single formula. In the bilaterals one can distinguish several different though overlapping stages of development and concepts of recognition.

1. Mutual acceptance of ministers as representative spokesmen for the communions to which they belong. This is one of the tacit presuppositions of bilateral conversations and can be seen as, at least, an application of the principle of par cum pari for purposes of dialogue.

2. Agreement on the essential or on important aspects of the doctrine of the ordained ministry, without yet deciding whether or to what degree these beliefs are embodied in the ministerial structures of both parties. The A-RC Canterbury statement contains a succinct formulation of this position both as a necessary methodological procedure and as an indication of the stage reached in that dialogue: "Agreement on the nature of Ministry is prior to the consideration of the mutual recognition of ministries" (no. 17). The latest A-RC/usa statement on the subject (1969) represents the same stage; but it envisages mutual recognition as the next step, since the consultation had achieved agreement on the Church as a eucharistic fellowship, the theology of the celebrant, and the nature of eucharistic sacrifice (ARC-DOC I, p. 16).

3. Partial recognition of the ecclesial character of the other church, implying an acknowledgement of the presence of the Holy

Spirit in its administrations, but leaving open the question of recognition of ministries. The R-RC/usa consultation deliberately avoids using the terms "validity" or "mutual recognition of orders" in the current state of their discussions because of the remaining differences. But "... we cannot but recognize the Risen Christ present and at work for the healing of his people in the ministry and Eucharist of each of our traditions", and the consultation goes on to suggest that this realisation be publicly recognised ("Ministry in the Church", 1971, no. 10).

4. Acknowledgement that the other church also possesses apostolic ministry, justifying qualified recognition, with the understanding that further agreements have to be reached in related areas before full recognition can be envisaged. The participants in the A-L conversations - both at the world level and in the United States - recognise in each other's churches "a true communion of Christ's Body, possessing a truly apostolic ministry", although the Anglican members cannot foresee full integration of ministries apart from the historic episcopate (A-L, nos. 85ff., 90f; A-L/usa, pp. 20ff.).

A startling avant-garde position is taken by the former arch-antagonists, Lutherans and Roman Catholics. The American commission recommends that the authorities of the participating churches should consider recognising the validity of each other's ministries and the real presence of Christ's body and blood in each other's celebration of the eucharist (L-RC/usa, nos. 35 and 54). On the Lutheran side this recognition is based on the conviction that in the Roman Catholic Church there is a responsible proclamation of the Gospel, that there are sacraments which are administered in accordance with our Lord's intention, that there is a wide agreement in the christological and trinitarian dogmas and in the understanding of salvation by grace alone, and that there is a considerable convergence in the understanding and practice of the eucharist (nos. 23ff.). On the Roman Catholic side this recognition is based on the conviction that the New Testament does not give a clear, definite picture of the ministry, that Vatican II has acknowledged the ecclesial character of other communities, that the Lutheran churches by their devotion to gospel, creed, and sacrament have preserved a form of doctrinal apostolicity, and that there is a wide agreement in the understanding of the eucharist (nos. 36ff.).

The international commission takes the same position, pointing out among other things that Vatican II can be interpreted as implicitly recognising other ministries (L-RC, nos. 63ff.).

5. Full mutual recognition as communions and as ministries, partaking together in the one Church of Jesus Christ (L-R-U/eur, Leuenberg Agreement, nos. 33f.). The formulation used in the Leuenberg Agreement - with its implication of the ministry in Word and Sacrament - is characteristic of the Reformation position: "... that they accord each other table and pulpit fellowship; this includes the mutual recognition of ministries and the freedom to provide for intercelebration" (nos. 33ff.).

In other reports the problem of recognition has either not yet been broached or been raised only in the form of preliminary questions.

Intercommunion. In past discussions the question of intercommunion was very closely linked with that of recognition of ministries in particular. The bilateral conversations tend to see the problem of intercommunion and its solution in a wider and more complex context of agreements and convergences. Thus it is usually for a combination of reasons that the reports, excepting the Leuenberg Agreement, do not yet see a sufficient basis for full eucharistic sharing (explicitly so L-RC/usa, no. 59; R-RC/usa, no. 11). At the same time most of them propose that intercommunion should be allowed on special occasions as a means of grace and a sign of unity already existing and promised.[1] In the present context, however, the specific problem is that of intercelebration. This is explicitly recognised only in the Leuenberg Agreement, and presented in the final text as an option because of the resistance to be expected in certain churches. It is possible, nonetheless, that some of the reports which favour mutual recognition of ministries as well as increasing intercommunion tacitly regard intercelebration as an implied concomitant.

Comment

In comparison with discussions on the ministry in Faith and Order, at least in the past, certain new elements can be observed in the bilaterals. The participation of the Roman Catholic Church has introduced the problems of indelible character and the papacy and

---

1. See section above on "Eucharist and Intercommunion".

given added weight to the question of the valid eucharistic celebrant. On the other hand, the traditional problem of apostolic succession in the form of the historic episcopate is now treated in a more flexible manner and its acceptance is no longer regarded as an absolute pre-condition for at least mutual recognition, not even by Roman Catholics (L-RC; L-RC/usa). The historicity and therefore variety and change-ability of ministerial structures is emphasised much more than in the previous discussion. Special problems relating to two particular churches (as e.g. Apostolicae Curae, or the ministry in the Reformation Confessions) can be investigated in greater detail, and above all, the decisive step of recommending mutual recognition of ministries can be achieved more easily in bilateral than in multilateral conversations.

On the other hand, all conversations reveal and sometimes explicitly confirm that they have been greatly enriched by the Faith and Order studies on the ministry which on their part are deliberately drawing on bilateral findings. A comparison of these statements and the successive versions of the Faith and Order study paper on "The Ministry" [1] shows manifest parallels in such essential matters as the interrelation of the general and the special ministry, the functions of the special ministry, apostolic succession, and ordination. Clearly the task for the future is to extend this interpenetration of varied approaches to the ministry, including that of church union plans.

1. One Baptism, One Eucharist and a Mutually Recognized Ministry: Three Agreed Statements. Geneva: World Council of Churches, Publications Office, 1975.

5. Unity and Union

Sources [1]

A-L	Anglican-Lutheran International Conversations Report ... 1970-1972
A-L/usa	Lutheran-Episcopal Dialogue: A Progress Report, 1972
A-RC	Windsor, 1971, Agreed Statement on Eucharistic Doctrine Canterbury, 1973, Ministry and Ordination
A-RC/usa	Documents on Anglican/Roman Catholic Relations (ARC-DOC I and II), 1972 and 1973
AB-RC/usa	Growing in Understanding, 1972
CC-RC/usa	An Adventure in Understanding, 1974
Ev-O/frg-r	Zagorsk, 1973, Die Eucharistie, 1974
L-R-U/eur	Leuenberg, 1973 "Agreement ("Konkordie") among Reformation Churches in Europe", The Ecumenical Review XXV, 3, 1973, 355-59
L-RC	Malta Report, 1971, "The Gospel and the Church", Lutheran World XIX, 3, 1972, 266-70
L-RC/usa	Papal Primacy and the Universal Church, 1974

The bilateral dialogues are manifestations of the ecumenical search for unity and at the same time a distinct approach to it. Unity is their central concern. Yet as already a study of the topic frequencies indicates, there are comparatively few among these conversations which deal thematically with the subject, asking the question: What is the shape of the unity we seek? The aims are usually more proximate and limited: mutual understanding, theological and pastoral examination of particular divisive issues, cooperation in specified areas.

This is not to say that the bilaterals are not bursting with a seething mass of formative convictions and ideas about unity. A moment's reflection on the multiple relationships of interaction in which such dialogues are placed, makes this abundantly clear. Each dialogue is part and parcel of the universal movement of ecumenical thought, and by virtue of the collective experience and knowledge of the participants, it becomes a point of collision and confluence

1. While all the bilateral reports are pertinent to the subject, the present bibliography is limited to documents referred to in the text.

of innumerable notions of unity. [1] Each dialogue is further, in itself, a field of interaction between three forces: the positions of the two partners (with their internal diversity of corporate and personal convictions) and, thirdly, the impulse of convergence which springs from the encounter, acquires a momentum of its own, and transcends and transforms the initial positions.

Because of the fluid and evolving state of this multiverse of ideas, they can be ranged in several different patterns of interpretation. But the earlier analysis of the aims of the dialogues furnishes a broad scheme of categorisation which is usable here too. [2] One may accordingly roughly distinguish between four sets of unity ideas in the bilaterals; in many instances they do at the same time form overlapping phases of a progressive search.

1. <u>In the Fellowship of the Spirit</u>. Common to all bilaterals is their matrix - a group of persons, professing Christ through their divided traditions, bound together by a shared purpose, growing in a committed fellowship of prayer and trust, of mutual understanding and respect for truth. To mention this may sound like a superfluous truism, but it is of paramount importance for understanding the inner history and the sometimes astounding achievements of the bilaterals. This experience of communion in the Spirit - with its paradoxical tension of unity-in-disunity - bears out the truth of a statement by the New Delhi Assembly of the World Council of Churches suggesting, in a cautious formulation, that "<u>koinonia</u> in Christ is more nearly the precondition of 'sound doctrine' than vice versa". [3]

There are frequent and sometimes deeply moving testimonies to the unity in spirit and love growing in such groups. Significantly, this experience is not confined to dialogues among spokesmen of traditions already allied in outlook and history; it occurs no less in dialogues among partners standing far apart. Thus the American Baptist-Roman Catholic group speaks of "an experience that came from the discovery that the same Christ in whom we believe is the Savior to whom others have also committed themselves; and that in Him we share far more than our deeply felt differences would suggest" (<u>Growing in</u>

---

1. The latest Faith and Order documents on the subject provide illuminating analyses of current thought; cf. <u>What Kind of Unity</u>? and <u>Uniting in Hope, Accra 1974</u>. Geneva: World Council of Churches, Publications Office 1974/75.
2. See pp. 124ff.
3. <u>The New Delhi Report</u>, 1961, p. 126

Understanding, p. 1). In a similar vein the Disciples-Roman Catholic report asserts: "For us, this experience of the Spirit was the most dramatic and moving sign of the unity which, in His grace, was already ours. It provides us with the motive to continue our efforts toward the goal of a fuller unity which in His way will be accomplished" (_An Adventure in Understanding_, p. 10). And this is re-echoed from another part of the globe in joint statements from Orthodox-Evangelical Lutheran dialogues, referring to "the atmosphere of mutual brotherly understanding and the spirit of Christian love", characterising the conversations (e.g. Zagorsk, 1973, _Die Eucharistie_, p. 21).

2. _Mutual Understanding among Churches_. Initially, and in a way all through, bilateral dialogues are an exercise in comparative theology and ecclesiology. They aim at mutual acquaintance and exchange of information about the life and thought of the participating churches, including their conceptions of unity. This is an encounter which produces a double effect. Each partner is here confronted with a different understanding of the Church and its unity, which challenges its own self-understanding and which intensifies the awareness of the existing differences - sometimes indeed irreconcilable - in worship and teaching, in church order and life style. At the same time elating discoveries are made of unexpected affinities, previously concealed by ignorance and prejudice, but now evoking a fresh appreciation of each other's treasures of grace. When, for example, Orthodox and Quakers discover their kinship in mystical spirituality or Methodists and Roman Catholics their shared concern for holiness of life, their visions of unity inevitably become richer and more wide-angled.

Mutual acquaintance does not yet necessarily imply any ecclesiastical commitment, at least not in the sense that the encounter would seriously put in question the self-identity of the churches involved, prompting them to ecumenical repentance and change. The future relationships between the two are not prejudged. The hopes expressed for "a fuller unity" are consequently still open-ended and ambivalent, not to say ambiguous. For one partner it may mean a unity which will, in some unforeseeable way, transcend and transform the self-understandings acquired by the two communions in their history of separation. For another, that fuller unity can only be conceived as a fulfilment of the unity preserved in his own tradition, by the grace of God, as a trust for the greater Church to come.

It is a sign of the strength of the ecumenical "hope against hope" that in several instances these two incompatible positions nevertheless are joined together in the same bilateral dialogue.

3. Theological Divisions and Convergences. In the search for fuller unity, a more advanced stage is reached when a dialogue proceeds from the level of exploratory exchange and rapprochement to a critical and reconstructive probing of those specific issues that keep two communions apart. The step is taken from a "dialogue of love" to a "dialogue of faith (truth)", to use a distinction already referred to. Most, if not all, of the dialogues sooner or later engage in such deliberate efforts to remove the causes of separation and to trace out the areas of common faith and practice. Even when the issues are treated seriatim without any explicit framework of unity, the very choice of topics does nonetheless furnish an indication of what the two partners regard as its essential requirements.

There is no need to dwell further on this type of unity effort since it is amply illustrated in the preceding sections.

4. The Shape of the Unity we Seek. Finally, there exists a number of dialogues which from the outset are aiming at the achievement of some definite form of ecclesial communion acceptable to both partners, and accordingly they structure their studies of specific subjects as parts of an integrated process. Here the bilateral conceptions of unity appear in their most explicit and instructive form. It will be appropriate, therefore, to devote the major part of this section to dialogues of this kind, and in order to outline their individual profiles more sharply, they will be presented singly and not in a cross-conversational synopsis. The presentation draws obviously to a large extent on the same material as that already cited in earlier sections, but here it is arranged in a different framework to illustrate coherent conceptions of unity.

The analysis covers three international dialogues, with a sideglance at parallel national developments in the USA, and a regional one. These have been chosen because they represent the most advanced level of theological interpenetration and because they furnish an opportunity to see three dialogue partners each functioning in two dissimilar relationships.

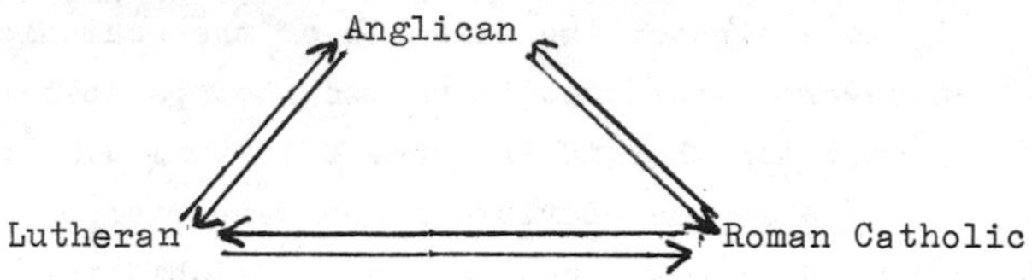

The fourth example, the Leuenberg Agreement, represents a regional model embodying a Lutheran-Reformed-United and thus an intra-Reformation concept of unity.

A. <u>Anglican-Lutheran Conversations</u>

The Anglican-Lutheran International Commission set as its aim to explore the conditions of "mutual recognition and fellowship between the two churches". To provide an adequate theological basis, the commission discussed a number of subjects in five areas: sources of authority, the Church, Word and sacraments, apostolic ministry, worship, "always in the context of the general mission of the Church to the world". The report registers substantial and explicit agreements on all these subjects with certain qualifications concerning episcopacy. The divergences are seen not as separative but as reflecting differing historical circumstances.

With respect to church unity, the concordant views of the two churches are stated as follows:

> " Both traditions agree that the unity of the Church, God's gift and our task, must be manifested in a visible way. This unity can be expressed in different forms depending upon the particular situation. Accordingly, there can be various stages in the mutual recognition of churches, in the practice of intercommunion and in the reciprocal acceptance of ministries. The goal should be full 'altar and pulpit fellowship' (full communion) including its acceptance by the individual members of the Churches, and structures that will encourage such fellowship and its acceptance." (no. 53).

The commission expressly endorses the "need for more rapid movement towards organic union" felt "in those countries where Anglicans and Lutherans are working side by side for the spread of the gospel, or where there are churches with close relationships with our two Communions..." (no. 99).

In the crucial part on "Apostolic Ministry", the sequence of the sub-sections already suggests the approach which the commission is adopting: apostolicity and apostolic succession, the ministry, episcopacy. In other words, the historic episcopate is not presented in isolation as an Anglican shibboleth; it is seen as one of the manifold forms of the apostolicity of the Church. "Thus apostolicity pertains first to the gospel and then to the ministry of Word and sacraments ..." and "the succession of apostolicity through time is guarded and given contemporary expression in and through a wide variety of means, activities and institutions ..." The report goes on to recognise that "all who have been called and ordained to the ministry of Word and Sacraments in obedience to the apostolic faith stand together in the apostolic succession of office" (nos. 73-77). Episcopacy too has been exercised in a wide variety of ways, episcopal and non-episcopal, and both communions have preserved it, though in different forms.

After this catena of agreements, there follow parallel declarations by the two delegations on the historic episcopate. The distinctive convictions of each tradition are presented, but in such a fashion that, while now in part incompatible, they do not exclude mutual recognition. The Anglican participants "gladly recognize in the Lutheran churches a true communion of Christ's body, possessing a truly apostolic ministry", and although they cannot foresee "full integration of ministries (full communion) apart from the historic episcopate", this does not in their view preclude increasing intercommunion (nos. 85, 87). The Lutherans express a similar recognition of the Anglican communion and its apostolic ministry, but while declaring that Lutheran churches are free to accept the historic episcopate "where it serves the growing unity of the church in obedience to the gospel", they insist that it "should not become a necessary condition for interchurch relations or church union" (no. 89).

The United States commission likewise focused its attention on the nature and forms of apostolicity as a basis for agreement on pulpit and altar fellowship. It concluded that "the essential apostolicity of the Church" had been maintained by both communions - a recognition particularised in the agreement between Episcopalians and Lutherans on the following fundamentals of church life and doctrine: (a) the primacy and authority of the Holy Scriptures; (b) the doctrine of the Apostles' and Nicene Creeds; (c) justification by grace through faith as affirmed by both the Lutheran Confessions and the Anglican Book of Common Prayer and Thirty-Nine Articles of Religion; (d) the doctrine and practice of Baptism; (e) fundamental agreement on the Holy Eucharist, though with some difference in emphasis (p. 23).

The commission frankly faced the problem posed by the historical fact that the two communions embody partly differing interpretations of apostolicity. The obstacle was overcome by acknowledging that the apostolic gospel is mediated and addressed to every new generation in multiple ways and that "within the one church, both the Anglican continuity of the apostolic order, and the Lutheran concentration on doctrine, have been means of preserving the apostolicity of the one church". Each respecting "the right of the other to honor the distinct history which mediates its apostolicity ...", the two communions should recognise each other's ordained ministry and sacramental administration as truly apostolic (pp. 20ff.).

Rejecting the sterile dilemma of whether intercommunion is to be seen as a means or a goal of unity, the commission placed the issue in the context of a growing fellowship: "Are we able mutually to affirm the presence of the Gospel and apostolicity in our respective communions sufficiently to agree that the renewal of the church is more likely to come in communion with one another than out of communion with one another?" (p.13). The following key passage among the recommendations forms a provisional answer to this question:

> "Subject to the consent of the appropriate local authorities ... Commendation of communicants of each communion to the Eucharistic celebrations and gatherings around the Word of the other, including intercommunion between parishes or congregations which, by reason of proximity, joint community concerns, and/or activities, have developed such a degree of understanding and trust as would make intercommunion an appropriate response to the Gospel." (p. 23f.).

B. Anglican-Roman Catholic Conversations

From the outset, the deliberate aim of the conversations was to work for organic unity of the two communions. At a meeting in 1966 between Pope Paul VI and the Archbishop of Canterbury, the two leaders issued a joint declaration which set the tone by speaking of the inauguration of "a serious dialogue which, founded on the Gospels and on the ancient common traditions, may lead to that unity in truth for which Christ prayed", and which would remove the obstacles that stand in the way of "a restoration of complete communion of faith and sacramental life".

Acknowledging that unity in the faith must precede organic union, the international commission set out to prepare common declarations of faith in three areas which have been principal sources of division: ministry, eucharist and authority. The eucharist was taken up first because it was felt that the question of ministry could not be resolved without prior agreement on the former subject.

The commission has thus far produced two agreed statements on eucharistic doctrine and on ministry and ordination, and is currently grappling with the question of authority in the Church, including papal primacy. The Windsor statement on eucharistic doctrine presents a "substantial agreement", notably on the two chief issues of controversy, namely the relation of Christ's sacrifice once-for-all to the celebration of the eucharist and Christ's sacramental presence. The disputed doctrine of transubstantiation is divested of its divisive force by the jointly accepted statement (in a footnote) that the term should be seen as affirming the fact, but not explaining the mode, of the mysterious change taking place. The significance of the consensus is underscored in the concluding sentence: "It is our hope that in view of the agreement which we have reached on eucharistic faith, this doctrine will no longer constitute an obstacle to the unity we seek" (no. 12).

The Canterbury statement on ministry and ordination interprets the ordained ministry in the wider context of the apostolic ministry of the whole Church to the world. The impasse caused by the Roman Catholic rejection of the validity of Anglican orders appeared insoluble, but the commission was able to break the impasse, if not yet resolving the problem of recognition, by adopting a fresh approach. Avoiding getting mired in the doctrinal and canonical debates of the past, it reexamined the question in the light of "biblical teaching and the traditions of our common inheritance" (no. 1). Leaving aside for the moment the derivative matter of recognition, it has instead successfully endeavoured to reach consensus on the prior question of the nature of the ministry. "Agreement on the nature of Ministry is prior to the consideration of the mutual recognition of ministries" (no. 17). Thus the report discusses the unity and diversity of ministerial services in the New Testament Church, the distinctive role and function of the ordained ministry in relation to the common priesthood of all believers, the divinely inspired emergence of the threefold pattern of order, the meaning of ordination and of apostolic succession. The controverted issue of the criteria of unbroken succession is resolved by the recovery of the ancient conception of a succession of apostolic teachings and teachers in the episcopal sees, rather than by means of an uninterrupted transmission of power from one bishop to another. The outcome is a remarkable consensus "on questions where agreement is indispensable for unity" (ibid.).

The United States commission, set up already in 1965, has served as a spearhead both in theological inquiry and in encouraging local implementation. At its 1969 meeting ("ARC VII"), it detailed "three possible steps in the restoration of full communion between our churches":

1. Re-encounter through Personal Exchange and Dialogue
2. Growing Together: Interim Steps
   a) A common declaration of faith
   b) Mutual recognition of ministry
   c) Partial eucharistic celebration
3. Towards Full Communion and Organic Unity.

The following passage indicates the general direction of thought:

> "Full communion must not be interpreted as an agreement to disagree while sharing in the Eucharistic gifts, nor may organic unity be understood as a juridical concept implying a particular form of Church government. Such a unity is hard to visualize, but would include a common profession of faith and would mean a sufficient compatibility of polity to make possible a united mission to the human family. Whatever structural forms emerge, it is hoped that cultural and liturgical variety will remain so that the values of both the Roman and Anglican ethos will survive and develop" (ARC-DOC I, p. 18).

The advance made thus far is marked by a number of substantial agreements on such subjects as baptism, the Church as a eucharistic fellowship, eucharistic sacrifice, the theology of the valid celebrant, the mission of the Church. Like its international counterpart, the commission is currently studying the authority structure of the Church. According to present plans, a comprehensive consensus document on doctrinal and pastoral aspects of full communion is to be completed by 1976, and, hopefully, later enacted at first on a regional basis in the USA with the approval of the appropriate authorities of the two world communions.

C. Lutheran-Roman Catholic Conversations

The Lutheran-Roman Catholic split in the 16th century was a tragic event, which in turn released a chain-reaction of fissiparous tendencies throughout the centuries. It is therefore natural that the two churches, when now they meet again in fraternal dialogue, should do so with a special sense of solidarity and of joint responsibility for healing the ancient rift, while fully aware of the depth of the separation. The so-called Malta report of the international commission reflects this sentiment.

The dialogue is aiming at a theological consensus sufficiently broad and solid to provide a basis for a qualified mutual recognition and occasional reciprocal intercommunion - leaving open such critical questions as ministry and papacy for further clarification. The report starts out at the very point where the separation once occurred, namely, the meaning of the Gospel and its soteriological and ecclesiological consequences. "The unity of the Church can be a unity only in the truth of the gospel" (no. 14). On two of the focal points at issue - the authority of Scripture and the doctrine of justification - the group achieved an astounding degree of consensus (nos. 21, 26ff.). The authority of the Word of God over and in the Church is affirmed and the doctrine of justification and sanctification is reconceived in its original New Testament setting, correcting the polemical misconceptions persisting in Lutheran as well as Roman Catholic teachings.

It is no doubt symptomatic that the longest part of the report is devoted to the ministry. "The question of the office of the ministry in the Church, its origin, its position and correct understanding represents one of the most important open questions between Lutherans and Catholics" (no. 47). But that here too the positions are coming closer together is evidenced by the references to the diversity of spiritual gifts, ministries and orders in the New Testament period; the historicity of church structures; the primary emphasis in the early doctrine of apostolic succession on the "substance of apostolicity, i.e. on succession in apostolic teaching", with the uninterrupted line of transmission of office being understood as "a sign of the unimpaired transmission of the gospel and a sign of unity in the faith" (no. 57); and converging reinterpretations of the priestly character and the task of the ministerial office. On the basis of the weighty evidence, both Roman Catholic and Lutheran participants felt justified in requesting their respective authorities to "examine seriously" the question of recognising each other's ministerial office (nos. 63-64).

The report closes with a section on "The Gospel and the Unity of the Church", but it limits its discussion to the two questions of papal primacy and intercommunion. With regard to intercommunion, the group acknowledges the necessity of a process of gradual rapprochement with various stages. In the present situation, it recommends that the church authorities "on the basis of what is already shared in faith and sacrament and as a sign and anticipation of the promised and hoped for unity, make possible occasional acts of intercommunion as, for example, during ecumenical events or in the pastoral care of those involved in mixed marriages" (no. 73). Some slight rapprochement is perceptible also in regard to the historic stumbling-block of papal primacy. This has been facilitated by the reassertion of episcopal collegiality at the Second Vatican Council, which placed the primacy in a new interpretative framework. The Lutheran participants on their side did not exclude the office of the papacy "as a visible sign of the unity of the churches ... insofar as it is subordinated to the primacy of the gospel by theological reinterpretation and practical restructuring" (no. 66). Although both sides reached out as far as possible in presenting bridge-building interpretations of their positions, the decisive question remained unresolved "whether the primacy of the Pope is necessary for the church or whether it represents only a fundamentally possible function" (no. 67). Yet here too a qualifying note is added which in cautious form suggests a new opening: "It was nevertheless agreed that the question of altar fellowship and of mutual recognition of ministerial offices should not be unconditionally dependent on a consensus on the question of primacy" (_ibid_.).

The United States commission has reached similar conclusions on baptism, eucharist and ministry. In its study of the eucharist as sacrifice, it felt justified in concluding that "Despite all remaining differences in the ways we speak and think of the eucharistic sacrifice and our Lord's presence in his supper, we are no longer able to regard ourselves as divided in the one holy catholic and apostolic faith on these two points" (_The Eucharist as Sacrifice_, p. 198). And the joint report on eucharist and ministry culminates in recommending to the authorities of the participating churches that they recognise the validity of the ministry and the eucharistic administration of the other communion (nos. 35, 54ff.).

The area where the commission has advanced farther than other dialogues is the constructive rethinking of the Petrine office as a symbol of unity in the universal Church. Placing the issue of papal primacy in this broader context, the commission calls attention to the ecumenical problems raised by the growth of a world Christian community. Despite the preliminary nature of the discussion, a number of agreements were reached, the most significant of which are:

> "Christ wills for his church a unity which is not only spiritual but must be manifest in the world;
> promotion of this unity is incumbent on all believers, especially those who are engaged in the Ministry of word and sacrament;
> the greater the responsibility of a ministerial office, the greater the responsibility to seek the unity of all Christians; a special responsibility for this may be entrusted to one individual Minister, under the gospel;
> such a responsibility for the universal church cannot be ruled out on the basis of the biblical evidence;
> the bishop of Rome, whom Roman Catholics regard as entrusted by the will of Christ with this responsibility, and who has exercised his Ministry in forms that have changed over the centuries, can in the future function in ways which are better adapted to meet both the universal and regional needs of the church in the complex environment of modern times" (no. 22; Papal Primacy and the Universal Church, p. 22).

In conclusion, the report addresses a series of searching questions to both sides. The Lutheran churches are asked to consider "the possibility and desirability of the papal ministry, renewed under the gospel and committed to Christian freedom, in a larger communion which would include the Lutheran churches". The Roman Catholic Church in turn is asked to consider "the possibility of a reconciliation which would recognize the self-government of Lutheran churches within a communion" and the acknowledgement of the "Lutheran churches represented in our dialogue as sister-churches which are already entitled to some measure of ecclesiastical communion" (ibid., no. 33).

D. Agreement between Reformation Churches in Europe : The Leuenberg Agreement (Konkordie)

The Leuenberg Agreement, envisioning the realisation of a Europe-wide fellowship among the churches issuing from the 16th century

Reformation, represents again another conception of unity. Carrying a marked confessional note, the fellowship involves full mutual recognition among the participating churches as having "part together in the one church of Jesus Christ" (no. 34). Church fellowship means that "on the basis of the consensus they have reached in their understanding of the Gospel, churches with different confessional positions accord each other fellowship in word and sacrament and strive for the fullest possible cooperation in witness and service to the world" (no. 29). It is thus neither a variant of federal or organic union, nor does it on the other hand constitute merely an institutionalised form of practical cooperation.

Consonant with Reformation principles, the Agreement traces the convergent intentions informing both partners back to the common soteriological centre, the Gospel of Jesus Christ. This is the foundation of the Church and consequently of its unity. For the Reformation Churches this implies that there exist two, and only two, criteria for church unity. " ... agreement in the right teaching of the Gospel and in the right administration of the sacraments is the necessary and sufficient prerequisite for the true unity of the Church." Nothing less, nothing more. It is in this central perspective that the Agreement proceeds to sketch out the proposed fellowship in three successive steps: the common understanding of the Gospel, agreement in respect of the doctrinal condemnations of the Reformation era, and the declaration and realisation of Church fellowship.

The Gospel is described as "the message of justification as the message of the free grace of God," communicated in the acts of preaching, baptism and Lord's Supper. Like the reformers themselves once did, the Agreement maintains that justification is no particularistic Reformation doctrine but consonant with the ancient creeds and with Scriptures. It makes claim to apostolic continuity and catholic breadth. "In this understanding of the Gospel, we take our stand on the basis of the ancient creeds of the Church and reaffirm the common conviction of the Reformation confessions that the unique mediation of Jesus Christ in salvation is the heart of the Scriptures and that the message of justification as the message of God's free grace is the measure of all the Church's preaching" (no. 12).

The condemnations contained in the 16th century confessional writings presented an awkward problem. Carrying confessional dignity, their abrogation would be unacceptable to most of the churches concerned on both doctrinal and constitutional grounds. On the other hand, their reaffirmation would form an insuperable obstacle to reconciliation. It is this dilemma which the Agreement seeks to transcend by asserting that the condemnations "no longer apply to the contemporary doctrinal position of the assenting churches" (no. 32). They have not become irrelevant, "but they are no longer an obstacle to church fellowship" (nos. 27, 33). The controversies which once led to these condemnations related especially to the doctrine of the Lord's Supper, Christology and the doctrine of predestination. On all three issues, the Agreement succeeds in presenting formulations that have proved acceptable to both Lutherans and Reformed.

Distinguishing between declaration and realisation of church fellowship, the Agreement sums up the elements of the act of declaration as follows:

> "In assenting to this Agreement the Churches, in loyalty to the confessions of faith which bind them or with due respect for their traditions, declare:
> (a) that they are one in understanding the Gospel ...
> (b) that ... the doctrinal condemnations expressed in the confessional documents no longer apply to the contemporary position of the assenting churches; (c) that they accord each other table and pulpit fellowship; this includes the mutual recognition of ordination and the freedom to provide for intercelebration." (nos. 30, 33)

There are two points in the statement which deserve attention for they mark historically important shifts. First, the stereotyped identification of confessional and ecclesial fellowship is abandoned; fellowship in the one Church is seen as compatible with a plurality of confessional positions within the common understanding of the Gospel. Secondly, church fellowship is seen as a process of growth toward ever fuller fellowship in all spheres and at all levels of church life. Full consensus de doctrina is thus no longer regarded as a precondition of ecclesial communion.

The relation of such a fellowship to organic union is left open; it is not a necessary later step, but neither is it precluded. "The question of organic union between particular participating churches can only be decided in the situation in which these churches live" (no. 44).

Comment

It has been suggested by critics of the bilateral dialogues that they are nothing but a convenient escape for churches which, for some reason or another, desire to avoid the threatening challenge of church union. This may or may not be a concealed motive, but, if so, the churchmen entertaining such a thought - as well as the critics - operate with a false alternative. As the above examples demonstrate, the two undertakings can and do in effect overlap; and it is likely that the bilaterals, as they face the demand to correlate their short term and long term goals more stringently, will increasingly come to include a consideration of optional church union models in their own planning. Freer and more flexible than official church union commissions, they can indeed perform a valuable reconnaissance function by exploring alternatives and testing their viability. But the interlocking of church union plans and bilateral unity discussions demands fuller development if it is to be effective. At present it is sporadic and fragmentary. The insights and experiences gained in one field deserve immediate transference to the other. It should be self-evident that, in areas where they co-exist, bilateral dialogue groups include representatives of church union commissions and vice versa.

Another requirement is the need for bilaterals to look beyond the limited scope of their own divisions, steadily to keep in mind the total scene, and to grapple creatively with the question of how their own partial conceptions of unity should be reshaped to serve the unity and the mission of the whole Church. Geared to overcoming some specific division, the bilateral concepts of unity themselves inevitably reflect the disunity of Christendom - a disunity exhibited in the conflicts and competition existing between different goal images. For their own sake, therefore, the bilateral unity discussions require a constant interchange with the multilateral ones.

A further observation of a different order is of a more serious nature. It concerns the rare appearance of any awareness that a unity of two separated communions, which over the centuries have developed in divergent directions, of necessity involves a sacrifice of self, a readiness to relinquish cherished practices and beliefs if this is necessary for the sake of growing together into the oneness of Christ's Church. There is little of radical self-questioning. It is rather assumed that any change in relationship and especially a future union must preserve intact what each partner regards as the historically distinctive - and not only the essential - features of its own life. The very appeal to apostolic continuity or to some inviolable confessional identity can serve as a shield against the challenges of change. But bilateral conversations are, in fact, no less dangerous than are church union negotiations in that they also present a choice between the security of established traditions and the vulnerable certainty of a renewing faith. The Unity statement of the New Delhi Assembly contains a stern reminder, not to be forgotten: "The achievement of unity will involve nothing less than a death and rebirth of many forms of church life as we have known them. We believe that nothing less costly can finally suffice."

6. Worship and Bilateral Dialogue

The centrality of worship in Christian life and consequently also in the search for unity is an inalienable ecumenical conviction - though perhaps honoured more with the lips than in acts. The Faith and Order World Conference at Montreal in 1963 named as one of the most important recent blessings of the ecumenical movement "... the current 'rediscovery' of Christian worship - of the twofold service to God and to the world which is expressed in the biblical term leitourgia - as the central and determinative act of the Church's life".[1] The mixture of darkness and light which the phrase "current rediscovery" suggests is no less true of the bilaterals.

The blessings and difficulties of ecumenical worship engage the bilateral conversations in four ways:

(a) Insofar as different types of worship hinder or facilitate the growing together of divided churches, they form a necessary object of bilateral inquiry. The dialogues have thus far concentrated attention on one cardinal issue in sacramental worship: eucharistic doctrine and the legitimacy of intercommunion. Non-sacramental worship, on the other hand, does not appear as a subject; it is no longer regarded as a matter of ecclesial division since the practice of sharing in prayer and devotion (communicatio in spiritualibus in contrast to communicatio in sacris) is accepted today virtually everywhere.

The subject of worship is further coming to the fore in another, broader context, namely, the increasing preoccupation with styles of spirituality and the ways in which these inform the Christian traditions and generate awareness of a unity of heart and mind deeper and more powerful than doctrinal, institutional and other divergences. The fecundity of such explorations is widely acknowledged but they are still in their beginnings - partly because of the diffuseness of the term "spirituality" which is used to denote such diverse things as the life of interiority, piety, religious otherworldliness, or a particular mode of apprehending the Gospel as, for example, the Franciscan spirituality. But insomuch as the term refers to a life of holiness and love, in the regenerating and unifying power of the Spirit, its specific affinity to devotion and worship is plain (cf. M-RC; M-RC/usa).

---

1. The Fourth World Conference on Faith and Order, Montreal 1963, p. 69.

(b) Worship is not merely a topic of bilateral inquiry, but its matrix. Because of their particular purpose, the dialogues are themselves an exemplary opportunity to express and to grow in spiritual ecumenism. For here the participants are invited to enter humbly and gratefully into other, perhaps uncongenial ways of worship, to share the gifts of openness and trust, of patience and forbearance. They are invited to rejoice in the unity mediated to them in the midst of their divisions by him who is the Mediator, and to surrender themselves to the larger purposes of God for the world.

The difficulties are familiar: the temptation to regard worship unconsciously as an habitual frame rather than as the sanctifying and integrating atmosphere of the day's deliberations; and the restrictions still preventing eucharistic sharing when certain churches are involved - to mention just two examples. The paucity of testimonies about the worship life of the groups is no doubt also caused by the difficulty of translating such experiences into cold print, especially in formal reports. But in this respect the American Baptist-Roman Catholic dialogue in the USA has shown the fruitfulness of a different mode of communicating the intimate experiences of a bilateral group, which deserves imitating. "Our desire", it states, "was to hold these serious academic conversations in a context of honest and open faithfulness and quite literally to engage in a trilogue with Christ our Lord as the unseen but ever present partner." Accordingly, it includes in its report a series of personal reflections of the participants, centering in the question "How I discovered Christ in our dialogue" (Growing in Understanding, pp. 7-16).

(c) Discussions around the implementation of bilateral findings usually centre in educational programmes, doctrinal reorientations and ecclesiastical policies. But if the Christian community is primarily a worshipping community, the working out of bilateral agreements in the devotional and liturgical life of the churches becomes a matter of high priority. It would involve such things as an open-minded appropriation of each other's spiritual and liturgical treasures and, on the other hand, an elimination of uncharitable allusions, not to speak of condemnations, which perpetuate ancient antagonisms. The matter is important not least for the reason that liturgies and rites are the point where the scandal of disunity most immediately touches the life of local congregations. The marriage service and the eucharistic communion of mixed couples are a particularly sensitive example.

(d) Finally, to narrow the focus on a question of special relevance to the bilaterals, how does worship influence ecumenical theologising? To be sure, worship is not a utilitarian exercise, but since it informs the whole embrace of Christian life, it is legitimate to ponder its influence on particular human activities, thus also on theological reflection. More than others, the Orthodox have retained the ancient knowledge of the interdependence of liturgy and doctrine; but a similar recovery is now occurring in Catholic and Protestant thought. The bilateral dialogues, too, are carried forward by the conviction that in the prayerful grappling with problems of truth, the Illuminator does indeed enlighten the mind, opening fresh perspectives on the impasses and leading through the pain of conflict into deeper comprehension of the mysteries of God and man. This is a general conviction. But there exist also exceptional moments of spiritual and intellectual candescence, when members of a group may be overwhelmed by a sense of the almost palpable presence and leadings of the Spirit - moments of discovery and creativity when the wholeness of truth is suddenly seen new.

The brief references to such experiences that can be found in bilateral documents reveal tantalisingly little about the mysterious interplay of spiritualities, worship practices, and the dynamics and methodology of theological reflection at the encounters. Following the example of the AB-RC/usa report, we are therefore instead presenting here a series of statements by persons deeply immersed in bilateral conversations. The contributors were left freedom to develop their thought as they saw fit within the scope of the designated subject, drawing also on their experience of multilateral conversations. In their diversity, these testimonies vividly illustrate the strengths as well as the weaknesses of the life of worship in the dialogue groups. They should certainly stimulate reflection - and serious self-examination.

Edmund Schlink - Lutheran; Professor Emeritus of Theology, University of Heidelberg, Federal Republic of Germany; veteran of Lutheran dialogues with Roman Catholics and with Russian Orthodox; long-time member of the WCC Commission on Faith and Order.

Worship as the Crisis for Ecumenical Dialogue. To gather in worship is the central event of the Church's life. It is here that God gathers men out of the world and sends them back into the world - to serve in the world. It is here that God serves men, speaking to them through his Word and making them partakers of Christ's body and blood. It is here that he bestows forgiveness, renewal and authority. At the same time, it is here too that believers serve God: confessing their sins, giving thanks to him, praying to him, and confessing Christ.

Anyone who has taken part in ecumenical dialogues knows how much these dialogues benefit from listening to God's Word and from praying together - and also from the intercessory presence during the eucharist, even if the order of the other or one's own church does not permit actual reception of the sacrament. If we participate with true devotion in the worshipping event, then it is inevitable that we are, through God's love and command, called into question, stripped of all our security, humbled and judged. As we allow ourselves to be judged, we are also opened up, freed and awakened. The attitude of self-defence is being transformed into one of an alert searching for the one truth, even in other forms of church life.

The influence of worship on ecumenical dialogue, however, cannot be restricted to the change of inner attitude in which the dialogue partners meet. No less important are the consequences which are to be drawn from the central position of worship for the methodology of ecumenical dialogue. If worship really is the centre of the Church's life, then this will undoubtedly affect the ways in which the different dogmatic and canonical statements of the divided churches are compared to one another, and how the differences are defined, evaluated and, if possible, eliminated. A paradigmatic significance must be accorded to the intention and character of what is expressed in worship. Reflection on the worshipping event must be included in the methodology of ecumenical dialogue. Worship is the crisis of our inner attitude as well as of our ecumenical deliberations. In general, people are not aware of this, but it is no less important. This may be explained further by some examples.

(1) As dogmatic statements, the free will of the sinner (as stressed by the Greek Church Fathers) and the enslaved will of the sinner (as stressed by the Augustinian-Reformation tradition) stand opposed. But in the worshipping act of confessing his sins, even the Orthodox Christian knows that he cannot free himself from his guilt. (2) The doctrinal statement of the Reformation tradition that "the Christian is both sinner and justified" ("simul iustus et peccator") is rejected by Roman Catholic dogmatics. However, as an existential expression, this same self-judgment of the believer is also found in Catholic piety. (3) In the eucharist, there are different modes of stating the relationship between the bread and the body of Christ, between the wine and the blood of Christ. But the differences between the ancient and the mediaeval-scholastic understandings of the transformation of the elements and especially the difference between the doctrines of transubstantiation and consubstantiation become less important when one reflects on the eucharist in the actual act of reception. For in this act of receiving, the attention is wholly focused on the gift of the body and blood of Christ, and not on the theoretical explanations of the relationships of body to bread and blood to wine. Christ's words at the eucharist are words that accompany his gift, and not theoretical explanations. Many more examples could be added. The dogmas have grown out of the elementary act of confessing the faith. But in the development of dogmas, particularly in the west, there has been a movement away from the characteristic structure of statements made in the context of worship. An attempt must be made to translate these dogmas back into their original matrix.

The same is true for statements of church law. It has its origin in the order of worship. In the first place, it is meant to serve the event of Divine Service: in its rules for admission to baptism and eucharist and thus for church membership; for the leadership of the church; for the administration of church property; for the relation of the local church to the regional and universal church, etc. In the history of church law, this origin has fallen more and more into the background and the individual legal rules have obtained a momentum of their own. For example, if one compares in the different churches the canonical and the dogmatic statements on the ministries, the apostolic succession, and the relation of bishop to presbyter, one finds immense differences; and an ecumenical dialogue which limits itself to a comparison of these statements will remain stuck in fruitless confrontations. These differences, however, appear in another light and can be largely eliminated, if one considers the service which is actually carried out through those ministries, and compares it to the service committed to the Apostles. Only if they are translated back into the elementary functions of church life, can canonical rules be compared in a fruitful dialogue. For those elementary functions have their centre in the worshipping community.

If worship thus is seen as the crisis for ecumenical dialogue, many dogmatic and canonical differences may well lose their antagonistic character. The divergent formulae become transparent for the same saving activity of God, which they are intended to express, and the certainty arises that the same gift of the body and the blood of Christ in the eucharist is received in another church just as in one's own. But where this certainty has taken hold, would it not be disobedient to refuse each other access to the Lord's Table? In this case, worship thus becomes the crisis also of church division.

What does crisis mean? To be called into question by God, to be judged by God. There are crises which heal and those which make things worse; crises which lead to life and those which lead to death. He who bows under God's judgment and admits that it is right, will be declared free by him and renewed. Whoever opposes the judgment of God and refuses to yield to its consequences, will perish under this judgment. God has passed many judgments on Christianity in this century, through which the churches have been put to shame, purified and enriched. In dialogue, they have found a unity in Christ which had been previously concealed. The more this happened, the more reluctant some became to draw the consequences for the union of their churches. Today a polarisation is visible between those people who withdraw into the enclosure of their own dogmatic and canonical tradition, and those who declare the union of the churches in faith and order as being unimportant, and escape into political activities. Both of these attitudes express a resignation which evades the grace of God's judgment.

William R. Cannon - Bishop of the United Methodist Church, Atlanta, Georgia, USA; co-chairman of the Joint Commission of the Roman Catholic Church and the World Methodist Council.

The great events of the history of salvation are presented variously in our different traditions. The interpretation of them is multiple and manifold, reflecting oftentimes our own denominational origins, as well as the vicissitudes of our history in separation from one another. Perhaps there are elements in the peculiarity of our worship that intensify the pain of division. There are likewise evidences of the richness of diversity, so that each denomination brings its own treasures into the storehouse of ecumenical devotion and piety and thereby enriches and enlarges the spirituality of Christendom.

Each day during our conversations in the Methodist-Roman Catholic Commission, the Roman Catholic members of the bilateral celebrated the Mass. The Methodist members were invited, not as participants, but as spectators. To be sure, we heard the liturgy in our own language, and there were certain responses in which we joined with our Roman Catholic brethren. But we did not partake of the elements. We did not communicate. Even when we were invited to read the lesson from the Scripture, it was in the capacity of a lay person, not a clergyman, and it was from the Old Testament, not the Gospels.

At first, I am sure, our attendance at the celebration of the eucharist was little more than an opportunity for studying what was, to most of us, an unusual pattern of public worship. Its frequency, a daily act, seemed odd, for with us it is an occasional rite, observed once a quarter, or, at most, once a month, and generally always on Sunday in congregational worship. Having been brought up on the stately language of *The Book of Common Prayer* (the Methodist communion service in English is based on Cranmer's), I found the new English liturgies of the Mass too colloquial and sparse to suit my liturgical taste. I still preferred the Latin of the past.

I invariably attended the service each day; and, as time went on, I began to appreciate it for what it was in itself, an act of adoration and praise to God for his inestimable gift of his Son, who died on the cross for our salvation, and a vivid and vital response of the faithful who, in communicating, take unto themselves all the benefits of his passion and feed on his most precious body and blood, thereby being renewed unto everlasting life. If Holy Communion could come to mean for Methodists what Mass does for Roman Catholics, a whole new dimension with its power and grace would be added to our experience of worship. This is one new treasure of theirs that I wish we Methodists could appropriate from the storehouse of ecumenical piety and devotion.

Yet at the same time, it was at the Mass that we felt, both Roman Catholics and Methodists, the pain of division. The more we worked together, the more we came to know and appreciate and even to love one another, the more eager we were to share together in the eucharist, to break bread and to pour wine, and to receive the elements from each other's hands, kneeling together at the same altar.

This sense of pain, more even than the joy of the fellowship we had increasingly attained, made us concentrate on the meaning of this sacrament and led to what may be a "breakthrough" to agreement on it. Methodists went so far as to say: "Christ in the fullness of his being, human and divine, is present in the eucharist; this presence does not depend on the experience of the communicant ... This is a distinctive mode of the presence of Christ; it is mediated through the sacred elements of bread and wine, which within the eucharist are efficacious signs of the body and blood of Christ." Roman Catholics, on the other hand, agreed that the eucharist is not "another sacrifice, adding something to Christ's once-for-all sacrifice", nor is it "a repetition of it". It is "the sacramental expression of the same sacrifice". This does not mean that Christ is still being sacrificed, which would wound Methodist sensitivity. Methodists are willing to go beyond Zwinglian memorialism and Roman Catholics stop short of perpetual reenactment of the sacrifice of Christ on the cross in the Mass. Likewise, they are prepared to reconsider the Aristotelianism of the Tridentine doctrine of transubstantiation, which is that "through the consecration of the bread and wine, a change takes place of the whole substance of bread into the body of Christ and wine into the substance of his blood". Their stress now is on the affirmation of Christ's presence and of the mysterious and radical change which takes place, not on explaining how the change takes place. In this, the Methodist and Roman Catholic positions are exactly the same.

Though the Mass is the heart of the Roman Catholic worship, this is not true of Holy Communion in the Methodist worship. Methodists especially stress the preaching of the word. "The difference between Christ's presence in the eucharist and his presence in the other means of grace is a difference only in the mode of his presence, for where Christ is present, he is present in his fullness." That is why Methodists in the bilateral have hesitated to conduct a service of Holy Communion for the Catholics to attend. It is not typical of their daily practice. They prefer a preaching service or prayer meeting.

Yet the spontaneous prayers offered by the Methodist participants have greatly impressed their Roman Catholic colleagues who lately have begun to pray extemporaneously themselves. They are taking seriously Vatican II's statement: "He is present in his word, since it is he himself who speaks when the Holy Scriptures are read in the church. He is present also when the church prays and sings." On exploration, we have found how close kin Roman Catholics and Methodists are in their spirituality, both of whom encourage warm personal piety, moral excellence, and a perfection of life in this world. John Wesley praised the Council of Trent for its doctrine of sanctification, and he contended it was the major mission of Methodism to spread scriptural holiness over the face of the earth.

Unfortunately, however, in our bilaterals, Roman Catholics and Methodists have not worshipped together in a joint service. Instead, they have been content to attend and observe one another's services. This, in my judgment, has been a mistake and should be presently corrected. We should join together in producing a joint service of worship. When it is the Mass, a Methodist participant ought to be invited to preach the sermon, and some of the hymns of Charles Wesley should be sung in the service by the entire congregation. When it is a Methodist service, without Holy Communion, a Roman Catholic should preach, and prayers should be read from the Missal. Some services could be just prayer meetings in which participants on both sides could offer to God out of their hearts spontaneous prayers.

The more we worship together, the deeper will be our understanding and our appreciation of one another. Methodist polity is already closer to that of Roman Catholicism than it is to any of the other Protestant denominations, including even the Anglican Church, at least in the Methodist churches that are episcopally governed. In worship we will come to see the common source of our theology as well. Doctrines are always less apparent than structure and government. But even here, Methodists are closer in many ways to the Latin traditions of the Middle Ages than they are to many of the teachings of the main-line churches of the Reformation. Joint worship services will make it convincingly real to both churches how much alike we really are, and how even our differences can serve useful and constructive ends.

Nikos A. Nissiotis - Greek Orthodox; Professor of Philosophy of Religion at the University of Athens, Greece; for many years Director of the Ecumenical Institute of the World Council of Churches, Bossey, near Geneva, a world centre of ecumenical dialogue and education.

A Worshipping Ecumenical Movement. The current bilateral dialogues presuppose the existence of the ecumenical movement in general and the fellowship of the World Council of Churches in particular, and are one of its finest fruits. Common worship on an interconfessional basis has, right from the beginning, been the foundation element of its spiritual cohesion and growth, although we have failed to appreciate properly the great fact that our worshipping together is the most self-evident event of our being together in the one ecumenical movement. We invoke the Spirit together, we place our whole being and action together under this invocation as one ecclesial communion. The fact of not being able to proceed to full eucharistic communion between the great historic churches should not prevent us from appreciating the existing fellowship in worship. For churches prohibited by canon law to participate in common worship, the present development signifies a dramatic breakthrough of the historical confessional patterns. It seems to me that all other elements of ecumenical development have to be regarded as centered around this worshipping interconfessional fellowship. Without this, the ecumenical movement is empty and groundless, lacking in convincing power and ecclesial reality.

Only those who have experienced this worshipping fellowship can appreciate its impact on their ecumenical attitude and theological reflection. At the Ecumenical Institute of Bossey, worship is the pivotal event of all the training courses, specialised consultations and ecumenical conferences. Here the reality of the one Church gathered around the one Christ in the one Spirit is revealed with convincing power, helping us to overcome our prejudices and divisions. This has nothing to do with a superficial irenicism, on the contrary. For worship brings out the peculiar characteristics of each tradition, and it is therefore, at first, a deeply frustrating experience to join in worship with others whose prayer language, symbolic gestures and religious customs are alien to us. But it is precisely in these frustrations, challenging our deepest convictions, that we are drawn together and begin to receive together the many-faceted grace of God. The unity of the Church is built by worship, will be achieved through worship, and will finally be perfected in worship.

Interconfessional Worship and Ecumenical Spirituality. Interconfessional worship is filling the gulf created by the past separation between two church traditions and actualised in their negotiations in view of a reunion. It urges those who participate in dialogues to engage in a strenuous effort of sharing in the most intimate experience of the partner. Here they appear before God as one heart and one mind, united by the same prayers of praise and thanksgiving, the same act of repentance, and the same intercession. And this is precisely the purpose of authentic dialogue.

But what still is largely missing is the personal transformation of the participants into members of one another, as members of the same Body of Christ. This is surely the crucial problem. What is lacking is a genuine ecumenical spirituality. By this I mean a real commitment to enter into a new relationship with the partner as joint member of the one historic Christian community. It means a thoroughgoing transformation of one's whole existence, a radical change of heart and mind including all the preconceived ideas about one's own identity and tradition as well as those of the partner.

Certainly, the measure of this mutual belongingness to the one Body, in the Spirit, depends on the concrete circumstances, the degree of mutual desire to approach each other closer, the burden of the historic past, the alienation from each other's churches for centuries, the doctrinal disagreements as expressed in polemic catechisms and confessional statements. All these elements block the road towards a practical ecumenical spirituality, and they can be overcome only by a renewed and renewing worshipping community. Ecumenical spirituality, achieved progressively by worship, would signify the following:

(a) a total surrender to God, allowing him to use those engaged in bilateral dialogues as instruments of building anew the one Body of Christ;

(b) a questioning of one's own fidelity to this oneness by a readiness to sincere self-criticism and reexamination;

(c) an attitude of repentance for having disregarded the value of the other's tradition, missionary witness and total commitment to Christ;

(d) a renewed understanding of and dedication to the task of bilateral dialogue as being of the essence of the Church, and not simply a new mode of ecumenical theology, and

(e) frankness in dealing with all the difficult topics of disagreement without labelling others as being "modern" or "progressive" or "revolutionary".

Bilateral Dialogue as a Continuous Act of Thanksgiving. This kind of dynamic spirituality is missing in today's interconfessional dialogue. For worship is not simply a repetition of some prayers familiar to both sides or the reading of a biblical text and a short meditation following, concluded by the Lord's Prayer. A bilateral dialogue, as also the whole ecumenical movement, is primarily an act of recognition, of reception of God's grace. Therefore, the dialogue in its very essence is a continuous act of thanksgiving. This is the paramount act reserved for men by God. Those engaged in these dialogues should be conscious of this fact of faith and loyalty to Christ. It is only then that rigid doctrinal and ecclesiastical oppositions begin to change and lose their exclusive character.

Let me refer again to my experience at Bossey, where we for many years have conducted an annual seminar at Easter time on the worship and theology of Eastern Orthodoxy for non-Orthodox students. It is impossible to convey the spirit of Orthodoxy merely by means of a theoretical presentation in the classroom. But I have observed time and time again how a liturgical theology grounded in the worship life of the Church, coupled with attendance at Orthodox parish services, can render the Orthodox position understandable and familiar and, in the end, make it a source of joy and spiritual enrichment. Another illustration of a different kind is the theological conversations since 1964 between representatives of Eastern Orthodox and Oriental Orthodox (Armenian, Coptic, Syrian) Churches. Though separated by doctrinal misunderstandings and political conflicts during centuries, they are almost identical in their liturgical life. Here too, it was by living together as one worshipping community that we were able to recover the common faith underlying our theological debates about the doctrine of the two natures or the two wills of Jesus Christ.

My conclusion, therefore, is that the bilateral dialogues, to be genuine, must be rooted in a praying and worshipping community. In this respect, the new charismatic communities (if they can overcome their anti-institutional mood), as well as the religious orders both in the east and west, have a beneficial role to play. The Taizé community is a pointer in this direction. I am convinced that it would be of great significance if, in the Orthodox world, we could offer one of our many historical places of monastical life as a centre for ecumenical dialogue by establishing an interconfessional monastic community, devoted to prayer for unity.

The ecumenical movement is today rightly giving such a prominent place to socio-political action against injustice and violation of human rights and to the liberation of oppressed people. Both for this reason and because of the steady expansion of bilateral and multilateral dialogues in the service of church unity, the movement must reappropriate the worship treasures of the churches and itself grow ever more into a worshipping community. This is one of the most urgent tasks of today's ecumenism.

Joseph C. McLelland - Presbyterian; Professor of Philosophy of Religion, McGill University, Montreal, Canada; member of several dialogue groups.

The question of the place of worship in bilateral dialogue on reflection strikes one as surprising, indeed disturbing. In my own experience of several dialogue groups, of which I will report on three, there is so little "worship" - or even discussion of its theory - that our question must be a good one. In the groups I have in mind, the Lutheran-Reformed hardly mentioned (or practised) it, the Orthodox-Reformed (now Lutheran-Reformed-Orthodox) leave it largely as an academic topic, while only the Roman Catholic-Protestant made it an integral and important part. Although the last is not quite "bilateral" in the same sense as the others, its very constitution might have led us to expect that it would be less happy with shared worship than they.

Bilateral dialogue tends to be the preserve of theologians, i.e. academics. Such people are a special breed, used to the thin air of abstraction and theory; even liturgy becomes theoretical for us. Thus it is not so surprising, perhaps, that two sets of representative academics should meet in the atmosphere of a seminar room rather than sanctuary. Moreover, there is a certain reserve about one's worshipping community which inhibits the sharing of its habits (and foibles) except after considerable trust in the other's sympathy is established. Again, the historical situation for bilaterals is one of divisive if not libellous propaganda and caricature. Against such polemical history we tend to start as historians and bridgebuilders, creating an intellectual climate for a better and more unitive experience. All this suggests some reasons why worship may engage us as a topic while awaiting developments before becoming more practical.

The three dialogues mentioned reflect this reasoning. Lutheran and Reformed, despite their family resemblances, met in a strong consciousness of historical conflict and spent much time in a sort of mutual apologetic. Our agenda was dictated by our 16th century fathers, with almost no attempt to allow contemporary issues to provide a way round that old battle-line. The modern movement of "liturgical renewal" for instance (or the presence of some Roman or Anglican liturgists!) might have shifted our perspective from what is a very pedantic type of debate to a more dynamic uncovering of common issues. Professor Jaroslav Pelikan, for one, has over the years called for a re-reading of church history as history of exegesis, showing how biblical texts functioned in the life and worship of the Christian community. Such a reading would help us recall the dialogue of our theologians away from certain bad effects of academia to a truer horizon against which to view history and hope.

Orthodox, of course, have a tradition in which theology is related to doxology in an intrinsic way; their presence as partners shifts the focus much further toward an alternative way of seeing. Yet just because of their commitment to liturgical theology they must engage their western colleagues in a theoretical discussion of the implications of the two ways of doing theology. Our Orthodox-Reformed dialogue, in my opinion, began to move toward a more realistic and authentic grappling with the root issue: how we both share in the continuity of Divine Service.

In both groups, the actual experience of common worship was almost non-existent. Prayers to open and close meetings seemed sufficient - a fact that reveals the "academic" mood we assumed. Only with Roman Catholic partners have I encountered a conviction that worship forms an integral part of dialogue. Now it must be admitted that the circumstances of the three groups were different, so that "terms of reference" dictated our stance to a high degree. The first two bilaterals were formal, official and representative of large areas, both geographical and ecclesiastical. The dialogue with the Romans was more local and informal, a response to our Québec situation as well as to the Vatican II mood. Moreover, some were members of Orders noted for their unity of theory and praxis. Our meetings often began with a liturgy jointly prepared. My own share in such preparation has proved a highlight in my experience; to plan, to choose texts and music in company with this "other" is an instant encounter with a different spirituality. "Spirituality" is what I take Christian dialogue to be investigating: a quest for whatever "unity in holiness" lurks behind those ancient debates and all that historical theology. There is a contrasting spirit, style and intention between "debate" and "dialogue". Our modern ecumenism is an attempt to overcome the debating stance of our fathers on behalf of a dialogical encounter which will allow the unity-in-diversity of people who claim the same ultimate spirituality. Our dialogue was able to move from common worship more easily towards the hard issues between us in contrast with the more academic approach noted above.

The lessons to be learned from this brief reflection may not be so obvious as I am suggesting, given both circumstances, terms of reference and personalities in the three groups. Yet I would judge that something like the contrast holds true for every bilateral dialogue. The old motto seems to hold, that the way to Christian truth lies through prayer, since our "truth" is not dead but living and personal: lex orandi lex credendi.

Father Yves Congar, O.P. - Paris, France; pioneer in Roman Catholic ecumenical theology and ecclesiology and prolific writer on the subject; ecumenical expert at the Second Vatican Council.

Common prayer has always been given its proper place in our meetings and conversations. From 1930 to 1939, for example, this was the case in our Whit weekend meetings with students, and in the meetings organised by L'Amitié (members of various teaching orders), and following 1945 in our regular meetings with Lutheran pastors and Orthodox theologians; in every case there was an expressed wish that there should be common prayer. Where the meeting lasted longer than one day, this took the form of mutual attendance at each other's eucharistic celebrations, and not simply a kind of evensong. In the years before 1939, the participants sometimes had problems about this. Some Catholics were reluctant to attend the Protestants' Lord's Supper, and I remember our Protestant friends one Saturday evening at La Rochedieu discussing among themselves whether they should attend our Mass the next morning, although their 16th century ancestors died for refusing to take part!

In the years from 1930 to 1939, the basic need was to get to know one another. We saw that it was not enough just to read papers, however authoritative, or to listen to others explaining their position and to discuss it with them; one only really knew them when one had seen and heard them praying, for it is only in God's presence and in living relationship with Him that a Christian can fully express himself and truly be himself. We realised already then that theology needs a doxological soil, a climate of prayer and praise, if it is to unfold, blossom and bear fruit. In our meetings and conversations, therefore, it was not just a matter of academic exercises. We met together as Christians in obedience to the Lord who prayed for the unity of all who believe in him. It is <u>he</u> who reunites us. And when the purpose of dialogue is not simply to exchange information and to reach theoretical conclusions, but to build up our unity in Christ, discussion alone is not enough; we must also pray together.

This must not necessarily be in the context of a eucharistic celebration. On the Catholic side, there are inflationary tendencies so far as the eucharist is concerned. Certainly, the eucharist is the supreme act which the Church performs and which itself creates the Church; and this is why what is improperly called "intercommunion" or "intercelebration" is impossible, since it would be to profess we are the same Church. This impossibility, of course, does not exhaust the question, although we do not have to go into it here. Moreover, it is not the bilateral conversations at an official level which are guilty of irregularities in this matter nor is it Christians who have seriously pondered the right questions. But seen from the perspective of the total mystery of the Church, ecumenism, while tending towards its full realisation in accord with God's design, is still in a sense at the catechumenal stage, just as we speak of a "liturgy of the catechumens" preceding the "liturgy of the faithful" (i.e. the sacramental celebration) with which it is linked by the Credo.

There are in France a great many more or less informal ecumenical groups, others which are more structured, and even regular meetings between Catholic bishops and experts on the one side and pastors or Orthodox priests and theologians on the other. We always pray together, generally in the context of a liturgy of the Word - or of the Taizé office, or of the service of Hours, or of Vespers. Sometimes we begin with a twenty minute period of recollection and meditation on God's Word: a passage is read, silent meditation ensues, followed by a formal concluding act; sometimes we would recite a few psalms antiphonally at the end of the meeting.

As we go back to the Psalms and other Scripture passages, we realise the extent to which the Bible really is our common treasure. If there is a celebration of the eucharist, some role is found in it for the minister or members of the other communion, care being taken of course to respect the discipline of each church, even if it means finding solutions which are admittedly unsatisfactory. Yet by doing this, the existence of a real ministry among the others is recognised. Catholics can and do do this for their Protestant brothers while at the same time avoiding any equation of pastor and priest, which in any case Protestants do not ask of them.

Of the regular bilateral dialogue groups, the one which has met most regularly is the Groupe de Dombes - named after the Cistercian monastery where it has held most of its meetings - which started in 1937 and has continued to the present. The Groupe's working method was initially inspired by the Abbé Paul Couturier. The hallmark of their method is precisely the integration of theological discussion and prayer, and the fecundity of the Groupe is due to this interaction. When you have prayed together, your discussion takes on a new quality. You are changed by prayer. More than once at the Dombes meetings an impasse has been reached in the discussion, but then after we have prayed together again a way forward has opened up. A level is attained at which the spirit of self-justification and rivalry disappears. One of the dangers of intellectual work, and even more of engaging in theological dialogue, is that we become trapped in an attitude of self-assertion. Prayer delivers us from this. For here a third factor, beyond myself and the other, a factor which is Reality and not pure Idea and which is shared by us both, is disclosing possibilities which we had failed to perceive. Experience teaches us even at a purely human level that it is humility which makes it possible for us to be true and to have access to the truth, especially to that portion of the truth seen by others. As we dispose ourselves humbly in God's presence and before others, we prepare ourselves to receive the illumination and secret anointing of one and the same Holy Spirit. Theologians like to affirm that this Spirit is the same in Christ as in his members: it is he who establishes the unity of the body. And it is also in him that all glory is rendered back to the Father: _in unitate Spiritus Sancti_. Doxology is at the beginning and at the end of all striving for unity. It also accompanies it at every stage of the way.

VI

BILATERAL CONVERSATIONS – PROBLEMS AND POSSIBILITIES[1]

Introduction

The fact that we can register today a large number of bilateral conversations on different levels, with different aims and methods and topics, is a new factor on the ecumenical scene. Multilateral and bilateral forms of encounter between separated churches have, of course, co-existed since the beginning of the ecumenical movement. The agreement on full communion between Anglican and Old Catholic Churches in 1931 was a result of such bilateral conversations. There are many other examples. The co-existence of these two forms can also be seen in union negotiations.

For the past twenty-five years, the founding of the World Council of Churches and the extension of the work of Faith and Order, the rapid growth of local, national and regional councils of churches, and the multiplying of church union negotiations have clearly brought about a predominance of multilateral forms of dialogue and collaboration

It is undoubtedly the official entry of the Roman Catholic Church into the ecumenical movement since Vatican II that has been the main reason for the current proliferation of bilateral contacts. This may be explained in part by the fact that the Roman Catholic Church is not yet a member of the World Council of Churches and is only slowly entering into multilateral forms of ecumenical encounter. Other possible explanations are the structure of the Roman Catholic Church and its theological patterns of encounter, and a certain disappointment or dissatisfaction with the results of multilateral theological conversations on the part of other churches.

The new bilateral dialogues, especially at the world level, have enhanced the significance and weight of world confessional families They raise, therefore, not only the question of the relationship be-

1. Cf. the instructive discussions in John Deschner, "Developments in the Field of Church Unity", The Ecumenical Review XXIV, 4, 1972, 447-58 and Peter Hocken, "Bilateral or Multilateral? A Pressing Ecumenical Problem for the Roman Catholic Church", One in Christ VI, 4, 1970, 496-524.

tween bilateral and multilateral forms of encounter, but also the larger question of the relationship between the World Council of Churches and the confessional families.

Two presuppositions should be made clear right at the beginning. There is and can be no question of "either - or" with regard to bilateral and multilateral dialogues. Secondly, there is only one ecumenical movement, which requires a proper coordination, mutual correction and enrichment of different forms of encounter. The ecumenical movement is a dynamic and comprehensive movement in history. It cannot be tied down to just one method. These two presuppositions indicate already the problem to be considered, which may require a rethinking of the content, methods and structures of ecumenical dialogue and strategy, also within the work of Faith and Order.

Problems of Conversations at Multiple Levels

Theological conversations on a world level are generally criticised for not having sufficient relevance for the actual situations and interrelations of the churches on regional, national and local levels. This is not only a matter of communication and information. At least two other questions of a more basic nature are involved. Firstly, are there not, it is argued, theological questions which, though in principle universal, nevertheless are decisively shaped by the context (historical, religious, cultural) in which the churches live and encounter one another in a given situation? It often seems to be very difficult, therefore, to apply to these particular situations common approaches or agreements reached in worldwide conversations. Secondly, can theological conversations really be carried out vicariously and representatively for others? Are not a dialogue process and its results relevant only for those who have themselves shared in this dialogue - which is not merely an exchange of ideas, but also a personal experience? No satisfactory answers are yet in sight. Sometimes the dialogue levels function in fruitful interaction, in other instances they give the impression of being unrelated or even working at cross-purposes. Some examples may illustrate how complex the present situation in reality is.

The aims, topics and eventual impact of conversations at different levels depend, of course, on a number of factors, but prominent among these is the constitutional and functional structure of the sponsoring bodies. A basic difference appears here between supranational churches and, on the other hand, more or less loosely organised associations or families of autonomous churches.

Thus the Roman Catholic Church possesses possibilities of orchestrating its conversations at different levels in a manner not available to any other world Christian body. This remains true even under the post-Vatican II trend of a devolution of responsibilities to national hierarchies, although some of the national dialogues, notably in the USA, display an independence of initiative which does not shrink from pioneering proposals and resulting tensions. Moreover, thanks to its communications system, the Roman Catholic Church is able to inform and sound out bishops and diocesan agencies around the world about bilateral documents and thus to take into account a broad volume of opinion in shaping its attitudes.

Sharing a common apostolic tradition, the Orthodox Churches likewise attach great importance to a united stance. Its realisation, however, is proving to be a laborious and time-consuming process. Pan-Orthodox commissions have been appointed to conduct official conversations with three other communions, but major emphasis rests at present on dialogues pursued by individual churches on national or bi-national basis.

Among the other world families of churches, the Anglican Communion has been the most successful in developing a global network of national dialogues (with Roman Catholic partners) and encouraging a fruitful cross-fertilisation between the various levels. The national groups fulfill a variety of functions - commenting on the international reports, interpreting and applying them to the local churches, producing sectional papers for incorporating in the international documents, and sometimes pursuing independent projects related to their own situation.

Continental and other regional types of dialogue are based on the assumption that the churches living in a particular geographical or cultural area, because of this fact, possess certain common traits which make it natural and profitable for them to cultivate closer fellowship. Such continental dialogues have reached their fullest flowering in North America; some of these have indeed advanced well ahead of their international counterparts. The Leuenberg Agreement among Reformation Churches in Europe represents again a different type of regional dialogue. It is interesting to note in passing that, while this agreement has been hailed by some as a model of wide applicability, Lutheran and Reformed leaders in North America are instead seeking other solutions because of their vastly different religious and cultural situations. It is no longer accepted that what is good for Europe theologically and ecumenically is good also for the world, on the contrary. Among the other continents, only Latin America shows the beginnings of regional bilaterals.

These rapid glimpses of the problems involved in multi-level dialogues do not allow any firm conclusions, at most some pointers. As now a growing number of bilaterals are entering the phase of implementation, there will be an increased emphasis on national levels where the actual decision-making takes place. It can further be expected that the progressive regionalisation of the ecumenical movement, evidenced in the growth of continent-wide Conferences of Churches, will give a push to regional dialogues, no doubt mostly multilateral but also bilateral. But these trends do not and must not involve a downgrading of worldwide conversations. The more limited encounters are often in danger of a provincialism which may occupy itself too exclusively with domestic problems and partial solutions, thereby losing sight of the universal dimension of the Christian faith and the worldwide community of the Christian Church. And the world level conversations, if properly based and conducted, serve as a reminder and a sign of this wider dimension. Yet if they are to be an "effectual sign", their relation to the encounters on the other levels needs to be reconsidered and forms and structures developed which will enable a more effective inter-communication and mutual enrichment and reinforcement.

An Appraisal

There are two factors which go a long way to explaining why certain communions participate very actively in bilateral conversations while others are almost absent, at least on the world level: (a) bilateral conversations are easier to initiate and to conduct for those communions which are well organised at world, regional and national levels; (b) bilateral conversations are most congenial to those communions which possess a strong tradition of dogmatic theology, doctrinal decisions and formularies and/or a well structured and theologically articulated liturgical tradition. This holds true at least for the conversations as now generally conceived. But different types are likely to emerge with the increasing participation of Disciples, Pentecostals, and kindred traditions, favouring more experiential ways of expressing their faith and testing the spirits.

The advantages of these two factors for conducting bilateral dialogues will be taken up in the following paragraphs. But first a serious disadvantage should be mentioned: a considerable section of world Christianity is not participating in bilateral conversations. As a result these are deprived of many contributions which the less well organised and less doctrinally or liturgically orientated communions could make to the common search for truth and renewal, mission and unity. By contrast, these communions are making their contribution in the multilateral conversations. The question arises, therefore, as to how multilateral conversations may be more effectively related to bilateral ones so as to remedy this disadvantage.

Bilateral conversations have the advantage of filling a gap in the network of ecumenical relations. There are churches which are, as a result of historical developments, majority churches in a particular country. They do not live in a pluralistic interdenominational situation. This holds true for a number of Roman Catholic, Orthodox and Lutheran churches. Bilateral conversations on a world or international level provide an occasion for these churches to experience closer ecumenical contacts and relations.

There are specific controversial questions and even mutual condemnations which were and still are major dividing factors between two communions. Bilateral conversations have the advantage that they can select these particular questions for their agenda and deal with them in a precise and detailed manner. Moreover, in local situations where churches are locked in an emotion-filled conflict, their world confessional families may significantly contribute to a solution by setting the conflict in a worldwide context.

Because the area of topics is limited and only two partners with their particular traditions are involved, bilateral conversations are more likely than multilateral ones to produce agreements and concrete recommendations.

Although the delegations appointed for bilateral conversations possess the official authorisation of their churches or world communions they have no authority in themselves. Therefore, bilateral conversations cannot arrive at conclusions or decisions which are as such binding for the churches. The same holds true of the world confessional families. Nevertheless, it seems clear that bilateral conversations under the auspices of world confessional families possess a greater weight and urgency for the churches involved than do others. Because of the official appointment of the dialogue groups, their terms of reference, and their limited task of representing one tradition in relation to another, it is more likely that the individual churches will respond favourably to the results and recommendations of such a conversation.

The ecumenical theological dialogue has gone beyond the phase of comparative ecclesiology and has become a common search for truth which is christocentric in its basic approach. There might be a danger, however, that in a bilateral conversation, being a confrontation between two church traditions, the approach tends to become again predominantly comparative and ecclesiocentric.

In most instances, the encounters concentrate on divisive issues inherited from the past. Accordingly, some doctrinal issues receive much attention while other and more contemporary problems which constitute a challenge to all the churches today are only rarely taken up explicitly. The consequent danger of being too backward-looking is nevertheless in many bilateral encounters avoided by the fact that these encounters are to a high degree conditioned by the general theological thinking of today and by the problems which are confronting all the churches in the contemporary world. It is precisely because of these common problems and tasks that the effort is undertaken to overcome past divisions.

The fact that one particular church or confessional family is engaged in concurrent conversations with several other traditions raises the question of self-identity. Are the results of discussions, for example, on the eucharist with these different partners contradictory or are they different but not mutually exclusive? In other words, is a church presenting differing faces to different partners? This danger can only be avoided by a correlation of the dialogues in which a confessional family is involved, by certain persons being associated with more than one dialogue group, and by the participation of observers from other confessions.

The long history of multilateral discussions, especially within the Faith and Order Movement, has had definite effects on general theological and ecumenical thinking. Suitable methods of dialogue were tried out; theological problems were clarified and some commonly accepted terminologies established; important convergences were hammered out in understanding the faith and witness, the life and structures of the Church. The same holds true of the multilateral developments in interchurch cooperation. It hardly needs to be emphasised that bilateral conversations cannot ignore the changes in the theological and ecumenical climate which have been brought about by this history of multilateral encounter. And evidence is not lacking that the conversations have, in fact, derived ample benefit from the work of, for instance, Faith and Order. But the promising exchange already taking place merely gives added weight to the question of how this wider dimension of multilateral discussions and activities can be made even more fruitful for bilateral conversations.

VII

CONCLUDING REFLECTIONS

The preceding section has made an attempt to assess the values and limitations of the bilaterals, relating them to the more widely known movement of multilateral discussions. In a summary overview, we shall now gather up a number of elements germane to the bilaterals, which have been touched upon previously in varying contexts: significant discoveries and trends in ecumenical understanding and the reasons for them, common problems which require deeper penetration, and steps ahead.

Why this Upsurge Now?

The bilateral conversations around the world form a movement of theological exploration and discovery which indeed has yielded truly remarkable results. The advances and convergences that are taking place appear all the more striking when one considers the fact that in several instances they are bridging agelong chasms within Christendom, and that all this has taken place within the short span of a few years. It is a breakthrough in understanding and recognising the common faith that poses an intriguing question: why did this not happen generations ago? Why now? The basic answer is, of course, a reference to the mysterious workings of the Spirit "which bloweth where it listeth". Or to quote St. Paul, "the fullness of time is come". At the level of observable human affairs, there is a variety of factors that can be observed; only three of them will be noted here since their importance is often overlooked or at least inadequately appreciated.

The first factor is the decisional premise, the element of daring choice, in all ecumenical theologising. It is frequently acknowledged by participants in dialogue that no advance would have been achieved had it not been for the new climate of mutual trust and acceptance and the earnest desire to go forward together which pervaded the deliberations. Theological and doctrinal arguments for and against a particular position, which a generation ago were held to be unshakeable, are now suddenly regarded as negotiable or quietly set aside as invalid. Part of the reason for this is undoubteldy an increasing theological sophistication, especially the recognition of the historical and eschatological character of Christianity. But it is no less clear that these unexpected and unprecedented convergences must be ascribed also to proleptic thrusts of hope, leading to deliberate adoption of new approaches which then in turn induce new theological structures and ways of reasoning. If this is correct, it is a matter which deserves closest attention in the further development of the dialogue movement - above all in its motivating context of spirituality and worship.

A second factor is the historical and ecological conditioning of the perception and articulation of Christian truth. Confessional traditions, with their characteristic images of self and of others, originated at particular historical moments and in particular cultural milieus which have inescapably shaped their mental make-up and become so much a part of their self-understanding that it requires extraordinary efforts of imagination and discrimination for an observer to distinguish between essentials and accidentals in the faith of a church. But transplantation to a different habitat or drastic changes in the symbiotic society of the kind which are occurring today, generate revealing changes in confessional style and outlook; cultural idiosyncracies are modified or stripped off and replaced by new ones; essentials become more easily recognisable. As a result, a dialogue between two traditions holds fresh promises of success when their conversation is carried out on a larger cultural scene than before or transposed to an entirely different context. The Lutheran-Reformed Leuenberg conversations, expanded to the continental scale of Europe, and the Eastern Orthodox-Reformed dialogue in North America are eloquent instances. The transformation of confessional traditions "made in Europe" when implanted in Asia or Africa furnishes, of course, even more telling examples; unfortunately, these churches are still virtually "absent partners" in the worldwide bilateral dialogues.

A third factor to be mentioned here is the liberating and enabling influence of pioneering ecumenical events, whether great or small. The point has evidently a much wider bearing than the bilateral dialogues, but it is relevant in this field also. It is difficult, for example, to overestimate the radiance throughout Christendom of a man like John XXIII or of the ferment of the Second Vatican Council, and it is no historical accident that the present bilateral movement took its early beginnings at the time of the Council. The bilaterals themselves display a similar facilitating effect. Once a dialogue group has achieved a significant breakthrough, it has thereby vicariously paved the way for others to follow after and to push on further. Even if consensus statements only in comparatively rare cases obtain explicit ecclesiastical endorsement, the very fact that responsible spokesmen are speaking with one voice on such hitherto divisive matters as eucharist and ministry would suggest to church members that such convergent opinions henceforth may at least represent a permissible option - thereby opening wider doors for ecumenical experimentation and fellowship. The same holds true of the methodological advances made. In the bilaterals, ways of approaching and resolving disputed issues have been worked out and tested, which can serve as helpful models for other subjects and other groups. The trigger effect produces a cumulative impact.

Outstanding Agreements

The following is a list of significant agreements - obviously varying in substance and precision - which have been achieved in the conversations thus far and been submitted to the respective ecclesiastical authorities:

(a) Agreements concerning the relationship of Gospel, Scripture and Tradition (A-L II; A-L/usa I; A-RC II; L-R/usa I; L-R-U/eur Leuenberg; L-RC I; L-RC/usa I; R-RC/usa III).

(b) Agreements on eucharistic doctrine (A-L; A-L/usa; A-RC III; A-RC/scot; A-RC/usa IV; L-R/usa II; L-R-U/eur Leuenberg; L-RC/usa V; M-RC II; OC-RC/eur; O-RC/usa IV; R-RC IV).

(c) Full intercommunion (L-R/usa IV; L-R-U/eur Leuenberg).

(d) Partial intercommunion under consideration (A-L; A-L/usa VI; A-RC III; A-RC/saf; A-RC/usa V; L-R/usa; L-RC; L-RC/usa XI; R-RC/usa).

(e) Agreements on the nature of the ministry and/or full or partial mutual recognition of ministries (A-L; A-L/usa IV; A-RC V; A-RC/usa III; L-R/usa IV; L-R-U/eur Leuenberg; L-RC III; L-RC/usa XI).

(f) Discovery of profound affinities in spirituality and concern with sanctification (M-RC I; M-RC/usa II-III).

(g) Full or qualified mutual recognition as churches (A-L IV; A-L/usa VI; L-R/usa IV).

(h) Agreement on "church fellowship" (full altar and pulpit fellowship) on the basis of a common understanding of the Gospel, invalidation of the mutual condemnations of the sixteenth century, and mutual recognition as Church of Christ (L-R-U/eur Leuenberg).

These breakthroughs are of more than intrinsic significance. They mark forward steps which increase the sweep and momentum of the search for unity, and provide methods and models for resolving other similar problems that lie ahead. Whatever there may have been of uncertainty and doubt about the outcome, there resounds in the bilateral reports a confident hope. Sometimes it is expressed explicitly as, for instance, in the report of the Anglican-Roman Catholic international commission, which declares, referring to its agreement on eucharistic doctrine: "... we are convinced that if there are any remaining points of disagreement they can be resolved on the principles here established" (no. 12).

Evidently, to measure exactly the import and range of those breakthroughs would require an extensive commentary on the explorations and debates which have preceded the consensus, the obstacles which had to be surmounted, and the value which the participants themselves attach to their findings. Documentary material is lacking for such an analysis; and apart from this, the real test of the value of these convergences will anyway be their reception in the churches and the degree to which they prove capable of stimulating a genuine change of attitude.

Shifts in Self-Understanding

There exists, however, another way of assessing these findings and that is by asking: What new thrusts are discernible? What shifts of emphasis are here being proposed in the internal balance of a communion and in its interrelationships with other communions? Such an assessment, however tentative, would help the churches and the world confessional families to clarify their own stance and, at the same time, obtain a clearer picture of the evolving stance of their partners. The need for such a stock-taking has been expressed repeatedly. The critical review of the Roman Catholic conversations in the USA, sponsored by the Catholic Theological Society of America, is a response to this need, although it does not trace a composite picture of the Roman Catholic position in those conversations. The Ecumenical Research Institute of the Lutheran World Federation in Strasbourg is planning a comprehensive study of the Lutheran identity in ecumenical dialogues.

But before attempting such a sketch, it will be useful to make a rough classification of different kinds of change:

(a) A dialogue may simply adopt a change that has already occurred or is occurring in the theological climate of the churches concerned.

(b) It may draw inferences from previous shifts of orientation or emphasis, accenting certain trends or projecting new conclusions based on a combination of opinions accepted by theological and/or ecclesiastical authorities. The "exegesis" of statements from Vatican II or from assemblies of world communions in support of extended recognition of other communions is an evident example.

(c) The theological and ecclesiastical spectrum of a church embraces a plurality of options. By espousing one or more of these, a bilateral statement sets new priorities among the options and thereby indicates a reorientation of thought. In this manner new value scales are suggested among the prevailing kinds of options - that is, among the differing beliefs and practices which a communion regards as preferred, legitimate, tolerable, irregular, illicit, etc.

(d) In rare cases, a dialogue may set forth a position which conspicuously extends the hitherto accepted range of options and thus can be termed a genuine breakthrough. As an example one might suggest the question addressed by the Roman Catholic members of the L-RC/usa commission to their own authorities, "whether the ecumenical urgency flowing from Christ's will for unity may not dictate that the Roman Catholic church recognize the validity of the Lutheran ministry", or the recent statement by the same commission concerning a renewed and restructured papacy.

The following enumeration of apparent shifts in self-understanding is based on the published dialogue reports. They must not be taken, therefore, as an indication of the official teachings and policies of the communions concerned, nor do they allow drawing a complete profile since the bilaterals focus on selected divisive issues. The analysis is perforce limited to those communions and confessional families whose profile appears with sufficient clarity and precision in the reports to permit such an attempt.

Anglican Trends

The Church and the Churches:

- more positive and appreciative recognition of the presence of the Church of Christ also in Protestant communions
- the principle of comprehensiveness is being interpreted in a manner which is at once firmer and more relaxed than earlier, safeguarding against two opposite perils: an unprincipled, diffuse ecclesiology and a rigid, pre-ecumenical spirit in applying the tests of the Lambeth Quadrilateral
- greater readiness to enter into and give support to church union efforts.

Apostolic Succession:

- recognition that the stream of apostolic tradition is wider, richer, and more diversified than previously acknowledged
- it is admitted, for example, that there may exist complementary signs of apostolicity, one compensating, as it were, for the deficiency or lack of one other
- in contrast to onesided earlier teachings, it is fully recognised that apostolicity does not merely signify unbroken continuity with the apostolic age, but, as much, a dynamic forward-looking mission to all men of every new age.

The Threefold Ministry and the Historic Episcopate:

- the fluidity and multiformity of ministries in the apostolic and post-apostolic periods, and the crystallisation of the threefold order only in the second half of the second century, are accepted findings of historical scholarship. There is, moreover, an increased readiness to face the doctrinal consequences of this insight into the historical process
- consequently, the absence of apostolic succession in the form of the historic episcopate does no longer preclude recognition of the ecclesial character and efficacious ministry of certain non-episcopal churches. However, the historic episcopate would be regarded as essential to the fulness of the reunited Church of the future.

Ministry:

- the understanding of the Church as a ministering community, with a plurality of services and gifts, is reflected in a re-evaluation of the place and role of the laity in the total life of the Church.

The Eucharist:

- substantial agreement on the eucharistic faith has been reached with the Roman Catholics on the one hand and with the Lutherans on the other. Anglicans are acknowledging that the point of the Roman Catholic doctrine of transubstantiation is not to define the "how" but rather to assert the reality of the mysterious change taking place, and that on the other side the Lutheran celebration of the sacrament is valid
- eucharistic sharing as means or goal of unity is dismissed as a false alternative in favour of a different kind of question: "Are we able mutually to affirm the presence of the Gospel and apostolicity in our respective communions sufficiently to agree that the renewal of the Church is more likely to come in communion with one another than out of communion with one another?" On the basis of an affirmative answer,it is recommended to extend the practice of intercommunion, including not only individual communicants in special circumstances, or at ecumenical gatherings, but also between closely related local congregations (A-L/usa, Progress Report, pp. 13-23).

Lutheran-Reformed Trends (the close parallel of Lutheran and Reformed trends makes it natural to treat them together)

General Shifts in Theological Outlook:

- acceptance of the thoroughgoing historical character of the Church
- acceptance of a legitimate pluriformity in all areas of church life, including doctrinal expression and church order
- the relation of consensus de doctrina and koinonia is no longer seen as a one-way process, but as a genuine interaction; formulation and promulgation of doctrine is often the result of experienced renewal and fellowship

in the Church
- the saving act of God in Christ is too rich and many-sided to be fully comprehended in any single formula, such as "justification by faith".

The Church and the Churches:
- greater readiness to recognise the Church of Christ in other churches even if they do not articulate their faith in confessional formularies; such statements do not belong among the notes of the Church
- the terms "rightly" and "duly" in the definition of the criteria of the Church in the Augsburg Confession, Art. VII, are interpreted in a broader, biblical rather than a restrictive, confessional sense.

Apostolicity:
- reappreciation of the historic episcopate as a valuable, even desirable, symbol and instrument of apostolic continuity; provided it is not made into a condition for ecclesial fellowship.

Ministry:
- a reappraisal of the purpose and function of order in the Church, manifest on the Lutheran side in a recovery of the theological dignity of church order, and on the Reformed side in a recognition that the "Presbyterian" type of order possesses no exclusive biblical warranty
- a consideration of a reinterpreted and restructured papacy as a symbol and instrument of the universal Church.

Eucharist:
- substantial agreement on eucharistic doctrine (real presence and sacrifice) with each other and with Anglicans, Orthodox and Roman Catholics.

Church and World:
- recognition that the conventional contrapositing of the doctrine of the "two realms" and the affirmation of the universal Lordship of Jesus Christ (a) is largely a pseudo-problem, (b) cuts across the Lutheran-Reformed difference, and consequently is not a church-dividing issue.

Roman Catholic Trends

General Shifts in Theological Outlook:

- increasing recognition of the involvement of the Church in the changes of history
- increasing acceptance of a certain plurality of "forms" of church life within the essential unity
- exploration of the notions of a hierarchy of truths and of development and pluriformity of doctrine.

The Church and the Churches:

- a recovery of the vision of the Church as mysterion and as a community of the Spirit (koinonia), the people of God, counterbalancing monolithic and excessively institutional and hierarchical conceptions
- re-evaluation of the local church (in the sense of diocesan and regional church), coupled with a trend towards legislative and administrative decentralisation and a fresh emphasis on episcopal collegiality expressed for example in the Synod of bishops; acceptance of the legitimacy of different types of church life
- no longer a simple identification of the Church of Christ and the Roman Catholic Church ("subsists in")
- earlier theories of the relationship of the Roman Catholic Church and other Christian communities are being replaced by a recognition of their ecclesial character, with the difference being one of degrees of fulness, and, accordingly, degrees of proximity to the Roman Catholic Church (from "partial" to "almost total" communion)
- a restoration of relations of brotherhood between the Roman Catholic Church and the Orthodox Churches, based on the rediscovery of the sacramental communion existing among them.

Ministries:

- readiness to look at Anglican and Lutheran ministries as true, though partial, apostolic ministries
- dialogue on ministry and on eucharist has proved possible and fruitful in advance of explicit reference to the problem of primacy.

Eucharist:

- convergences of varying weight and substance on eucharistic faith (especially the real presence and sacrifice) with Anglicans, Lutherans, Methodists and Reformed
- the vocabulary of transubstantiation claims not to define the "how" but to affirm, in terms of a specific tradition of teaching, the reality of the mysterious change taking place
- more liberal Roman Catholic dispositions regarding sacramental reciprocity with the Orthodox and a more liberal access to the Roman Catholic eucharist, in defined circumstances, for non-Roman Catholics of the western tradition.

Partners in Asymmetry

When the Vatican II Decree on Ecumenism spoke of coming dialogues "on equal footing" (par cum pari), many Protestants greeted this as a historic acknowledgement of the ecclesial equality of separated churches, not realising that the principle referred primarily to a ground rule of ecumenical ethics and etiquette without which no dialogue would thrive. The ground rule is indispensable precisely because of the dissimilarity of the partners. And it is perhaps particularly indispensable and difficult to observe in the bilaterals as here the rugged individualities and peculiarities of the churches appear in sharper relief than in multilateral deliberations with their interest in the universals of a problem rather than in the physiognomy of individual participants. Over the years, the bilaterals have acquired a rich fund of experience concerning the asymmetrical relationships between churches and the unexpected misunderstandings and frustrations which they can provoke. It is a matter that deserves more serious attention than it receives for it has more than once been the unnoticed stumbling-block bringing an effort at rapprochement to the verge of defeat.

The following examples illustrate the point:

- the separation between the Eastern and Western parts of Christendom, manifest in differing ways of grasping the mysteries of God, of understanding the Church, and of reflecting and arguing theologically, which still makes it well-nigh impossible for them to entertain a real dialogue instead of merely pursuing parallel monologues

- the peculiar psychological and theological inhibitions that hamper churches repudiating infallibility, as they engage in dialogue with a church claiming the prerogative of infallibility - and vice versa no less
- the babylonian confusion of theological and confessional languages, which, by associating different meanings with the same term, perversely thwarts the efforts to fix religious equivalences and to recover the Pentecostal miracle of mutual understanding
- the wide differences in conceiving the status of a dialogue and its findings and likewise in the procedures of ecclesiastical reception.

Identity and Change

Whom do the participants in a bilateral dialogue represent? What should they represent? And more basically, what are the criteria, the normative givens, that serve to give balance and determinative shape to the explorations? The complexity of the problem appears with particular acuity in the bilaterals. They are by definition constituted by two partners, each of whom is supposed to be a definable entity; and this requirement is heightened by the official character of the conversations with its assumption that the participants somehow are representative spokesmen. Still more important than the ecclesiastical representativeness of the participants is that of their doctrinal and ecclesial posture. For here the question arises of what a communion or world confessional family ultimately stands for: its foundations of faith and the norm structure which, ideally and in fact, inspires and directs its life.

The question about representativeness, however, is but one aspect of a whole cluster of problems that are coming to the fore today, namely, the concern with identity. The intermingling of Christian traditions as a result of both the ecumenical movement and rising population mobility, the acceptance of diversity in expressing the faith, group psychology and sociology of institutions - these are some general factors that have brought a sharper awareness of the moving dynamics of ecclesial and confessional identities. The matter affects the bilaterals at two points. Whenever a communion is engaged in dialogue with different partners, the question naturally arises whether or not it maintains an identical stance or presents dissimilar self-images in differing contexts. And the question is sharpened by the transformations which the partners are undergoing in the process, and by a realisation of the still greater changes to come, which a consummation of ecclesial fellowship would entail. The situation points up several problems that demand clarification.

(a) An interchurch dialogue does not only stimulate greater openness and a sharing of the gifts of the Spirit. It does also have the opposite effect: a heightened self-awareness and self-assertiveness blocking the impulses towards a wider fellowship. The latter reaction is often made more intractable by the assumption that an identity forms a consistent, indissoluble whole, sometimes epitomised in a sacred code-word; and that even the slightest modification or concession at this point would mean betraying the faith. Scriptural inerrancy, papal supremacy, believer's baptism, justification by faith alone, glossolalia are well-known examples.

A way out of this dilemma is to be found in the recognition that the identity of an ecclesial body constitutes a composite reality, with a hierarchy of foundational, denominational, national and other components, possessing varying degrees of permanence and importance. The existence of a hierarchy of truths, acknowledged by the Second Vatican Council, is an obvious parallel. It is true that to recognise such a hierarchy does not offer any simple solution insomuch as the churches score the individual components differently. What is of the _esse_ for one, is of the _bene esse_ for another, and an _adiaphoron_ for a third. But there can be no doubt that by such a differentiating analysis, the partners are bound to discover - as the bilaterals convincingly demonstrate - that they basically have much more of a common identity than their subsidiary characteristics would lead them to believe. The distinctive features do not disappear, but, relativised, they tend to lose their divisive force.

(b) It is by seeing identity as a function of continuity and renewal that the problem appears in its proper perspective. For then it becomes unmistakably clear that no church or confessional family possesses an intrinsic and changeless identity of its own. It can lay claim to no other identity than that of partaking, together with other churches, in the body of Christ. Its identity is but an aspect of its apostolicity, that is, its participation in the apostolic tradition and the apostolic mission. And then it is seen that development and change, far from being a threat, on the contrary are a necessary condition for expressing the apostolic identity of the Church as it reaches out to living men in a world of change. The report of the Faith and Order consultation at Salamanca, 1973, has an appropriate word here, which applies as much to bilateral as to multilateral conversations:

> "The identity and unity of the Church have their ultimate and normative reality in Jesus Christ, who comes to us in the power of the Holy Spirit, calling His church to and empowering it for an ever-renewed testimony to His redeeming and reconciling work. In this living tradition we are one with the Church throughout history and at the same time we are liberated to articulate our witness within the conditions and demands of our present historical moment. Identity and change are not therefore opposed or contradictory. Rather our present identity is to be found as, from and within its whole tradition and out of its solidarity with the needs and hopes of the world, the Church undertakes to manifest the Gospel of our Lord Jesus Christ in thought, life and action." (*The Ecumenical Review* XXVI, 2, 1974, 298; *What Kind of Unity*? p. 126)

Magisterium and Decision-Making

Inherent in the bilaterals is another problem which likewise calls for concerted investigation in the years ahead - the norm structures and, as important, the decision-making agencies and procedures which shape the attitudes of the churches. As the Christian traditions confront each other and at the same time are challenged by the forces of modernity, the whole matter of truth-finding and decision-making *in* the Church, not to speak of the authority *of* the Church in its evangelistic and social witness in the world, is in a state of flux and confusion. The preoccupation with confessional identity, the clinging to inherited traditions and ways of life, are understandable reactions to this state of affairs. But, for any individual tradition to assert *its* norm system, and to present it as a common universe of discourse for all, does not lead out of the impasse. In a pluralistic ecumenical situation, none of the historic Christian norm systems provides a transcendent resolution of the dilemma; they are themselves part of the dilemma.

While the problem is general, it affects the bilateral at two points in particular. Most of them - and some more thoroughly than others - have reflected on the normative givens of the Christian faith and the differing ways in which these are apprehended and applied.

Usually this has been done in the form of discussions of Scripture and tradition, creeds and confessional documents. In recent years, however, some bilaterals have gone further, beginning to reflect on the agencies and processes by means of which the Church articulates and promulgates its corporate mind. As was to be expected, the matter came to the fore chiefly in conversations with the Roman Catholics, focusing on the teaching authority of bishops and popes. What prompted this renewed interest was the realisation that the churches are divided not only in what they believe and do but, no less, in the ways by which they develop and justify their distinctive beliefs.

The second point where the issue immediately concerns the bilaterals is, of course, in the area of the reception and implementation of their proposals. In many cases the response is negligible or excessively tardy, with the result that innovative impulses lose their transforming power. While the reasons are varied, one of them is undoubtedly the inadequate attention paid to the complex decision processes by which new insights are enfleshed in the realities of church life.

Churches in dialogue not only possess each their own norm structure, but in fact several: first, the professed, secondly the operational (or rather an inconsistent diversity of them) and, thirdly, subtle shifts, caused by ecumenical and other influences, in the interpretation of individual components and likewise in the general balance of the structure. It is this third element which is of special interest here. Advocates of bilateral proposals for change are wont to argue, for obvious reasons, that these proposals are entirely in accord with the normative tradition of their own church. But the fact cannot be denied that bilateral documents do reveal real shifts of emphasis in weighing and applying their authorities, signalising a convergence of norm structures which promises a new departure also in this field.

Significant among these signs is the general acceptance of (a) the primacy of the apostolic and post-apostolic witnesses over later witnesses (e.g. the founding fathers or confessional statements of divided churches); (b) the belief in the power of the Spirit to guide the Church into new truth today as in the past, liberating it from slavish bondage to outdated doctrinal and canonical rules; (c) the importance of the <u>sensus fidelium</u> in the learning/teaching church (extending in some sense the principle of "collegiality" to include also the laity); (d) the increasingly felt need for ecclesiastical structures of teaching and decision-making which not merely serve and preserve the churches as they have developed in their separate histories, but serve the upbuilding of the larger ecumenical community now being born.

It is difficult to overestimate the importance of the fact that today, for rapidly growing numbers of Christians, the present fellowship experienced in the koinonia of the Spirit across denominational barriers takes precedence over loyalty to doctrinal and canonical rules which institutionalise past experiences of that koinonia in separated communities, and which therefore are no longer felt to be binding or even relevant.

The partners in dialogue therefore need to encourage studies of their magisterial and decision-making structures, with a view to facilitating ecumenical coordination and cooperation in the exercise of the teaching office of the churches.

Wider Relationships

Stewardship of time and money, and shrinking resources, call for a much more deliberate and intensive coordination of efforts than has been attempted thus far.

(a) Cross-fertilisation between bilaterals: It would involve not merely an exchange of completed reports, but, more importantly, a regular sharing of work in progress among bilaterals dealing with similar subjects. The practice of personal linkages between national and international commissions by means of double membership, ad hoc consultants, and WCC observers also deserves further development. This should be done both vertically (within each world confessional family) and horizontally (among the world confessional families, between international commissions, and likewise between national and regional commissions).

It is likely that, by an analogical transposition of discovered convergences from one dialogue to others, quite new affinities may be discovered. Already now it is plain that substantial agreement on the doctrine of the eucharist extends over a much larger area of Christendom than could have been imagined ten years ago.

(b) "Multilateral" bilaterals: Some of the bilaterals described in the second chapter are in fact trialogues, but the terminology is nevertheless justifiable insomuch as the dialogue deals with two sides of an issue and the participants on one side are sufficiently close to function as one partner (e.g. the international L-R-RC commission on mixed marriages or the new L-O-R commission in the USA). This is a pattern worth extending wherever feasible, for reasons both of economy and efficiency. For example, the growing Lutheran-Reformed rapprochement, evidenced in the Leuenberg Agreement of Reformation Churches in Europe and in the LWF-WARC Joint Committee, would suggest the advisability of considering similar joint dialogues with other communions in other parts of the world as well.

Another such bilateral - of far greater complexity and dimensions - would be the much-needed dialogue, long advocated by Orthodox spokesmen, between the Eastern and Western parts of Christendom on their divergent ways of apprehending and articulating the Christian faith (epistemology and theological methodology).

(c) Beyond bilaterals: There are other patterns of dialogue, lying between bilaterals and omnilaterals, which deserve to be explored as they may prove to be better suited to handling certain problems. Thus, for instance, a conversation among Orthodox, Methodists, Quakers and charismatics on styles of Christian holiness would be of benefit to all.

(d) Church union negotiations and bilateral conversations: As both largely cover the same ground and moreover several bilaterals are deliberately looking toward organic union, a close cooperation is imperative. This would involve regular exchange of materials, and participation of church unionists in bilateral commissions and vice versa, in countries where churches are engaged in both endeavours.

An effective interchange of this kind would further require that, in cases where churches belonging to different traditions are engaged in church union plans, the respective world confessional families, too, enter into dialogue for the double purpose of assisting their member churches in suitable ways, if requested, and secondly, examining the implications of such a union for the two world families themselves, as well as for the other member churches. A dialogue between the Anglican Communion and the World Methodist Council is an example that immediately comes to mind.

<u>A Permanent Forum</u>

The proliferation of bilateral dialogues has undeniably resulted in wasteful overlappings and diminishing returns. The need is therefore increasingly being felt for a greater measure of coordination and exchange - covering all the stages of planning, execution, appraisal, and implementation - if the bilaterals are to yield maximum benefit. The World Confessional Families and the Faith and Order Commission are actively pursuing these ends, and several proposals have been advanced for equipping such efforts with some kind of permanent structure. The two bodies recommended already in 1971 that the Faith and Order Secretariat in Geneva assume a continuing clearing-house function, and later consultations have urged the establishment of a "permanent forum" or "an advisory board".[1] Without entering into a discussion of possible options, it would seem that the several interests involved might indeed best be served by (a) setting up a small advisory board, composed of representatives of world confessional families, bilateral dialogues, and the Faith and Order Commission, and (b) requesting the Faith and Order Secretariat to serve as a clearing centre. Such a solution would create a joint forum for consultation among interested bodies which are partly within and partly without the World Council of Churches; facilitate continuing review and overall coordination and planning; and ensure the much needed interchange between bilateral, multilateral and union conversations.

Reception and Implementation

It would be generally agreed that one of the weakest points of the bilateral movement is the area of reception and implementation. The findings of the bilaterals - partly of historic significance - have as yet hardly made a dent on the teachings and practices of the churches. The reasons are not difficult to find. Innovative and sometimes radical proposals have to fight against the inertia and resistance of immensely powerful ecclesiastical *faits accomplis*. Bilateral insights must, like other religious and theological insights, vindicate themselves in the open market place of ideas, and even if they gain a sympathetic hearing, the passage through bureaucratic, magisterial and legislative machineries is notoriously slow and cumbersome. And to make the *consensus fidelium* a requirement for ecumenical reform does, in the nature of the case, further lengthen the rhythm of change. It represents nonetheless a tremendous advance, for it helps to transform the bilaterals from a conversation among specialists into a communication among churches. Efforts by church authorities to en-

1. See Recommendations, below pp. 262f.

courage the widest possible dissemination and discussion of bilateral findings is, therefore, a necessary step before such proposals can receive official approbation and enactment.

The dialogues described in the present Survey suggest a number of ways in which the process of reception can be speeded up and to some extent directed. As they illustrate, it would be a false approach to think merely in terms of reception or implementation; what is required is rather a continuing process of cooperation and experimentation by which the sponsoring churches themselves are growing in dialogue and fellowship at all levels. [1]

The Challenge of the Bilaterals to Churches and World Confessional Families

As this Survey will have shown, the bilateral conversations are unquestionably performing a unique pioneering function in enabling churches and confessional families to tackle specific obstacles to unity and to actualise the universal dimensions of their ecumenical responsibility. Yet, however important their theological accomplishments may be, the real test of the relevance and value of the bilaterals is still to come. The test is again the reception of the unifying truths, which they are discovering, in the life and relationships of the churches involved. The responses are, as we have seen, conflicting and provide no clear indication. A special obligation rests here on the world confessional families - also for the reason that they are sponsoring the worldwide dialogues now being conducted and cannot escape the long-range implications of this involvement. In their diverse ways, they all claim to serve the universality and wholeness, that is the catholicity, of the Church of Christ. Yet many of them are still largely content with "doing their own thing", instead of assuming their joint responsibilities in today's world and urging their member churches to press forward together. While it is true that the world families, with one or two exceptions, possess no constitutional authority they can nevertheless rightly be expected to exercise bold and imaginative ecumenical leadership in the moral lead they are offering. A catholicity which is not shared and does not result in sharing, is a contradiction in terms.

---

1. See above pp. 140f.

This is the insistent challenge that the bilaterals are levelling at the churches and world confessional families. The future of the bilateral dialogues will finally depend upon one basic question. If they become an institutionalised expression of mere ecumenical good-will without a serious commitment to accept challenge, to take risks, to be willing to change inherited positions and attitudes, then they become a l'art pour l'art game and might as well be discontinued. But if these bilateral conversations can continue to arrive at concrete and honest agreements and if the churches and their authorities are prepared to consider these agreements with a positive and open mind, there will be an undoubted future for such conversations. They may then still be far ahead of large sections of the Church, but they will be pathfinders on a road which the churches can follow with good conscience and with assured hope.

VIII

RECOMMENDATIONS

In reviewing bilateral developments, various confessional and ecumenical consultations in recent years have summed up their assessment in specific recommendations for consideration by the appropriate bodies. Of particular importance in the present context are the following recommendations adopted by the Conference of Secretaries of World Confessional Families in 1971 (A and B), the Faith and Order Commission in 1971 (C), and the Conference of Secretaries of World Confessional Families in 1974 (D). The latter statement deserves special attention as it represents an amended version of a document submitted to the Conference by a preceding consultation convened expressly for the purpose of making a first international assessment of the bilaterals. Overlapping or now outdated recommendations in the earlier documents have been omitted.

A. The Conference of Secretaries of World Confessional Families at its meeting in Geneva, November 29 - December 1, 1971, after having discussed the following recommendations in the "Draft Survey of Bilateral Conversations", agreed:

"That the representatives present of the various churches and world confessional families concerned bring these recommendations to the attention of the respective bodies for possible implementation:

1. To accept responsibility for adequate documentation and information about their own bilateral conversations and those of their constituent churches.
2. To communicate this documentation and information on a regular basis, apart from their own constituency, to:
   (a) the executive officers of other world confessional families,
   (b) the Secretariat of Faith and Order.
3. To transmit the material from other world confessional families to their own bilateral groups in order to facilitate a continuing cross-fertilisation.
4. To urge their bilateral groups to take account of pertinent developments in Faith and Order and in the ecumenical movement at large and to encourage the exchange of views

between those taking part in bilateral and multilateral conversations, and suggest in suitable situations the exchange of participants and observers.

5. To take care, in the planning of dialogues, of a more adequate representation of their total constituency, with special attention to the problems and the churches of the Third World.
6. To assist in the coordination and interaction of bilateral conversations on the different levels - world, regional and national.
7. To encourage theological scholars and teachers to take due account of the processes and results of bilaterals in their teaching and writing.
8. To urge their member churches to incorporate the findings of bilaterals in their educational and opinion-forming materials.
9. To reconsider in the light of their new position as partners in a world-wide theological dialogue their self-understanding and their relationship to the World Council of Churches."

B. The Conference further received the following recommendations and transmitted them to Faith and Order for their consideration:

"1. Carry out a continuing (or periodical) topical analysis of the incoming materials, with cross-conversational comparisons with parallel church union documents.
2. Occasionally attend meetings of bilaterals.
3. Convene an international consultation on bilaterals (possibly combined with, or at the same time and place as, the next Faith and Order consultation on church union plans).
4. Encourage scholarly studies of the bilaterals and their contribution to ecumenical advance.
5. Communicate results of bilaterals to other relevant units ofthe World Council of Churches.
6. Incorporate into its own programme an adequate consideration of the concerns and findings of the bilaterals (e.g. in the projected study on models of unity and in the continuing studies on ministry, eucharist and intercommunion)."

C. The Faith and Order Commission at its meeting in Louvain, August 1971, adopted, among others, the following recommendations:

"In order to strengthen the relationship between bilateral conversations and union negotiations, the Commission recommends:

(a) The effective exchange of information and materials.

(b) The inclusion of participants in union negotiations in commissions conducting bilateral conversations.

...

The Secretariat of the Commission should:

...

- Provide a clearing house for the exchange of information and materials concerning bilateral and multilateral conversations, establish a repository of such materials, and prepare periodical surveys of the developing trends of such conversations.
- Make available to participants in bilateral conversations and union negotiations the final report of the project sponsored by the Conference of Secretaries of World Confessional Families on bilateral conversations." (1)

D. The Future of the Bilaterals and the Bilaterals of the Future (Statement approved for submission to the World Confessional Families and the World Council of Churches by the Conference of Secretaries of World Confessional Families at its meeting in Geneva, December 11-12, 1974.)

"1. Christian dialogue has its origin in our Father's will for his people. Its purpose is the unity of the Church through faith in Jesus Christ and His way of salvation in order that the world may believe. We are compelled by the Holy Spirit and His power. Christian dialogue is not an exercise in human ability to compare doctrines and traditions, but manifests the calling of the churches to respond together to the gracious activity of the Triune God. We pray that we will always be open to new ideas that He may give us. We do our work by faith, realising that in time He may displace these by new and better works of grace.

1. See full report in Faith and Order, Louvain 1971, pp. 234-238

2. The importance of the intensified ecumenical activity of the World Confessional Families is seen most clearly in the theological and pastoral agreements achieved through the bilateral dialogues. A worldwide survey of these dialogues, sponsored by the World Confessional Families in cooperation with the Faith and Order Secretariat of the World Council of Churches, contains an overview of these dialogues, their achievements so far, and the questions they raise. The Conference of Secretaries of World Confessional Families enlarged their meeting in December 1974, by the addition of persons involved in bilateral dialogues, and in consultation with them proposed the following considerations.
3. Bilateral conversations between representatives of churches or confessional families are a relatively new kind of theological discussion, running parallel to multilateral discussions, church union negotiations, and faith and order studies in general.
4. The general situation of the bilaterals is one of transition. Two phases are overlapping: the striving for theological agreements and the attempt at the same time to translate these agreements into ecclesiastical relationships. Furthermore, different bilaterals are at different stages. Their specific goals need spelling out clearly. There are also unofficial conversations which have been profitable and useful, but which must be officially accepted by ecclesiastical bodies if their contribution is to be effective.
5. Bilaterals have certain specific functions and values. There is in them the opportunity and necessity of transcending national boundaries in fellowship. They may clarify distinctions which historically have divided two ecclesiastical traditions and are often glossed over in multilateral conversations. Some bilaterals have the greater ecclesiological significance in that they are authorised by official church bodies and seek decisions from their churches. A danger is that they weigh two traditions too heavily as if they constitute a "cathol-

icity" which they can discuss in isolation. If the values are to be fulfilled, a number of questions arise, e.g, are the dialogues contributing to the unity of the whole body of Christ, and are they aiming to be fully representative of different cultures and traditions? The concern for catholicity, which is richer and larger than any particular bilateral, must be foremost. Perhaps when a bilateral dialogue reaches a certain stage of achievement it might possibly be enlarged by the participation of a third or even more partners. Churches ought not to be content to do bilaterally what they could more usefully do multilaterally.

6. Most bilateral consensus statements have been worked out by officially appointed commissions. These statements need to be widely shared and theologically tested at all levels of church life. The theological expression of the statements at times needs improvement. Reactions need to be invited from the partner churches in dialogue. Feed-back of this sort would bring maturity to the texts but might also raise new questions which would need answering. It is also essential to test the reception of the consensus statements in the light of the theological experience of the churches involved in the dialogue located in radically different cultural situations throughout the world.

7. Part of the testing of consensus statements in the churches is the task of communicating them to a wider readership. The statements should witness to the truth which they proclaim in ways that can be understood, and should preferably be accompanied by pastoral texts spelling out the implications of the new understandings reached for local situations. The statements must be "incarnated" in the lives of the local churches by developing their liturgies, catechisms, and constitutional documents, and by re-interpreting earlier texts of ecclesiastical condemnation. This process of translating these new agreements may well give rise to tensions in local, national and cultural contexts.

8. There is an encouraging increase of bilaterals. At the same time there are many areas where these bilaterals are not taking place. For example, ways should be found to encourage entrance into these conversations by those churches whose theological persuasion causes them to be reluctant to do so.
9. The bilateral conversations at the world level often lack adequate participation from Africa, Asia and Latin America. These different cultural and religious situations provide perspectives differing from those usually operative in bilateral conversations. There is urgent need for theological encounters between those engaged in bilateral conversations and those involved in new emerging theologies in these areas.
10. The final goal of the bilateral conversations cannot be clearly envisaged. It is therefore necessary to work with imperfect models and definitions. Multilateral conversations in the form of local church union negotiations tend to regard "organic union" as their model. Some bilateral conversations also regard "organic union" as their model. On the other hand, there are other bilateral conversations which tend to aim at mutual recognition, and to regard "reconciled diversity" as a model - in any case, further thought needs to be given to the definition and relation of these terms. There are other instances in which it is possible to set only proximate and intermediate goals as genuine for involvement in bilateral conversations.
11. University theology departments and church seminaries often do not give sufficient attention to faith and order discussions or bilateral conversations, or indeed to theological synthesis or to the relation of theory and practice in general. The bilateral conversations have, however, not only produced statements with valuable content, but have evolved a new method in which the emphasis is not on individuals but on corporate theologising. At the same time the bilateral conversations must pay full attention to the findings of the theological sciences.

12. Among topics which demand urgent consideration in the future and which, while they are common to many bilateral dialogues, need to be examined from different perspectives, are:

- Authority and decision-making in the Church
- The Role of the Scriptures
- Ministry, including forms of episcope
- The definition and relation of "organic union", "reconciled diversity" and "conciliarity"
- Christian holiness and spirituality
- Newly arising trans-confessional groupings which sometimes call into question existing ecclesiastical fellowships
- Marriages and inter-church marriages
- New divisive bio-ethical questions such as population control, genetical control, organ transplants.

But the principal topic for all bilateral dialogues will evermore be clearly seen to be a common vision of the unity of the Church at every level in obedience to the faith.

13. Some specific considerations:

(i) Continuation of the commitment by the confessional families to bilateral conversations by enlarging their effectiveness through:

- wider dissemination of publications addressed to various groups;
- wider participation at all levels of the Church's life in the bilateral process;
- interchange between different bilaterals at world, regional and local level;
- interchange between bilaterals, multilaterals, and church union negotiations.

(ii) Ways urgently need to be found to relate different bilateral dialogues to one another. This could be accomplished by more adequate sharing of consensus statements and other material. More significantly, however, this sharing and evaluation could be made effective in a forum devoted to this very task, which might also provide for an encounter of bilateral participants with a wider spectrum of dialogue partners. The autonomy of each church or World Confessional Family would nevertheless need to be fully respected and guaranteed. It is therefore recommended that the Conference of Secretaries of World Confessional Families invite the Faith and Order Commission, in consultation with the churches and the World Confessional Families, to convene an Advisory Group, which would need a clearly defined status and would be related in some way to the context of Faith and Order, to explore ways of interrelating bilateral dialogues, so that together they may contribute to the fuller unity of the Church."

IX

EDITIONS OF DOCUMENTS

Three editions of documents relating to bilateral conversations have begun publication and others are reportedly under consideration:

ARC-DOC I and II. Documents on Anglican-Roman Catholic Relations, compiled by the Bishop's Committee on Ecumenical and Interreligious Affairs in cooperation with the Joint Commission on Ecumenical Relations of the Episcopal Church. Publications Office, United States Catholic Conference, 1312 Massachusetts Avenue, N.W., Washington, D.C. 20005. 1972 and 1973.

Um Amt und Herrenmahl (On Ministry and Eucharist). Dokumente zum evangelisch/römisch-katholischen Gespräch. Okumenische Dokumentation I, im Auftrag des Instituts für Okumenische Forschung in Strassburg herausgegeben von Günther Gassmann, Marc Lienhard und Harding Meyer. Frankfurt/Main: Verlag Otto Lembeck, Verlag Joseph Knecht, 1974.

Vom Dialog zur Gemeinschaft. Dokumente zum anglikanisch-lutherischen und anglikanisch-katholischen Gespräch. Okumenische Dokumentation II, im Auftrag des Instituts für Okumenische Forschung in Strassburg herausgegeben von Günther Gassmann, Marc Lienhard und Harding Meyer. Frankfurt/Main: Verlag Otto Lembeck, Verlag Joseph Knecht, 1975.

Kyrkogemenskap (Church Fellowship). Kring samtalen mellan lutheraner och reformerta. En kommenterad dokumentsamling i redaktion av Lars Thunberg med inledning av Holsten Fagerberg. Konfessioner i dialog 1. Stockholm: AWE/Gebers i samarbete med Nordiska Ekumeniska Institutet, 1974.

Evangelium och Kyrka (The Gospel and the Church). Kring samtalen mellan lutheraner och romerska katoliker. En kommenterad dokumentsamling i redaktion av Lars Thunberg med inledning av Per Erik Persson. Konfessioner i dialog 2. Stockholm: Almquist & Wiksell i samarbete med Nordiska Ekumeniska Institutet,1974.

X

DIRECTORY OF AGENCIES

Anglican Consultative Council
The Rt.Rev. John W.A. Howe, Secretary General
32 Eccleston Street, London SW1W 9PY, England

The Archbishop of Canterbury's Counsellors on Foreign Relations
The Rev.Canon M.M. Hamond Moore, Chaplain
Palace Court, 222 Lambeth Road, London SE1 7LB, England

Ecumenical Office of the Executive Council of the Episcopal Church
Dr. Peter Day, Ecumenical Officer
815 Second Avenue, New York, N.Y. 10017, USA

Anglican Council of Latin America (CALA)
The Rt.Rev. J.W.H. Flagg, President of Anglican Council of South America (CASA)
Apartado 10266, Correo Colmena, Lima, Peru

Baptist World Alliance
Dr. Robert S. Denny, General Secretary
1628 Sixteenth Street, N.W., Washington, D.C. 20009, USA

Office of Ecumenical Relations
American Baptist Churches in the USA
Dr. Robert G. Torbet, Assistant General Secretary for Ecumenical Relations
Valley Forge, Pa. 19481, USA

Council on Christian Unity of the Christian Church (Disciples of Christ)
Dr. Paul A. Crow, Jr., President
P.O. Box 1986, Indianapolis, Indiana 46206, USA

Kirchliches Aussenamt der Evangelischen Kirche in Deutschland (EKD)
The Rev. Dr. Heinz-Joachim Held, President
Bockenheimer Landstrasse 109, 6 Frankfurt/Main,
Federal Republic of Germany

Lutheran World Federation
Dr. Carl H. Mau, General Secretary
Dr. Daniel F. Martensen, Secretary for Interconfessional Research
150, route de Ferney, 1211 Geneva 20, Switzerland

Institute for Ecumenical Research
Prof.Dr. Harding Meyer, Acting Director
8, rue Gustave Klotz, 67 Strasbourg, France

Division of Theological Studies of the Lutheran Council in the USA
Dr. Paul D. Opsahl, Executive Secretary
315 Park Avenue South, New York, N.Y. 10010, USA

World Methodist Council
Dr. Lee F. Tuttle, General Secretary
Lake Junaluska, North Carolina 28745, USA

Division of Ecumenical and Interreligious Concerns
General Board of Global Ministries
The United Methodist Church
Dr. Robert W. Huston, General Secretary
475 Riverside Drive, New York, N.Y. 10027, USA

International Conference of Old Catholic Bishops
The Most Rev. Léon Gauthier, Secretary
Willadingweg 39, 3006 Berne, Switzerland

Representation of the Ecumenical Patriarchate of Constantinople
at the World Council of Churches
The Most Rev. Emilianos Timiadis, Metropolitan of Calabria
150, route de Ferney, 1211 Geneva 20, Switzerland

Representation of the Moscow Patriarchate
at the World Council of Churches
The Most Rev. Makary, Bishop of Uman
150, route de Ferney, 1211 Geneva 20, Switzerland

Standing Conference of Canonical Orthodox Bishops in the Americas (SCOBA)
The Rev.Dr. Robert G. Stephanopoulos, General Secretary
10 East 79th Street, New York, N.Y. 10021, USA

Department of External Church Relations of the Moscow Patriarchate
The Most Rev. Juvenaly, Metropolitan of Tula and Belev, Chairman
18/2 Ryleeva, Moscow G-34, USSR

Conference of the Heads of the Oriental Orthodox Churches
P.O. Box 2171, Addis Ababa, Ethiopia

World Alliance of Reformed Churches
The Rev. Edmond Perret, General Secretary
The Rev. Richmond Smith, Secretary of the Department of Theology
150, route de Ferney, 1211 Geneva 20, Switzerland

The North American Area of the World Alliance of Reformed Churches
President James I. McCord, Secretary
Princeton Theological Seminary, Princeton, N.J. 08540, USA

Secretariat for Promoting Christian Unity
00120 Vatican City, Vatican

Bishop's Committee for Ecumenical and Interreligious Affairs of the
National Conference of Catholic Bishops
The Rev.Dr. John F. Hotchkin, Executive Director
1312 Massachusetts Avenue, N.W., Washington, D.C. 20005, USA

Department of Ecumenism of the Ecumenical Commission of the
Catholic Episcopate of Latin America (CELAM)
Father Jorge Mejía, Executive Secretary
Pacheco de Melo 2016 4° A, Buenos Aires, Argentina

Secretariat on Faith and Order of the World Council of Churches
Dr. Lukas Vischer, Director
150, route de Ferney, 1211 Geneva 20, Switzerland